The Daily Mail Book of
HOME MAINTENANCE
& IMPROVEMENTS

Harmony Books Ltd
Unit 11, Stirling Industrial Centre, Stirling Way, Borehamwood, Herts WD6 2BT
☎ 01-953 9292

First published 1989
© Christine Reeves

British Library Cataloguing in Publication Data
Reeves, Christine
The Daily Mail book of home maintenance and improvement.
1. Residences. Maintenance, repair & improvement
I. Title
643'.7

ISBN 1 85553 001 5

Cover Photo : Tiffany suite from Perrings

Designed and Typeset by Design 29, Dyfed
Printed and bound in Great Britain by Ashford Colour Press Ltd

BEST PLACES'

mmitment to retain the degree of customer
isfaction and loyalty so necessary in
otecting their high level of recommendations.

You might believe that one window or
or is so much like another but that's doing
urself a disservice and missing another
asterpiece.

So, for the best investment consult your
cal press or Yellow Pages, and seek our sign of
proval.

· DOORS · AND · WINDOWS ·

FOR THE COMPLETE COLLECTION

Coastal Aluminium Products Limited
Holton Heath Trading Park, POOLE, Dorset
BH16 6LE Telephone: (0202) 624011

FM 1491

The Daily Mail
Book of
HOME MAINTENANCE
& IMPROVEMENTS

HOW TO MAINTAIN, DECORATE & IMPROVE YOUR HOME

Christine Reeves

harmony
books

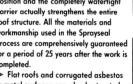

CONTENTS

APPENDICES

PART 1

HOW TO MAINTAIN YOUR HOME

HOME MAINTENANCE

It doesn't matter what the age of your home is, there will always be something you can do to improve it, from replacing the kitchen and fitting double-glazing to adding an extension and redecorating. However, as well as updating the amenities and decor, it's even more important that you look after the basic fabric of your home to ensure that the framework is kept sound and free of damaging damp, rot and insect infestation. Carry out regular twice-yearly checks, one in spring, one in autumn, to ensure you spot any problems as soon as they arise and deal with them immediately.

Whether you've been in your present home for many years or just moved in, it's worth spending some time carrying out these checks carefully, making a note of anything which needs to be done. Briefly the areas to look at are: roof, guttering, walls, floors, loft including roof timbers, wiring and lighting, plumbing, insulation, doors, windows and central heating. Then consider the kitchen and bathroom and the general state of decoration throughout.

The chances are that the older your property, the greater the number of jobs which need to be carried out. List them all, then try and place them in order of importance, for example it's sensible to fit central heating before you

update the bathroom. Also try to remember that some jobs will actually reduce the running costs of the house and ought to be given priority. Insulation for example will reduce the amount of heat lost from the building thus reducing your heating bills, so should be tackled before you start redecorating.

Many maintenance jobs are seasonal: exterior decorating is best done during a dry spell between the spring and autumn when the house structure has had a chance to dry out; interior decorating during mild, sunny weather to avoid condensation. Any building or concreting work, such as adding an extension or replacing windows, should be tackled in dry, frost-free conditions, whilst the central heating system should be checked during the summer months. Check guttering and for water penetration and damp during prolonged rainy periods.

ROOF CHECKS

Your first step should be to inspect the roof for faults which could result in rain getting into the roof timbers. Use a pair of binoculars to check from outside the house. Look for slipped, damaged or missing tiles and ridge tiles, also check the flashings (the strip of material which seals the gap between the roof and any vertical walls) and valleys of the roof. Go up into the loft and, using a torch, check for dampness — the best time is during a heavy rainstorm when dripping water will be easier to detect.

Check your first- (or top) floor ceiling. If there are tell-tale damp spots on it, it's almost certain your roof has a leak. The water may not be getting into the roof at the point immediately above the stain, but in another area and then running along the roof timbers or joists, so check the entire roof area with care.

If you live in an old property where the roof is in a particularly bad state of repair you may have to consider re-roofing. Contact a professional company such as Redland for advice, they offer a useful booklet *Redland Guide to Re-roofing* which is available free by phoning Freephone Redland, or by writing to them direct.

As an alternative to totally re-roofing, particularly a roof where the slates or tiles are in good condition but the nails or pegs have deteriorated, consider a professionally applied roof repair treatment, which will both renovate and insulate the roof area.

A specially formulated foam is applied to the underside of the roof tiles and this forms a permanent bond which holds and supports the tiles or slates ensuring they don't slip and preventing wind, rain, snow and dust entering the loft space. This treatment is carried out by Thermabond Roofing, a Cheshire-based roofing contractors and thermabonding specialists and ISL Ltd (Insulation Contractors) who are based in Hampshire.

Whilst you're up in the loft check the insulation there should be at least 100 mm (4″) of insulation between the joists and ideally 150 mm (6″). If there is no insulation at all, get the job done as a matter or priority. If you have less than the recommended amount, top it up with more.

GUTTERS AND DOWNPIPES

The rainwater and melting snow that run off your roof are collected in the gutters and the downpipes. The next time we get a downpour, don't see it as our climate playing tricks again. Instead, seize the opportunity to go outside, and check that your gutters and downpipes are effectively doing their job of conveying the water safely to the drains. If they are not, it could mean that the outside of your house is getting an unnecessary soaking, with the risk of damage to the masonry, rot being introduced into the woodwork and damp penetrating to the inside of your home.

For the past 25 years, rainwater disposal systems, (as the builder calls them — he refers to gutters and downpipes collectively as rainwater goods) have been invariably made of plastic (uPVC, in fact). Before that they were in cast iron, although during the 30s a few asbestos systems were fitted. You are more likely to come across faults if you have a cast iron system, because this material is prone to rust — which is hardly the perfect material to come into contact with rainwater. Regular maintenance will keep rust at bay, but we don't always paint the outside of our homes as regularly or as thoroughly as we ought. We particularly skimp the back of downpipes and the inside of gutters. And you can't - of course - treat the inside of downpipes. Rust can develop in all of these places.

Here are some of the more common problems, and what can be done about them.

Blocked gutter Blockages are more likely to happen where the gutter turns a corner, or meets up with the top of a downpipe. If you get a blockage use a garden trowel, or shaped piece of card, to scrape out the debris and scoop it into a bucket hung from a ladder. Bung up the top of nearby downpipes to stop the

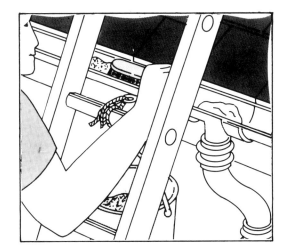

Blocked downpipe You can tell when a downpipe is blocked by looking at the join between sections. Water will bubble out here if it cannot proceed on its way to the gulley. So this is also a clue to the whereabouts of the blockage – it must be lower down than this point.

You clear a blockage by poking a length of stiff wire or a long pole down the pipe. If your house, like most, has an overhang or offset – that's the short sloping section that takes the pipe under the eaves - you will have to use wire, which can negotiate the bend. A pole can be used on straight sections, such as you get on garages and extensions.

In both cases, cover the gulley grating so that you do not push rubbish into the drains.

debris from falling down them. Flush the gutter through with clear water and clean plastic systems with a cloth, cast iron ones with an old brush. This flushing may be your first indication that you have a blocked downpipe.

If the blockage is a stubborn one, you may have to dismantle the downpipe – it is held loosely in place – then clear it with a wad of rags on the end of a pole. Reassemble once you have cleared the blockage.

Blocked hopper You will have to clear this with your hands, so wear thick rubber gloves as protection. There may be sharp twigs, even broken glass in the hopper. Once again, take care not to push debris down the pipe.

Overflowing gutters Water gathers in pools in a gutter and in extreme cases flows over the sides, because the slope is not sufficient to carry it away. You may spot this happening when flushing out a blocked gutter you have just cleared. On a plastic system, remove the brackets and move them along slightly (the existing screw holes will stop you from getting a proper fixing unless you reposition) placing them to give the correct slope. Fill the old screw holes and spot-paint to stop water from entering the woodwork. Iron brackets can often be bent upwards to raise the gutter to the correct position. Otherwise drive small wedges between bracket and gutter.

Rust may have caused complete failure of an iron bracket. In that case fit a new one (make sure it's the right size). The new bracket need not be cast iron. You can buy a plastic bracket and paint it to match.

With both plastic and iron, finally flush with clear water to check that the 'fall' is correct.

Leaks at gutter joints With some makes of plastic gutter, lengths are joined up by a clip. In other cases the joint is solvent welded. Check that all the parts are properly located. If the seal has failed, apply a non-setting mastic. It could be that the clip has broken, and is not compressing the seal properly. Buy and fit a new one. Remake a solvent-welded joint with fresh solvent.

On iron, reseal the joint with a bituminous mastic. You might have to remove the bolt that holds the two sections together. Of course, it will be corroded. First, apply penetrating oil and, if that does not free the bolt, saw through it with a hacksaw. Next coat the mating parts with mastic, and fit a new nut and bolt.

Leaks in downpipes If the leak is at a join, it may be an indication that there is a blockage at a lower level. Leaks elsewhere should be dealt with as for gutters.

Leaks elsewhere You are not likely to get these on plastic unless there has been accidental damage. Rust can cause cracks and small holes on iron. On both types, you can seal with a waterproofing tape, or a glassfibre repair kit.

Damaged gutter section If it's plastic, remove the section from its clip, and fit a new one. Keep sound bits of the old section for future minor repairs, which you can make by clipping or solvent-welding short lengths in place.

You will find it very difficult to buy a new cast iron length, but you can fit plastic into an iron system using a special adaptor, which you buy where you get your gutter. Paint the plastic to match the iron.

Damaged downpipe A cast iron section may be so badly damaged by rust that you decide complete replacement is called for. That's easy enough. Buy a length of plastic pipe, take out the old iron one, cut the plastic to the same length and insert it in the joint. Downpipe joints are not sealed, so that water can escape if there is a blockage.

Length of gutter or pipe missing entirely Most likely to happen with cast iron because the component, or the bracket holding it in place, has rusted away. Fix new components, as above.

There may be so much wrong with your rainwater disposal system that the only sensible thing to do is replace it completely. This is a big job, but is by no means beyond the abilities of a competent do-it- yourselfer. First, though, you have a fair amount of planning to do.

There is no doubt that your new system should be in plastic, for it has so many advantages over the only possible alternative, cast iron. In fact, one of the main disadvantages of cast iron is tracking down a supplier, for it has become so unpopular that hardly any is manufactured nowadays. Plastic rainwater goods are cheaper to buy, longer lasting, do not rust, require no painting (although you can paint them if you want to change their colour), are lighter to handle and easier to fix. In fact, the only reason for choosing cast iron would be if you are restoring a period house, and want to stick to traditional materials. But once painted, plastic is indistinguishable from cast iron.

A rainwater system is made up of a series of components that are put together to suit the needs of your house. So get the catalogues of a few manufacturers, study what is available and, using the components, plot a system as close as possible to the one you have at present. Plastic guttering comes in a range of shapes – or profiles to use the correct term. You do not have to stick to the profile you have at present. But you must stick to the same size, or its equivalent in a profile change.

The capacity of the system was calculated by the architect or builder who designed your house in the first place, to be sufficient to take the water that would run off a roof of the size and slope that you have. If yours is a terraced or semi-detached house, and your gutters join up with those of your neighbour who is not contemplating replacement at the same time, make sure that your new system can be linked up to his. Adaptors are available to allow plastic to join cast iron, but make sure that the profiles are compatible, too.

Here is a selection of some of the components you will find in the catalogues:

Brackets Used to support lengths of gutter. Usually fixed by being screwed to the fascia board – the timber that neatens off the top of the house walls. Types that fix to the rafters, for sites where there is no fascia, can also be bought.

Floating union Used with many systems to join sections together. The word 'floating' indicates that it is a component on its own. In some instances, some of the following components – even a length of gutter – may incorporate a union.

Gutter bends Used to take the gutter round a corner. Various angles are available – 90°, 112° and 135° are typical.

Hopper head Receives water from upper-floor waste pipes and conveys it to the gutter, sometimes by linking up to a downpipe.

Outlets Used to link gutters to a downpipe – they have a short length of pipe that sits inside the top of the gutter. The one shown on page 14 is a running outlet i.e. it is intended to be fixed in the middle of a length of gutter.

Overhangs On houses (but not small buildings such as sheds and garages) the downpipe has to pass under the overhanging eaves on its way from the outlet to the straight run of pipe. The name given to this stretch is the overhang or offset (in builders' slang because of its shape, it is also commonly referred to as a 'swan's neck'). Some manufacturers sell a complete overhang; others offer the components to allow you to make your own of the correct shape and size.

Pipe bends To take a pipe round a bend. You would use these in making your own overhang.

Pipe brackets Two types are available. The most common also acts as a union, to link up two lengths. But clips to hold the pipe to the wall in the middle of long lengths can also be bought.

Pipe branch Connects a 'branch line' pipe to the main run.

Shoe Shaped component at the base of the pipe that throws water clear of the wall and into the gulley.

Stop ends Used to close off a length of gutter. Since there is often a downpipe at the end of a run, some companies offer a top end

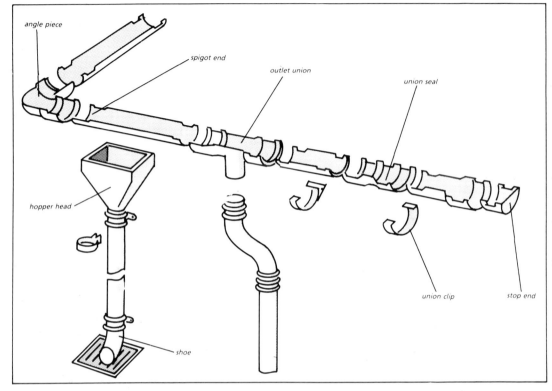

angle piece

spigot end

outlet union

union seal

hopper head

union clip

stop end

shoe

with outlet; others would expect you to make up this item yourself.

Straight guttering Comes in various lengths − 2, 3 and 4m − are typical. As far as possible, you should make full use of standard lengths, although here and there you will have to cut to size.

Straight pipe It's what downpipes are made of.

BRICKWORK & WALLS

One of the most common faults with a brick wall is that the mortar between the courses will start to wear away, under the action of wind and rain. It's hardly likely that things will get so bad that the bricks are not held together properly, but the wall could become less weatherproof, and bad pointing (as it is known) makes your home look down-at-heel.

The process of renewing the mortar is known as **repointing**. This is not all that difficult a skill, but to repoint a house is a major undertaking that will require lots of time and energy − plus proper access equipment, for you cannot just tackle small sections of the repointing and leave it at that. Once you start, you must finish, otherwise the new mortar contrasting with the old will merely be drawing attention to the fact that you have had a problem.

Repointing smaller walls − such as you might get on a brick-built garage, or even a garden wall − is a much less awesome undertaking, and could be a good practice ground before you started on the main house.

Equipment

The repointing is done with a mortar of one part of cement to four parts of sharp sand, mixed with little water to a stiff consistency. The mortar is placed on a tool the builder calls a hawk. Modern hawks consist of a sheet of galvanised metal about 300 mm (12″) square with a handle underneath. You can make your own from a piece of plywood or blockboard, and a 300 mm (12″) length cut off the end of a broom handle. Fix the handle by driving a nail or screw into it through the blockboard.

You will also need a small pointing trowel and a tool the builder terms a 'frenchman'. You improvise this by taking an old kitchen knife, filing it to a point, and bending the tip at right-angles.

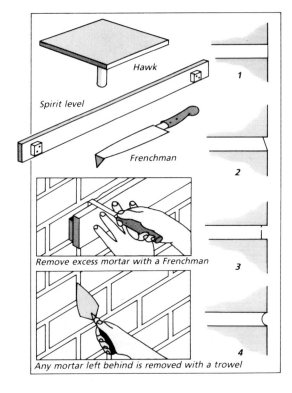

Hawk

Spirit level

Frenchman

1

2

Remove excess mortar with a Frenchman

3

4

Any mortar left behind is removed with a trowel

Method

1. Begin by raking out about 12 mm (½″) of the old mortar, using an old thin chisel and a hammer, then brush out all the dust and loose material. Work on about a square metre of the brickwork at a time, soaking it first by brushing in clean water, so that the masonry will not dry out the mortar too quickly.

2. Place some mortar on your hawk and smooth it. Pick up some on the back of your trowel, hold the hawk close to the wall and as you push the trowel forward, tilt the front of your hawk upwards, and lift the mortar clear.

3. Treat the verticals first, pressing the mortar well into the joints. You will be left with a

thick surplus at the outside of each joint. Chop this off when a section of vertical is completed.

4. Now you can finish off the section by treating the horizontals, pressing the mortar home from the top of the joint.

5. The chopping off of the excess in this case is done with the 'frenchman' drawn along a straightedge. Any mortar left behind is removed with your trowel.

6. The sketches show the various finishes you can give to the mortar. To form *1*, rub the mortar with sacking, taking care not to spread it over the brickwork; *2* is formed with the 'frenchman'; *3* is scraped out with a pointed rod, then smoothed with a stick when the mortar has hardened slightly; *4* is raked out with a metal bar. The last two are completed when the mortar has hardened slightly.

Rendering is a word used to describe a coating based on sand and cement that is applied to the external walls of a house, usually to make them more weatherproof or to cover up poor quality brickwork. You will see it a lot, for instance, on the solid walls put up during the 30s. However, even sound walls of cavity construction can be rendered as a decorative feature.

Renderings are usually applied in two or three coats, and there are various finishes:

Smooth The top coat is polished with a wooden float trowel to give the smooth effect that its name suggests. In early Victorian buildings, it may have been scored to represent stonework. This type needs regular painting.

Textured finishes have a pattern applied to the final coats by the use of a gauging trowel, banister brush, steel float, decorator's comb or a roller (e.g. diamond effect).

Roughcast (also known as Tyrolean) contains gravel in the final mix. It is sprayed on to the wall by means of a machine known as a Tyrolean projector.

Pebbledash or **Spardash** features small stones in the final coat. The pebbles are cast into the wet mortar from a shovel and pressed home with a wooden float.

These rough finishes are better at shedding water than the smooth and repainting is not called for so frequently. It usually becomes necessary eventually, however.

Rendering is a highly skilled craft, and except for small patches is not suitable work for the do-it-yourselfer. However, you can carry out the maintenance on them.

Rendered walls require more maintenance than brick. All mortar mixes shrink to some extent as they dry out, and this can cause tiny cracks to appear. On top of that there will usually be movement of the building and that too can affect the rendering. All of this will not matter too much if the building is painted regularly. But the trouble is that redecoration tends to get neglected and water enters any cracks. As a result it can cause the cracks to enlarge and, especially as it freezes during winter, weaken the adhesion between rendering and masonry. As a result blisters of loose material can develop, and bits might even fall off, leaving bare patches.

It is important to repair these defects, not only because they look unsightly, and thus lower the value of your house, but also damaged rendering is not doing its job properly of keeping the house weatherproof.

Cracks Hair-line cracks will be covered by an exterior wall paint. But larger ones will need to be filled. Exterior-grade fillers are sold for this work, but where a lot of repairs are called for it will be cheaper to buy one of the small bags of ready-mixed mortar, just needing the addition of water. Or you can, of course, mix your own mortar. The mix should be quite stiff.

Clean out the crack with the point of a trowel or filling knife to get rid of all loose material, then push the filler home.

Blisters You locate these by tapping the surface with, say, the handle of a trowel or hammer. A hollow sound will indicate that the rendering is not adhering properly to the underlying brickwork. Hack it off, with a hammer and bolster chisel, right back to the brickwork. Begin in the centre of the blister, getting rid of all loose material, and work outwards until you are sure you have reached a sound edge.

The resulting hole is filled with a mortar mix – 1:5 of cement and sharp sand is suitable.

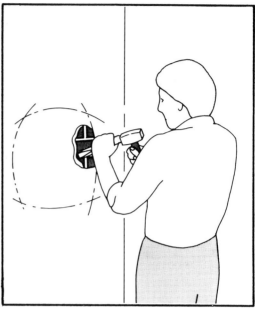
Begin at centre of blister

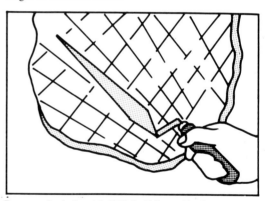
Prepare the hole with PVA building adhesive

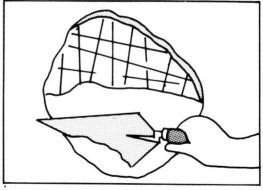
Begin at the bottom of the hole and spread upwards

First brush the masonry with pva building adhesive, and add adhesive to the mortar as detailed on the instructions.

The mortar is applied from a hawk, by means of a steel float, in two coats. Begin at the bottom of the hole, push the mortar from the float on to the wall, and spread it upwards. Leave this coat for about four hours then scratch it with the point of a trowel to provide a better key for the second coat. This first coat is often described by builders as being the 'scratch coat'.

Leave overnight, then apply the final coat. Do not work this final coat too hard, otherwise you risk bringing the cement to the surface and it will not dry properly.

Bare patches There may still be loose material adhering in the middle of the patch. Chop this off, and chop all round the edge of the patch, with a hammer and cold chisel, until you are absolutely sure you have a sound edge. Then treat as for blisters.

With both bare patches and blisters, the final mortar coat should be smoothed or textured — or pebbles added — to suit the rest of the wall.

All your repairs will be immediately obvious, so the rendering will need to be painted right away.

You might see a white powdery substance forming on the outside walls of your home. This is nothing to worry about. It is called **efflorescence**, and is caused by salts coming to the surface as moisture in the brickwork evaporates. Eventually it will disappear of its own accord. If you don't want to wait, you can remove it with a stiff brush. But don't use water. That will only make matters worse.

Efflorescence indoors is another matter. It could be a sign that you have a damp problem.

If the bricks of your house wall are too porous, rainwater will soak into them. Trouble arises when this freezes, for the water will then expand and cause the face of the bricks to crumble. This process is known as **spalling**. If only one or two bricks are affected, you should replace them. It's an easy enough job. You chop out the mortar holding the brick in place, and withdraw it. Then you take a new brick and mortar it in place with a 1:3 mix of cement and soft sand. Soak the surrounding brickwork with clean water to stop it from drying out the

mortar too quickly. Spread the mortar on the bottom and sides of the opening, and on top of the brick, then push the brick in place. If you have cavity walls, take care not to drop old or new mortar into the cavity.

If you cannot find a new brick to match, turn the old one round so it's inner face is now on the outside. Mortar may ooze out on to the face of the wall. Leave it to harden for about half an hour, then flick off the dried bits with your trowel.

Where spalling is extensive, a complete cover-up might be called for - with rendering or wall tiles, etc.

The **damp-proof course** is a barrier inserted in the walls of your home, ideally about 150 mm (6″) above ground level, to stop moisture in the ground from rising up them. It is an important precaution, for rising damp, as it is known, can enter the interior of your home, doing damage to both the house itself, and the health of its occupants.

The earliest dpc's — installed say, a hundred years or so ago — were of slate. Later, copper and lead, bitumen or felt, were used, and in more modern times thick black polythene is installed.

Some of the earlier dpc's have now failed, and need renewing — you will soon know if rising damp is entering your home. They can be replaced, and indeed a dpc can be installed in a home that does not have one.

There are four main methods:

1. Cut out a thin band of masonry all round the house and insert a dpc, then fill in with mortar.

2. Install an electro-osmosis system which uses a minute electrical charge to divert the dampness back to earth.

3. Fit porous ceramic tubes, which increase the evaporation of moisture, thus preventing it from rising.

4. Inject a silicone-based chemical which transforms the bricks themselves into an impervious layer.

None of these, except perhaps the injection method, is suitable for non-professionals, and if your house requires the installation of a dpc, you should call in the experts.

However, if your home does have a dpc, the important thing for you is to ensure that you do nothing to affect the efficiency of it. Obviously, take care not to cause it physical damage, but also avoid piling materials – garden soil, a bulk delivery of solid fuel or sand - up against the wall. For that could convey the damp into the wall higher up, a process known as 'bridging the damp-proof course'. And this will let rising damp into your home just as surely as if the dpc did not exist.

For the same reason make sure any patio or path you install adjacent to the wall is at least two courses of brickwork below the dpc.

Cracking of timbers caused by Dry Rot fungus

DEALING WITH DAMP

Damp can wreak havoc to the structure of your home and can enter your house in many ways – through the roof, the walls, door and window frames and via the floor. If you think any house timbers are affected by rot, push a sharp knife into the wood, they will feel soft and spongy if rot is present. As there are many types of damp, establish the cause of the problem before you carry out any repairs.

Severe Dry Rot attack to timbers and masonry

Dry rot thrives on moist timbers in poorly ventilated areas and has a cotton wool appearance, which turns a rusty red colour once the fungus gains control. Usually found in floor timbers, once established it is difficult to eradicate and needs to be professionally treated. All the affected timbers will have to be replaced.

Wet rot is a result of timbers becoming completely saturated, the affected timbers wrinkle and eventually crack along the grain. Fortunately wet rot will die out as soon as the cause of the damp has been removed, although any affected timbers will need to be replaced.

Rising damp is caused by water travelling up from the ground into the walls of the house and may be the result of a defective damp-proof course (dpc). As the moisture rises so it

The fungal strands of the Wet Rot fungus – Photos courtesy of Rentokil

collects salts from the bricks which crystallise on the internal plaster. Check to make sure that the dpc has not been bridged, for example by soil piled up against the wall and covering it.

Penetrating damp is usually caused by an exterior fault, for example, gutters or downpipes blocked by leaves and other debris so that during a storm water soaks into the adjoining wall. This eventually shows up as a damp patch on the inside wall. Alternatively the gutters, particularly if they are relatively old and made of cast iron, may be leaking. Clean gutters and downpipes regularly and replace any which are damaged or broken.

Condensation is a problem usually found in modern homes, it is the result of warm moisture-laden air (steam) condensing into water droplets when it meets a cold surface. If this is allowed to happen over a long period mould may develop on the affected wall or ceiling surfaces. Insulating your home may help to reduce the number of cold surfaces,

although improved ventilation in the rooms where the steam occurs – usually the kitchen and bathroom – will also help.

Recently a product called Sempatap was introduced to the DIY market to help combat the problems of condensation. It comprises a high grade latex foam bonded to a tough non-woven glass fibre surface which is fixed to the problem wall or ceiling in much the same way as you would fix wallpaper. The Sempatap lining raises the temperature of the covered surfaces by 2-3°C which is enough to inhibit the formation of condensation.

If there is damp in your home and you are in any doubt at all about the cause or how to deal with it, call in a professional company, such as Rentokil, to make a diagnosis and, where required, carry out the necessary treatment.

INSECT INFESTATION

Many homes may be affected by various insect pests, some are completely harmless, although others can cause a lot of damage. At the first sign of any insect infestation try to identify the cause and eradicate the problem as quickly as possible.

Woodworm is caused by the grubs of all wood-boring insects, although the most common is the furniture beetle. The female beetle lays her eggs in cracks and crevices in the timber of badly-fitting joints, when the grub hatches it burrows into the timber eating its way along the grain. When it eventually emerges two or more years later, leaving the familiar round flight hole about 2 mm (1/16″) in diameter, it's as an adult. These holes are often the first sign you have of infestation, although there may be several generations of beetle active inside the timber.

The furniture beetle is thought to inhabit three-quarters of British homes so most outbreaks of woodworm are almost certainly due to this particular pest. Other wood-boring insects which can cause even more damage include the deathwatch and long-horn beetles

Damage caused by Death Watch Beetle

which bore larger holes from 3 to 6 mm (1/8″ to 1/4″) in diameter.

If you think you have woodworm, contact a specialist company for advice, as they will be able to tell you the extent of the damage.

WINDOWS & DOORS

Door and window frames have to withstand moisture from both inside and out so, if the timber is not properly protected, dampness may occur causing the wood to gradually rot. Regular painting or staining is the preventative treatment required to stop this happening although, because they can be such time-consuming jobs, they are often not carried out properly. If you discover minor outbreaks of rot in any door or window frames, it can be treated using proprietary products such as Ronseal's Wood Repair System. If the timbers are badly decayed there is probably no alternative but to replace them.

Replacement window frames are available in a number of different materials, requiring the minimum of maintenance: aluminium and plastic (uPVC) as well as timber. Whatever your preference, it's well worth opting for double-glazing which will help reduce your fuel bills and make the house warmer.

The front door is usually the first means of entry for burglars as well as invited visitors so, if it is in a bad condition it will offer little resistance. Check both your front and back doors; if they were made from an inferior timber they may be badly warped or the timber frames may have rotted away. In both cases a replacement door is the answer. From a security point of view at least, all external doors should be made from good quality hardwood such as sapele, mahogany, iroko or rosewood. A large range of styles is available from DIY outlets such as Wickes and Magnet, but do try and choose a door which will be in keeping with the age of your property.

ELECTRICS AND WIRING

One area of your home which needs to be checked carefully at least once every five years is the wiring. A defective cable can start a fire or electrocute someone, so you could be dicing with death if you don't ensure that the wiring is in good condition. An old system, which uses rubber-covered sheathing is probably at the end of its useful life so should be replaced as soon as possible. If you have any round light switches or round pin sockets it is likely to indicate an old system. If you are in any doubt have the system checked by a qualified electrician who is on the roll of the National

Inspection Council for Electrical Installation Contracting (NICEIC). Many are also members of the Electrical Contractors Association. A modern system, with PVC-covered wires and cables should last at least 25 years.

If your wiring does need to be replaced it's well worth having a residual current circuit breaker (RCCB) incorporated with the mains switch in the consumer unit to protect all socket outlet circuits.

INSULATION

Despite all the advertising campaigns to save energy there are still many homes with inadequate insulation. Considerable savings can be made on the heating bills if your house is properly insulated, also the right insulation will help reduce draughts, making your home a more comfortable place to live.

From a cost-saving point of view, double-glazing is one of the least effective energy-saving measures, unless you opt for one of the DIY systems. However it does offer a number of benefits which are worth paying for: increased comfort, reduced noise and reduced condensation.

HEATING

Most homes these days have some form of central heating, and whatever system you have it should be serviced regularly. Ideally these services should take place during the summer when the heating can be switched off with the minimum of inconvenience and there is plenty of time to wait for any replacement parts to arrive. If your heating has not been serviced recently, get it checked immediately by a member of the Heating and Ventilating Contractors' Association.

As well as these regular maintenance checks, existing central heating systems may well benefit from being fitted with more modern and efficient controls, this is particularly true if your system is at least ten years old.

Despite the increasing importance of central heating, the traditional fireplace is regaining its popularity. In older properties the fireplaces which were boarded up during the 60s and 70s are now being opened up again to provide an attractive focal point for a room, whilst in modern properties more and more people are installing fires complete with special chimney flues.

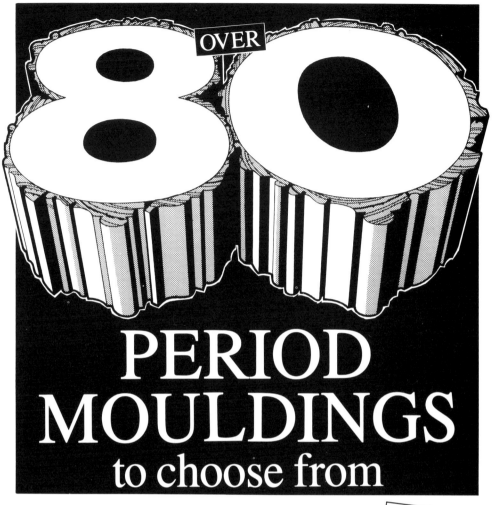

OVER 8O PERIOD MOULDINGS
to choose from

Regency, Georgian, Victorian, Edwardian, Gothic, Wren, Adams, now you can bring back the warmth, elegance and charm of bygone eras with this unique range of mouldings from Champion. All of them can be delivered to anywhere in the U.K.

Each moulding faithfully matches the exact profile of the original. They are all carefully machined from prime quality softwood or selected hardwood. They can be painted, polished, stained or clear varnished with little waste and virtually any quantity can be ordered.

Champion has a long established reputation as a timber specialist. All these mouldings are produced in our own mills using the latest machine technology, from timber selected and imported directly by us.

SPECIAL PROFILING SERVICE
If you need to match an existing moulding Champion can produce it from a sample or a drawing very economically. Alternatively, you can design your own.

CHAMPION
Leadership in Timber

CONTACT US FOR A LEAFLET

TIMBER MOULDINGS SPECIALISTS
Champion House, Burlington Road, New Malden, Surrey

UNDERSTANDING THE ELECTRICS

Although it is best to leave complex wiring jobs to a qualified electrician, it's worth understanding how the system works. Electricity is potentially dangerous and should be treated with the greatest of respect. However, provided you understand how the system works and take all the obvious precautions beforehand, such as switching off at the mains before you carry out any tasks, there is no reason why you can't tackle some of the simpler wiring jobs.

Electricity is supplied to your house through the **service cable** which goes to your **meter** through the **service box** which is fused. This is sealed by the Electricity Board and must never be touched. If the fuse in this box fails, call in the Electricity Board.

From the meter, the electricity goes to the **mains switch** which contròls the supply to your house. This is where the supply is turned off and on. In older homes, the mains switch may be located in a separate box; in modern homes it is part of the **fuse box** or **consumer unit** where the supply is split into separate circuits for power, lighting, cooking and so on, each with its own fuse. The electrical equipment and

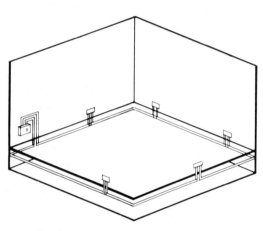

Ring Circuit

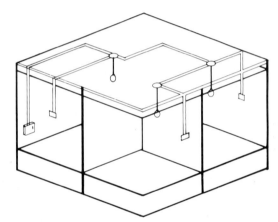

Loop-in lighting system

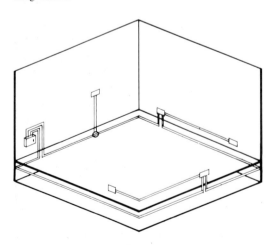

Ring circuit with spurs

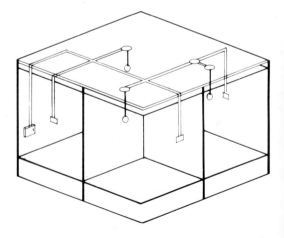

Junction box lighting system

wiring, from the meter onwards, is your responsibility.

Many homes are now being fitted with a **residual current circuit breaker (RCCB)** or **earth leakage circuit breaker (ELCB)** which notices any sudden change in the current flow and automatically switches it off. RCCBs may be incorporated with the mains switch in the consumer unit or be fitted elsewhere to protect one circuit. For safety, if you do not have an RCCB, it would be worth having one fitted.

Leading from the fuse box are several **circuit cables**. The circuit supplying the 13 amp socket outlets and plugs in most homes, and certainly all modern ones, is known as the **ring circuit**. This is a ring or loop of cable which goes from the consumer unit, 'visits' each socket in return and returns back to the consumer unit. It is protected by a 30 amp fuse.

There is no limit to the number of socket outlets which can be fitted to this circuit, so long as it does not serve a floor area of more than 100 square metres; the maximum load that can be taken at one time is about 7,500 watts. If you want to increase the number of sockets on the ring main, you can add extensions known as **spurs**. Regulations allow each spur to serve one fused connection unit for a fixed appliance or one single or double socket outlet. You can have as many spurs as there are sockets on the original circuit.

THE SYSTEM

A **radial circuit** feeds a number of socket outlets or fused connection units, but instead of returning to the consumer unit its cable stops at the last outlet. Any number of socket outlets can be supplied by one of these circuits but the size of cable and the fuse rating changes accordingly.

Domestic lighting circuits use a radial system, but can be one of two types. A **loop-in system** has a single cable running from ceiling rose to ceiling rose, terminating at the last one on the circuit, with a single cable running from each ceiling rose to the light switch. The second, older, type is the **junction box system** where each light has its own junction box with a cable running from this box to the ceiling rose and another from the box to the light switch. In practice most lighting systems are a combination of these two methods.

FUSES

There is a limit to the amount of current that can pass through a conductor such as a wire. If more current flows along it than it is designed to carry, it could get overloaded and get dangerously hot, possibly even burst out in flames. To prevent this happening all domestic circuits are fitted with **fuses** which are deliberately designed to be the weak spot, so will melt or 'blow' before any damage can be done. For safety it is vital to always fit a fuse of the correct rating for a particular appliance or circuit and never replace a fuse with another of a higher rating or with any substitute piece of metal.

Basically there are two types of fuses used in household circuits:

Cartridge fuses, ceramic tubes containing fuse wire packed with fine sand, fit into rectangular three-pin plugs and come in three ratings: 3, 5 and 13 amps. All fused plugs are sold containing 13 amp fuses, so always check the rating of the appliance before fitting the plug and change the cartridge fuse if necessary. Always keep a supply of spare fuses. If a replaced fuse blows again as soon as the power is switched on, there is a fault or the circuit is overloaded − for example, there are too many appliances being used at the same time. Sort out the problem − fast.

FUSE COLOUR CODE

COLOUR	MAX. RATING	APPLIANCES
3 amp Red	750 watts	radio, clock, lamp, black & white tv
5 amp Black	1,000 watts	fridge, iron, hair dryer, toaster
13 amp Brown	3,000 watts	fire, kettle, washing machine, heater

Rewirable fuses have a porcelain fuse bridge fitted with two brass screws to take fuse wire. They fit into the fuse holder installed in the fuse board or consumer unit near the meter. Always keep spare fuse wire close to the fuse box. If one of the fuses blows it will need to be replaced with new wire of the correct amp rating. Never insert fuse wire which is heavier than the gauge intended for the circuit. Don't stretch or strain the new wire as you tighten the screws.

Whatever type of fuse used, they are rated in the same way. Cartridge fuses are colour coded and marked with the appropriate amp rating for a certain type of rating. Fuse wire is bought wrapped around a card which is clearly labelled.

Some consumer units will be fitted with **miniature circuit breakers (MCBs)** instead of fuse holders, which are amp-rated just like fuses. When you want to isolate a circuit, instead of removing the MCB you just switch it off. When a fault occurs the circuit breaker will switch off automatically, you just press the switch down – or the button in – to reset it. If it does not stay in the 'on' position there is a fault on the circuit. MCBs should not be confused with an RCCB. An MCB only works in the case of an overload where there is too much current; an RCCB operates when there is a change in the current flow.

CABLES AND FLEXES

Cables are used to carry the electricity supply to the socket outlets. They are oval in shape and meant to be permanently fixed. They are made of three conductors or wires, one is covered with red insulation (live), one with black (neutral) and the third, called the earth continuity conductor, is left bare. These wires are thick and fairly rigid.

Flexes, which connect the plug to the appliance, are also made up of three conductors and are known as three-core flex. They consist of lots of fine wire strands so that the flex is pliable and bends easily. The insulation coverings are different colours from those used on cables: live is brown, neutral is blue and earth is green and yellow. The outside insulation of most flex is made of plastic, although some appliances may be covered with rubber wrapped with braided linen, irons for example.

SAFETY

Whenever you are dealing with electricity always follow these guidelines:

■ Always switch off the power at the consumer unit and remove the circuit fuse carrier before inspecting or doing any work on any part of an electrical installation.

■ Turn off and disconnect any portable appliance or light fitting which is plugged in a socket before you start working on it.

■ Before you turn the power back on always double check all your work, especially connections.

■ Always use the correct tools for the job and use good quality materials.

  Wire cutters or diagonal cutters for cutting cable and flex to length.

  Wire strippers for removing insulation from individual wires – not the outer sheath of cable.

  Sharp knife to score the outer sheath of cable – be careful not to cut through the insulation of the wires inside.

  Thin-bladed screwdriver for unscrewing and screwing the brass terminal screws found in many electrical fittings.

■ Fuses are a vitally important safety device. Never fit one that is rated too highly for the circuit it is to protect. Never use any other type of wire or metal in place of a proper fuse or fuse wire.

■ Wear rubber soled shoes when working on any electrical installation.

UNDERSTANDING THE PLUMBING

If there was a leak in one of the pipes in your house would you know what to do? Whether or not you are willing to tackle your own plumbing – and increasingly more people are prepared to carry out minor repair and installation jobs – it is well worth while understanding the plumbing system in your home. Find out where the valves, stopcocks and draincocks are situated and turn them occasionally, so that if you're ever faced with an emergency you'll know where they are situated and they won't be too stiff to use.

WATER SUPPLY

Quite simply, cold water is supplied to the home from the public mains via a service pipe. At the point where the pipe enters the house, just above floor level, it is fitted with a main stopcock, which enables you to turn the water supply off and on. Just above is the draincock, which allows you to drain the house system if necessary. From the stopcock upwards, the plumbing becomes the responsibility of the householder – you!

Your home will have one of two systems:

Direct systems are only found in older properties. All the cold water taps and the toilets are fed directly from the rising main. The one plus point of such a system is that drinking water can be drawn from all the cold water taps in the house.

Indirect systems are found in most homes and are certainly fitted in all modern homes. The cold water supply enters the house under mains pressure and goes directly to the cold water storage cistern – usually located in the loft – via the rising main. Most of the cold water taps in the house, any appliances and all

The Moritz bathroom suite from Armitage Shanks

the toilets are indirectly supplied from this cistern under gravity pressure. The one exception is the cold water tap in the kitchen which is supplied via a branch pipe from the rising main to give a supply of clean drinking water.

Indirect systems have a number of advantages.

1. If there is a failure in the mains supply, there should always be a supply of water to flush the toilets.
2. Because the major part of the supply is under relatively low pressure, the system is fairly quiet; a high mains pressure can cause 'water hammer' as the water tries to go round the tight bends.
3. Because very few outlets are connected to the mains, there is less likelihood of the mains supply becoming contaminated.

WASTE

A drainage system is designed to carry dirty water and toilet waste to the main sewer via underground drains. All the different branches of the waste system are protect by U-bend traps full of water which are designed to stop sewer and drain smells entering the house. Depending on the age of your home, it will be fitted with one of two waste systems:

A two-pipe system is the most common and found in older properties. It uses two separate waste systems. Waste water from baths, sinks and basins drains into a waste pipe which feeds into a yard gully located at ground level; a separate kitchen sink waste pipe normally drains into the same gully. Meanwhile, toilet waste is fed separately into a large diameter soil pipe. Both the yard gully and soil pipe discharge into an underground inspection chamber, or manhole, which provides access to the main drains.

A single stack system is found in most modern homes dating from the 60s. All waste from basins, baths and toilets drains into a single vertical soil pipe or stack which, unlike a two-pipe system, is often built inside the house. The only possible exception may be the kitchen sink, which may still drain into a gully located at ground level.

REGULATIONS

Your local water authority insists that certain regulations are followed if you alter any existing installations, or if you install new plumbing, to ensure that you do not contaminate the water supply. Building Regulations cover the design of waste systems to ensure there is no danger to health. So, if you want to make any alterations to your water supply or waste, first seek the advice of your local water authority (their address will be on your water rates bill) or council.

For example, if you want to change a tap it must satisfy the requirements of the local water byelaws – and some taps don't. Also, your local water authority needs seven days' notice, in writing, of any proposed alteration you intend to make.

WATER SOFTENERS

When rainwater falls on to the earth, it is absorbed into the soil. In many areas of the country this water passes through certain types of rock, such as limestone and chalk, picking up various minerals as it does so. It is these minerals, now dissolved in the water, which cause hard water, the bane of many a householder. Hard water is a nuisance because not only does it cause an unpleasant scum to form around baths and wash basins, but it also furs up kettles, water pipes and showers, greatly reducing their efficiency.

If you live in a hard water area, a domestic water softener provides a cost efficient solution to the problem. They work on a process of 'ion exchange'. Most units are fitted to the incoming water supply above the main stopcock. As the water passes through the unit so the damaging calcium and magnesium minerals are trapped on a bed of synthetic resin and replaced by sodium salts. In time the resin will have become totally saturated with these unwanted minerals and will need to be rejuvenated by washing with a solution of sodium chloride or common salt. Most modern softeners automatically regenerate the resin bed, although you will need to put in fresh supplies of salt occasionally.

Water softeners come in a vast range of sizes, depending on the amount of water you use, and specialist companies such as Kinetico or Permutit, offer a range of softeners for all domestic appliances and will be able to advise you on what you need.

ADVICE

If you are in any doubt about making any alterations to your water system, seek the advice of a professional plumber. For a list of registered plumbers in your area contact the Institute of Plumbing, 64 Station Lane, Hornchirch, Essex RM12 6NB. ☎ 04024 72791.

A GUIDE TO INSULATION

You can't prevent heat loss from a building, but it can be reduced. If the insulation standards required in today's new houses were applied to a typical pre-World War II dwelling, the amount of heating needed could be cut by 35%

As a guide, an average pre-World War II semi-detached house with cavity walls loses heat as follows:

35% through the walls

25% through the roof

15% into the ground

15% through draughts and door openings

10% through window glass

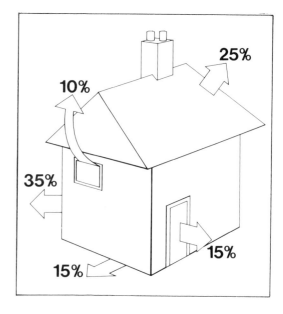

Many insulation methods are possible, but not all are practical or effective and the pay-back period for others may not justify the expense. Draughtproofing, for example, will repay its cost most quickly, followed by hot water tank lagging, loft insulation, cavity wall insulation and double-glazing – in that order. Measures with the shortest pay-back period are those you can do yourself for materials' cost only. Any increases in fuel costs relative to insulation costs will shorten the pay-back periods.

DRAUGHTPROOFING

This is simple and effective and DIY draughtstrips and sealants to fix around doors and windows are inexpensive to buy. Choose from foam or rubber tube strips and a variety of products for letterboxes and keyholes. The cost of draughtproofing will probably be repaid in one year. Don't forget that a fully fitted carpet is an effective way of reducing draughts through floorboards and under skirtings.

Constructing an external porch or conservatory will create an air trap which reduces heat loss, but reduced heating costs alone will not justify the expense. A simple measure, such as closing internal doors, will reduce draughts, so fit door-closing springs or rising butt hinges.

HOT WATER TANK

Lagging the hot water cylinder is one of the insulation jobs most rapidly repaid – it can save the cash equivalent of 16 baths a week. Special jackets, made to British Standard 5616, will do the job perfectly, provided you buy the right shape for your cylinder. Remember the thicker the lagging, the greater the savings.

LOFTS

Loft insulation should be at least 100 mm (4″) thick and preferably 150 mm (6″). Use either glass-fibre matting between the ceiling joists, or a loose-fill material such as vermiculite or expanded polystyrene granules. Loose-fill materials need to be laid to a greater depth (150 mm/6″ or 225 mm/9″) than glass-fibre matting to achieve the same insulation level. Blown-fibre insulation is another alternative, but you will need to use a specialist contractor for the job. Use a combination of materials where access problems prevent you putting glass-fibre in tight corners. You can also add extra roof insulation by fixing bitumen-bonded paper to the underside of roof tiles. Do take care to maintain ventilation levels in the loft by leaving open the space at the eaves, which permits air circulation. If you don't, moisture could accumulate, resulting in condensation and rot. Investment in roof insulation can be repaid in as little as two years.

HOW TO INSULATE YOUR LOFT

If your loft does not have any form of insulation

New look Micafil the perfect home insulation is an entirely natural mineral product.

In today's world when natural (Green) products and produce are in much greater demand, Micafil stands out as the perfect product for safe home insulation.

Unlike many other forms of insulation, Micafil contains no man-made chemicals, is non-irritant, clean and hazard free.

More and more people are taking a new look at Micafil and discovering for themselves the many advantages it has over other forms of insulation. This versatile product can be used in the conventional insulation of lofts (simply pour in between joists and level to required depth, or top up existing insulation using the same technique).

Alternatively, Micafil can be put to use in a number of other areas – use it between partition walls and floors to reduce sound, or mix with portland cement (see bag for details) to create a perfect thermal barrier for floors, backboilers and flues.

Everywhere it seems, there are new and exciting applications being found for this remarkable and natural product.

Insist on the natural choice for your home.

Micafil is available from all major builders merchants.

The Natural Choice For All Round Insulation

MICAFIL

It's Only Natural

DUPRE VERMICULITE (A Division of Microfine Minerals Ltd) Tamworth Road, Hertford, Herts, SG13 7DL. Tel: (0992) 582541

at all, you are literally throwing money away – some 25% of your heat escapes through the roof and you could make significant savings on your heating bills if it was insulated properly. Even if there's already some insulation there it could be worth 'topping up' - anything less than 25 mm (1") is not enough; you should aim for a depth of 150 mm (6").

One of the most popular ways of insulating a roof is using mineral wool insulating blanket which comes in rolls to fit between the joists. To calculate how many rolls you'll need, count the number of spaces between the joists and multiply by the width of the roof, and don't forget to include the top of the loft hatch!

Because the loft space will be colder after you have insulated, you will also need to insulate any water tanks in the loft as well as all the pipes. Measure the water tank and the lengths and diameters of all the pipes, including overflows.

EQUIPMENT

- Mineral wool blanket
- Nose and mouth mask (mineral wool insulation can act as an irritant, always wear a mask to protect against nasal irritation)
- Pair of protective gloves (to avoid skin irritation)
- Torch or inspection lamp
- Planks (to stand on)
- Pair of scissors or sharp cutting knife
- String
- Drawing pins or nails
- 25 mm (1") thick polystyrene sheeting (to cover water tanks)
- Split foam pipe lagging
- Insulation tape

METHOD

1. Clean out the loft as much as possible to give yourself a large working area. Remove any 'walking' boards placed over the joists.

2. Make good any cracks or holes in the ceiling between the joists. They could allow warm, moist air to get into the loft, resulting in condensation.

3. Put on your mask and protective gloves and lay down the planks.

4. It is vital that there is unobstructed ventilation at the eaves to prevent condensation. As you work, always cut the end of the blanket, which fits between the joists at the eaves, into a wedge shape.

5. Starting at one end of the loft, close to the eaves, kneel on one of the planks and start unrolling the blanket between the joists where the roof and floor meet. Don't push the blanket right into the edge.

6. Continue unrolling the blanket, being careful not to compact the insulation or press it down into awkward corners. When you get to the far end, cut the blanket into a wedge so that it fits loosely into the eaves.

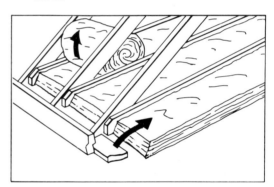

7. Continue working in this way making sure that where one roll ends and another starts, they butt up closely to one another.

8. Don't forget to insulate the top of the trap door. Cut the blanket to size and fix with dabs of adhesive, then hold it in place with lengths of string attached with drawing pins or nails.

9. The only part of the loft floor which should not be covered is the area directly beneath the cold water storage tank. This will allow heat from the house to come through and help prevent the tank freezing in cold weather.

10. Take the insulating blanket up the sides of the tank and tie firmly in place with string.

11. Cut the polystyrene sheet to fit the top of the tank and place over the top.

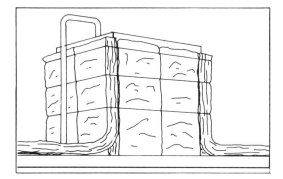

12. To insulate the pipes, simply open the foam lagging along the split and slip over the pipe. Secure the split with insulation tape. Where two lengths of foam butt up to one another, seal the join with tape.

13. Pipes which are difficult to reach are easily tackled. Slip the foam lagging on an easily accessible part of the pipe, secure with tape and push it along until it reaches the awkward area. It should be flexible enough to go round most bends.

14. Pay particular attention to tee joints in the pipes. The lagging should be mitred to fit and secured with tape.

NB If you are increasing the thickness of your loft insulation, say from 100 mm (4″) to 200 mm (8″) simply 'cross lay' the second layer of blanket at right-angles to the joists. However, you will need to place planks of wood at right-angles to the joists, on top of the insulation, to walk on.

No matter how light you think you are, never stand on the floor area between the joists — you are likely to go through the ceiling!

An alternative to mineral wool blanket is the Rockwool Multi Purpose Slab which gives excellent thermal and acoustic insulation

WALLS

More heat is lost through walls than anywhere else, but, unlike roof insulation, wall insulation cannot be carried out using inexpensive DIY methods. Cavity walls − which account for most of the houses built this century − can be filled with an approved material by an approved firm. Urea formaldehyde foam, blown mineral fibre or polystyrene/polyure-thane pellets of foam are the materials you can choose from.

ADVICE

For a list of registered installers in your area contact the National Cavity Insulation Association, P.O.Box 12, Haslemere, Surrey GU27 3AM. ☎ 0428 54011

WINDOWS & DOUBLE-GLAZING

Windows can be double-glazed, which has the added advantage of reducing draughts as well as cutting out dust and noise, although it is possible that it will increase condensation within the house. Professional double-glazing can be very expensive and although it will cut window heat loss (as distinct from draughts) by half, this will only represent an overall 5% saving on your fuel bill. The same money spent on a more modern heating boiler, or extra controls, may save you more. Obviously, fitting one of the cheaper DIY secondary glazing kits would be more cost effective.

The benefits of double-glazing are well known. It will help cut down the amount of heat loss through your windows − reducing expensive heating bills; will virtually eliminate draughts through window frames; will considerably reduce any outside noise; and act as a dust insulator. In addition, it will also increase the air temperature in the area of room close to the window, making it more comfortable to be in, thus increasing the amount of usable room space during colder months.

Double-glazing works by trapping a layer of air between two panes of glass − the optimum air gap is around 18 mm (¾"). Broadly speaking there are two systems to choose from:

Secondary double-glazing is simple and inexpensive, but should only be considered if your existing window frames are in good

Replacement double-glazed window from Magnet

condition. It simply involves fitting a second pane of glass - or possibly an acrylic sheet or plastic film − over the existing window, either over individual panes (which is the least effective method as the draughts will still come through the window frames), or over the entire window itself. Whole window systems can have panels which slide open or are hinged, although their biggest disadvantage is that they will impede the opening of the outer window.

Primary double-glazing is where the normal single pane of glass is completely replaced with two panes which have a hermetically sealed air gap between them and is the more favoured method, although more expensive. Because air cannot circulate in the gap, very little heat is transferred from the inner pane to the outer pane and cold air cannot be transferred from the outer pane to the inner one. As a result little heat is lost through the glass.

Some companies are now filling this gap with inert gas to reduce the amount of heat which can cross the cavity, improving the efficiency of the double-glazing unit. Others use low-emission glass which has a special coating on the inside of the outer pane to prevent the heat in the room escaping by 'reflecting' it back into the room. Solar control glass is also a fairly new development and will help to keep the room cool in summer by reducing unwanted 'solar gain'.

If you opt for primary double-glazing, you need to give some careful thought to both the window style and the material the frame is made in. Basically there are two types of window:

Casement where the window frames are fitted with hinged sashes (the name given to the section which opens).

Sash which has vertically sliding (up and down) frames. If both top and bottom sashes open they are known as double hung sash windows.

You can get both of these types as replacement windows and many have lockable catches and projecting hinges which make them more secure and easier to clean than their predecessors. Wherever possible try and choose a window style which complements the period of your property – many a house has been ruined by an insensitive choice of replacement window. Nowadays you can get small Georgian paned windows, leaded lights and bow windows for single glazed replacement windows as well as double-glazed units. As the choice available is extremely wide take your time looking at what the different manufacturers offer. For example, would a top-hung window be more beneficial than a conventional casement window? If you're thinking of patio doors, would a tilt-and-slide door be more practical than a single two-panel slider?

When it comes to choosing the frame material, the option is between timber, aluminium and plastic, or a combination of these materials.

Timber is the traditional material for window frames. Choose hardwood if you want a natural wood finish, softwood which has been impregnated with timber preservative if you want a painted finish. The cheaper frames are made from a paint-grade softwood; next up the scale come frames made from a superior softwood, such as Douglas fir, which can be painted or stained. Most expensive are hardwood frames, such as mahogany. Timber is

a good insulator and will provide good thermal performance. Also, as it is a strong material, it will provide good security and can be fitted with quality bolts and locks if required. The one disadvantage is that it will need to be regularly maintained, either painted or stained. Timber-framed, double-glazing units are available in standard sizes or can be made-to-measure.

Aluminium is a very popular choice for replacement windows as it's virtually maintenance free. It has either a silver-grey anodised or grey, black or white acrylic finish and has to be fitted to a subframe, made of either hardwood or uPVC. Anodised aluminium only needs to be cleaned occasionally with a mild detergent solution, although the wooden frame will need to be regularly repainted or stained. Aluminium frames used to suffer badly from condensation, but this problem has now virtually been resolved and companies are either fitting a thermal break between the window and frame or coating the aluminium with plastic. If you are thinking of buying aluminium, check before you buy. Another disadvantage is that aluminium is a relatively soft material so could be forced by intruders, ensure they are fitted with good locks. They're available in some standard sizes, but are mostly made-to-measure.

Plastic (unplasticised polyvinyl chloride or uPVC) is fast becoming a popular choice for replacement windows, although it is likely to be the most expensive option. It has good insulating properties, has no subframe which needs to be maintained and only needs an occasional wash down. However, it could be vulnerable from a security point of view so ensure that the frames are reinforced internally. Plastic may lose its shiny surface after prolonged exposure to the sun, can discolour in bright sunlight and could become brittle. It's mostly available made-to-measure.

When you're choosing any type of double-glazing do give some thought to safety. In an emergency it may be necessary to escape from the room via the window so never install a completely fixed double-glazing system or one which only has a small top-hinged window. Ensure that at least one of the windows in the unit is either hinged or sliding and can be opened quickly for an escape.

Another important safety aspect to consider is the glass you use. Every year there are around 27,000 accidents requiring hospital treatment involving glass doors and windows. Accidents will happen but you can make sure that you reduce the risk of serious injury by ensuring that you use safety glass, particularly if there are young children in your family. There are two types of safety glass:

Toughened or **tempered** glass is up to five times as strong as ordinary glass, so is extremely difficult to break. When it does break, it turns into thousands of small granules which are relatively harmless.

Laminated glass is a 'sandwich' of two sheets of glass with a layer of plastic in between. On impact the glass may crack, but the plastic interlayer holds the pieces together, so there is unlikely to be any dangerous fragments of glass to cause any injuries. As laminated glass remains whole, even after it breaks, it will also continue to provide an effective barrier to keep out the elements and intruders.

Replacing a window should not require planning permission, but if you significantly alter your windows, by enlarging the opening for example, you would be well advised to consult the Building Control Officer at your local authority. You will certainly need permission if you live in a listed building or conservation area.

Contrary to popular belief, fitting replacement windows is a job which can be carried out by a competent DIY enthusiast. Single glazed replacement window kits and sealed double-glazing units are readily available from branches of W.H. Newson, Magnet and Wickes.

Whether or not you are willing to tackle such a job really depends on your own capabilities. If you are in any doubt – and you must remember that double-glazed units can be very heavy and unwieldly - perhaps it would be a good idea to leave it to a reputable company. The double-glazing industry has suffered badly in the past from 'cowboy operators' but any company which belongs to the Glass & Glazing Federation has to follow a strict code of ethical practice for the way their members should treat the public. They also operate a deposit indemnity fund and a scheme for settling customers' complaints. Write to them at 44-48

UPVC horizontal sliding secondary double-glazing from Polycell

Borough High Street, London SE1 1XB for a list of members in your area.

SECONDARY DOUBLE-GLAZING

Secondary glazing is an effective way of reducing heat loss through your windows. In very simple terms, it comprises a pane of glass or sheet of acrylic, which is fitted to the inside of an existing single-glazed window. It works by trapping a pocket of air between the outer layer and the secondary (inner) layer, which produces an insulating effect. The secondary glazing can be glass, plastic sheeting or even plastic film. It's not the thickness of the material used to provide the glazing which matters, but the air gap between the two layers, so the larger the gap the more effective the results.

Where possible you should aim for a gap of about 18 mm (¾"), although if you are troubled by outside noise, a bigger air gap – of between 100 and 200 mm (4" to 8") – will be necessary.

Secondary glazing can be fitted in several places:

- To the sash frames, which will reduce heat loss through the glass and enable the window to be opened, but will not stop any draughts.

- To the window frame, which will reduce heat loss and stop draughts. With a fixed panel system, this will prevent the window from being opened.

- Across the window reveal where it literally sits on the window sill to reduce heat loss and stop draughts. Once again with a fixed panel system the window cannot be opened.

Perhaps the simplest and cheapest type of secondary glazing is plastic film (the kind used for wrapping foodstuffs). However, this should only be regarded as a short-term treatment, suitable for one winter at the most.

Equipment

- Double-sided sticky tape

- Kitchen film of the appropriate width

- Sharp knife

- Hair dryer

Seasonal double-glazing film from Sellotape

Method

1. Clean the window frame thoroughly, using a clean cloth and washing-up liquid to remove any grease, rinse with clean water and wipe dry.

2. Apply the double-sided tape to the frame edges and peel off the backing paper.

3. Starting at the top of the window, stretch the film across the top of the frame and let it adhere to the tape.

4. Holding the roll steady with one hand, carefully unwind the film applying light pressure only until it is correctly positioned, then rub down on to the tape all round.

5. Carefully cut the film against the frame with a sharp knife.

6. Use a hair dryer to shrink the film and remove the crinkles. Start at an upper corner and move diagonally across the film with the dryer about 6 mm (¼") away from the surface.

7. Once the film is taut, cut off any excess using the sharp knife.

FIXED PANEL SECONDARY GLAZING

More versatile than plastic film are the various DIY panel systems, some are designed to be permanently fixed, others come with fixed and hinged panels, others have sliding panels. Most are designed to be used with plastic sheeting or glass, which can be taken down and stored during the summer months, although the fixings remain in position. There are different methods of fixing but here we describe a system using a plastic edging strip which slots over the edge of the glass or rigid plastic panels.

Equipment

- Rigid plastic sheet or glass panels - for sizes see below

- Extending metal rule

- Straightedge

- Pencil

- Sharp knife

- Proprietary plastic edging strip and fasteners

- Scissors

- Screws

- Screwdriver

Method

1. Measure the windows to work out the size of the glass or plastic sheets. Treat fixed and opening windows separately. Where appropriate one sheet can be fixed across the whole window recess. The glass or rigid plastic should overlap the window by about 10 mm (⅜") on each edge.

2. If using rigid plastic, and it has to be cut to size, mark the size with a pencil, then hold a straightedge along the line and use a sharp knife to score the line several times. Snap the sheet over the edge of a table.

3. Press the edging strip on to the glass or rigid plastic all the way round, starting at the middle of one side. Don't cut off the strip at the corners, but mitre it by cutting a V-shaped notch with scissors or a sharp knife. (A special mitre block may be supplied to do this.)

4. Clean the inside of the windows thoroughly.

5. Now hold the glass or rigid plastic panel in position over the window and get someone else to mark the top and bottom edges on the frame for the fastener positions.

6. Loosely screw two fasteners on both top and bottom edges of the frame at the intervals specified for the type of edging strip you're using.

7. Hold the glass or rigid plastic panel in position against the frame, tighten the fasteners securely to hold it in place. Now fit the remaining fasteners.

8. Repeat for all other windows.

Before you install any secondary glazing ensure that:

- You can escape from the room in an emergency - rigid plastic sheet does not break easily.

- You can open at least one window in the room for ventilation.

- There will be enough air in the room to supply air burning fires — open fires, gas fires or cookers and flued boilers.

SAFETY

A word of warning. Never block air-bricks in the wall or permanent ventilators in windows. Kitchens and bathrooms need ventilation to prevent condensation, whilst ventilator bricks allow air to circulate under the floor to discourage rising damp and rot. Permanent ventilators in closed fireplaces should also be left free to keep chimneys dry. Most important of all, gas, oil and solid fuel heating systems need a certain amount of air to burn safely. Unless you're all electric, or your boiler has a balanced flue, for safety you should allow adequate ventilation in any room where there's a fuel-burning appliance.

A GUIDE TO CENTRAL HEATING

What are the options when it comes to choosing a new central heating system and how can you improve and update an existing system? The main purpose of a central heating system is to make your home feel comfortable. For most people that means a temperature of about 21°C (70°F) in living rooms and 15 to 18°C (60 to 65°F) in bedrooms, bathrooms and the kitchen. However, individual requirements will vary widely.

If you are out at work all day and have no children, your heating is probably only required twice during the day. If you have a large family, you will use more rooms in your home as well as more hot water, whilst invalids and the elderly need a higher room temperature than is normal. So, if you are planning to install central heating, a system designed specifically for your needs will always be better and more efficient in the long run than an off-the-shelf package which requires a low initial outlay.

In simple terms you can choose between a 'wet' system, which uses a boiler, pump, pipes, hot water cylinder, radiators and controls and can be based on any fuel, or a 'dry' system, using gas convector heaters or electric storage heaters.

Wet systems are the most commonly chosen. They comprise:

A **boiler** in which the fuel is burnt, which can be wall-mounted or freestanding. Some gas boilers are so compact that they can be concealed inside an ordinary cupboard. If you don't want a boiler in the kitchen, one alternative is a back-boiler which fits into an old fireplace with a solid fuel or gas fire which can be used independently of the boiler. If you opt for a back boiler it may be necessary to increase the number of radiators in the rooms to maintain the required temperature when the fire is not in use.

The water is heated in the boiler and then pumped round the system through a series of **pipes** to the **heat emitters** - the engineer's term

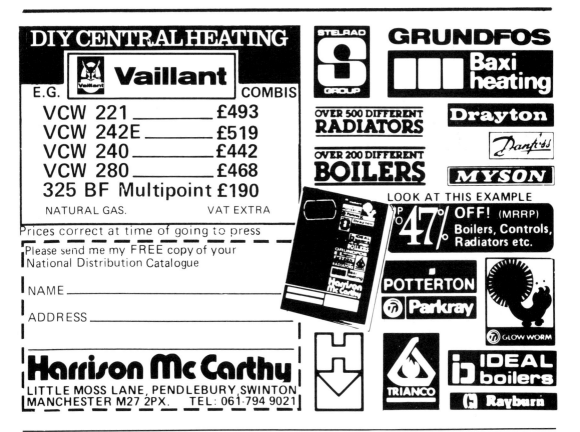

The 'Sculptur' towel radiator from Zehnder

those by ThermalPlus, are increasingly popular and can provide over twice the heat output of any ordinary single panel radiator of the same size, so you can have all the heat you want from a radiator half the size.

You feel warm at lower room temperatures with radiant heat, so in order to get maximum radiant heat avoid placing furniture in front of radiators and don't allow curtains to hang over them. Radiators are best positioned under windows, as this helps reduce the cooling effects of the window and reduces down draughts and cold spots in the room.

Skirting heaters are very unobtrusive but relatively expensive. This is partly due to the need to insert 'dummy' sections where heating is not required. Without these dummies the room may appear unbalanced. The big advantage of skirting heaters is to minimise draughts by spreading heat evenly throughout the room.

Automatic controls can be incorporated into even the most elementary central heating system. Basic controls consist of a boiler thermostat, timer or programmer, room thermostat, radiator valves and a hot water cylinder thermostat. Additional controls are available and will help keep your fuel bills down. These include thermostatically controlled radiator valves, such as those by Danfoss and Drayton, which take over the job of cutting off hot water flow to individual radiators when the room is warmed by strong sunlight or by 'waste' heat from the cooker, tv or the presence of lots of people. Zone valves, will cut out whole sections of the house at certain times (the south side during sunny weather or bedrooms during the day time) and room thermostats which provide individual temperature control to each room. A frost thermostat will protect your pipes in the coldest weather.

for radiators and convectors. A new generation of attractively styled radiators is available to fit in with almost any choice of decor. Runtalrad for example offer a range of colours and designs, whilst Zehnder have one shaped like a ladder designed to act as both a heat emitter and drying rack. Convector radiators, such as

WHICH FUEL?

The cost of installing central heating can vary a good deal, depending on the amount of work involved and where you live. Never take the unsupported word of one of the fuel suppliers - they have a clear interest in selling more fuel — and always try to compare at least two fuels.

Carefully consider which fuel is best suited for you needs. All fuels may not be available in all areas, although in most circumstances you will have a choice of at least two.

Gas is by far the most popular choice of heating fuel and is widely available. It requires no storage facilities and is ideally suited to automatic control. Boilers are available with virtually every required heat output and come in both floor-standing and wall-mounted models, some of which are very compact. They can have a conventional flue (chimney) or be room sealed (balanced flue) where the boiler has to be located on an outside wall. If you are not fitted with a mains gas supply your local gas region is obliged to connect you if your house is within 23 metres (25yds) of an existing main and it is required for ordinary domestic consumption.

LPG Liquefied petroleum gas can be a useful option if you cannot be connected to mains gas. However a large storage tank is required and the overall cost will be higher than natural gas.

Oil is chosen today mainly by users who have no access to gas but who require more automatic operation than is possible with solid fuel and are not prepared to pay for on-peak electricity or risk power cuts. Oil is also popular as a standby for boilers which are adapted to burn more than one fuel. Its main disadvantage is that it requires a large storage tank in an accessible position.

Solid fuel used to mean coal and smokeless fuels like Coalite, but today it also includes wood, either in log or woodchip form which can be used in fires such as those by Jøtul. Open fires have been regaining some of their traditional popularity and will provide a room with an attractive focal point, however, they have a low heat output – about 3kW maximum – will only provide radiant heat and should only be considered alongside a full central heating system. An enclosed roomheater with a back boiler burns fuel more efficiently and has a heat output of up to about 12 kW. This is sufficient for smaller three-bedroom houses. It is possible to turn down enclosed roomheaters to a tick over level when heat is not required.

Solid fuel can also be used (like any other fuel) to fire a remote freestanding central heating boiler; most boilers of this type are gravity (hopper) fed. Solid fuel systems are not suited to automatic control as they react slowly to temperature changes and will require a separate fuel store. They also need regular maintenance.

Electricity is an attractive alternative to oil and solid fuel, because it is very clean, requires no fuel storage and, unlike other types of heater, does not need a flue. Off-peak electricity, known as Economy 7 is used to heat insulated storage heaters, which give out the heat during the daytime; these heaters can usually be positioned anywhere within a room. The biggest drawback is when extra heat is required in very cold weather during on-peak hours to maintain the heat output, which adds considerably to the running costs.

UPDATING YOUR HEATING

If you already have a central heating system fitted, which is over ten years old, it is well worth having it surveyed by a competent heating engineer. This will reveal if it is as efficient as it could be. It's a fact, whether you use gas, oil or solid fuel, that a modern replacement boiler and updated controls could slash your central heating bills. Savings of 25p in every pound are usual and 35p is possible. Irrespective of the savings, you can be sure of improved comfort and reliability. So what's changed in the past few years to make these savings possible? Quite simply the answer is technology. A modern boiler uses less fuel to produce the same amount of heat than its predecessors and its output can be matched more exactly to your particular heating and hot water needs than was possible in the past.

It's up to you to decide what temperatures you find comfortable and how long to run your central heating. The actual cash you save will depend on these and several other factors:

■ The age and condition of your old boiler, generally the older it is the more wasteful it is of energy.

■ The type of new boiler you are interested in; gas boilers in particular have been made more efficient and the ultra-modern condensing boiler, which is suitable for many applications can give exceptional fuel savings.

- The type of fuel you use at present (the cost of some fuels has risen more than others).

- The types of fuel available to you for future use.

- The existing controls. Some old systems may only have an on-off timer and boiler thermostat.

- The new controls you could fit.

- The level of insulation in your home.

One option is to have a new boiler, where lower fuel costs is only one of the benefits. A new boiler is smaller (leaving you more room), simpler to operate and safer than its older counterparts, it's also cleaner, quieter, more reliable, more elegant and compact. It's worth remembering, too, that an old boiler which has not be maintained regularly could suffer from safety problems, including defective gas valves, a blocked or corroded flue or faulty automatic ignition.

It's hard to believe that many central heating systems installed some 12 to 15 years ago had no controls other than a timer, so you could either have the heating on or off. Make sure your system has a room thermostat as a minimum, and consider additional controls as well.

To be sure of maximum fuel cost savings you need good controls. With modern automatic controls the beauty is that you can forget the ritual of switching on and off. Once you've set the temperature and time you can just sit back in comfort. The following are examples of the types of money saving controls now available:

Hot water thermostat will control the operating temperature of the water supply leaving the boiler and stops the water from boiling.

Room thermostats automatically control room temperature and will switch off the heating system when your home reaches the pre-set temperature you've chosen for your comfort. If the temperature falls below this level, the system starts up again. Consider both a centralised room thermostat, for the whole house, as well as separate thermostats for each

The Drayton Tempus Four programmer

room. The latter will switch off the heat where it's not wanted (bedrooms, for example) when it's not wanted.

A programmer or **time switch** allows you to completely control when your heating switches on and off. Modern seven-day programmers for example allow you to pre-set the on/off phases of the heating and hot water separately and at a different time for seven days. Programmers should always be used in conjunction with a room thermostat and hot water cylinder thermostat.

Thermostatic radiator valves cut off the flow of hot water to individual radiators to maintain the desired room temperature. They automatically compensate for any extra heat which may occur, for example through sunlight streaming through the window or if the room is full of people.

ADVICE

If you would like impartial advice, either about a new central heating system, or updating an existing one, consult an independent heating installer who will be able to help you assess the needs of your family and your property. The Heating and Ventilating Contractors' Association is the officially recognised organisation representing central heating contractors. For the name and phone number of your nearest HVCA installer write to: Heating and Ventilating Contractors' Association, 34 Palace Court, London W2 4JG. or 23 Heriot Row, Edinburgh EH3 6EW. Or 543 Antrim Road, Belfast BT15 3BU. Or telephone the Home Heating Link Line: 0345 581158, which will only cost you the price of a local call.

PART 2

HOW TO DECORATE YOUR HOME

BE YOUR OWN INTERIOR DESIGNER

Colour is probably the single most important factor in decorating. Used properly it can make a small room seem larger or a dark room lighter; it can visually alter a room's dimensions and can completely change a room's mood and atmosphere. Unfortunately, most of us are not very good at using colour properly, we're unable to imagine how colours will look and, as a result, are often scared of making a drastic change just in case it proves to be a disaster. Instead we wistfully look through home decorating magazines, admiring the imaginative schemes and then tend to play it safe and opt for pale colours which will go with anything.

First, let me assure you that there's no magic formula to using colour successfully; at the end of the day the right way is to do what pleases you most. But if you would like to be more adventurous with your decor, you need to know how to plan a decor scheme and to learn exactly what colour is, how it relates to its surroundings and how it can be used. Once you have grasped the basic principles you are half-way there.

Whether you're creating a colour scheme from scratch or updating an existing one it's important to plan it properly. The best piece of advice is to take your time. You are likely to be living with your choice for many years to come so be patient, that way you should avoid mistakes. Never rush into buying a particular wallcovering or fabric just because you like it without first planning the rest of the scheme. Instead use a sample of the design and plan a scheme around it (see 'Creating a Scheme'). But before you commit yourself to anything, sit down and work out the constraints.

■ What furnishings do you have to retain: carpet, furniture, curtains?

■ Does the room have any good or bad features? Which ones do you want to emphasise and which ones need to be disguised?

■ What is the style/age of the room and house? Are there any distinctive decorative features?

■ How practical does the decor have to be? If you have children or pets it needs to be very hardwearing; less so if it's for a guest bedroom.

■ What is the room's aspect and does it get a lot of natural daylight?

■ What is your budget?

Now start thinking about the mood you would like to achieve: warm and cosy, cool and bright, cheerful, pretty, stylish or restful. If you need inspiration there are a number of ways you can get help. Look through home interest books and magazines. Look at other people's homes, as well as decor ideas used in window displays, restaurants, even stately homes. Look through wallpaper books and visit interior design shops and showrooms. Consider the colour combinations used in the latest fashion collections.

You may find it will help in the planning stages to make a rough diagram of the room to be decorated and to list all the relevant information, which can then be kept for future reference. Put down the room's dimensions, window position(s), aspect and direction of the sun, doors, radiators, etc., together with any existing furnishings and features.

THE COLOUR WHEEL

It has been said that the human eye can distinguish over 10 million different colours, although every single one is based on the colours of the rainbow: red, yellow, orange, green, blue, indigo and violet, plus black and white. So it's not surprising that we get confused about choosing a colour scheme. A good starting point in learning how colours relate to one another and how they can be used is the colour wheel, which is made up from the colours of the rainbow arranged in a circle.

The **primary colours** red, yellow and blue, are the three key colours. They are known as primaries because they are pure colours, you cannot mix them from any other colours.

Secondary colours orange, green and violet, are mixed from equal amounts of two primaries: red + yellow = orange; yellow + blue = green; blue + red = violet. In between come any number of intermediate colours all mixed from their neighbouring colours.

Tertiary colours are made by mixing a primary colour with its adjacent secondary colour, such as blue and green mixed to make aqua.

Within each colour, variations can be achieved by adding black or white (which strictly speaking are not colours at all, scientifically

white is made up of all colours and black is the absence of colour). A **shade** is a colour mixed with black; a **tint** a colour plus white; a **tone** is a blend of a tint and a shade. So pink is a tint of red and white; maroon a tone of red and black. A **muted** effect is a colour mixed with grey.

When it comes to devising a colour scheme, there are basically three options. Firstly, **monochromatic** schemes based on different tones of the same colour. Blue, for example, can range from powder blue to deep navy, green from pale lime to dark olive. Monochromatic schemes produce a positive result, which is both welcoming and relaxing, but it can also look dull.

Related or **harmonious** schemes use colours found next to each other on the colour wheel. Because they share a common base colour, the result can be very pleasing.

Contrasting or **complementary** schemes use colours directly opposite one another on the wheel: red and green, violet and yellow, orange and blue. Used in their purest form they have a strong, almost jarring, effect on one other – yellow and violet for example – but if you use tints instead, such as lilac with primrose, the visual effect is quite different.

PSYCHOLOGY

Because of their association with heat, red, orange and yellow and their derivatives are known as warm colours; while greens, blues and violets are considered cool colours. But these colours also have other properties which can have a psychological effect on the occupants of a house and ought to be given some consideration.

Red is a hot, bold colour. Associated with fire and heat, it can stimulate the pulse and excite – or irritate. It will make a room appear warm and welcoming, but it can also cause you to become irritated more quickly than other colours. In its purest form, avoid using it in large amounts in rooms where you spend a great deal of time, the living room for example, and unless you want a fiery relationship with your partner it's not recommended as the main colour in a bedroom. Use it in small quantities as an accent colour, for cushions and accessories rather than as the main wall or floor colour.

Orange is a warm, earthy, reassuring colour associated with nature – just think of autumn leaves and sunsets. Because of these associations it creates a sense of solidity, serenity and reassurance and can be cheerful and stimulating. It would be suitable for dining rooms as it should make guests feel comfortable, whilst stimulating conversation. However, used in large quantities in its purest form it can be tiring and irritating; schemes using orange tones of peach and apricot are easier to live with.

Yellow, the colour of the sun and spring flowers, is friendly and cheerful, hence the phrase a sunny disposition. In its purest form it exudes warmth, giving a friendly feel. It is one of the happiest colours and can be used to great effect to brighten up and warm a dull room, a north-facing bedroom for example. But some tones can look unappealing, particularly under artificial light, so make sure the colour stays true in all forms of light.

Green is the colour of nature and of life itself and, as a result, is a very flexible and adaptable colour which goes well with almost every other. It is the most restful colour to the eye, being cool, fresh and elegant, representing stability and security, so makes a good choice for living rooms.

Blue is the colour of the sky, representing loftiness and depth. It creates a cool, fresh, restful look which can be used to make rooms appear larger. The peacemaker amongst the colours it is the one to use to calm down the emotions, in a bedroom for example. Because of its associations with water it is considered a clean colour and is often used in kitchens and bathrooms to give the rooms a fresh, hygienic look.

Violet, the result of mixing vibrant red with cool blue, is a colour which causes conflicting emotions – you either love it or hate it. It indicates a depth of feeling, sensuality and richness, but it can cause confusion and be unsettling. Its variations, such as lilac, are easier to live with and are particularly appealing in a bedroom.

WATCH POINTS

Colours will change in different types of light, so it is very important that you try out large samples of your chosen fabrics, paints, wallpapers, etc., in the room in which they will be used, under all lighting conditions. When light falls onto an object the surface absorbs some of the colours in the light and reflects others; this determines the object's actual colour. For example, a blue object absorbs all colours except those in the blue spectrum, which it reflects. Some colours change under artificial light, such as tungsten and neon, because these artificial lights do not give out quite the same balance of the light colour spectrum as natural light. For example a red, which has a blue tinge when viewed under artificial strip lights, may look warm and clear when seen in a naturally sunny room. A rich blue viewed in a dark room may seem perfect, but used in a sunny room it could lose much of its intensity.

Colours affect the colours next to them so be careful how you use them. For example, although you may love a particular shade of orange and a beautiful blue, which both look stunning on their own, they may clash if used together, so always try out colours together before you make a final decision. At the same time certain 'neutral' shades of beige and grey, which can look dull on their own, may look wonderful when used with a bright red or pink.

How much there is of a colour will affect how you see it. For example, if you completely decorate a room in a particularly vivid shade of yellow or pink, it may be difficult to live with, although the same colours used in small doses can make an all-white room stunning.

CREATING A SCHEME

We would all love to be able to start a room scheme from scratch, but usually we have to retain a carpet, sofa or some other item. Sofas can always be recovered, but a carpet will have to be the 'fixture' for the new scheme and used as a starting point. Start with a sample of your 'fixture'; if you can't find an exact match, look for one which is close in colour and texture. Now start collecting fabrics, wallpapers and paint shades in the colours you would like to use. At this point don't worry about how well they go together. You may find that it's helpful if one or two samples contain some of the 'fixture' colour to help to tie the whole thing together. Don't restrict yourself to just one range of tones, but combine different colours in different tones.

Together with colour, texture also plays an

important role in a successful scheme, because too much of the same sort of finish can be overpowering. For example, gloss paint, highly polished floors and furniture and shiny chintz curtains are too similar in finish to work well together. Conversely, a scheme which is totally lacking in any texture will look flat.

Once you have collected all the samples you like, go through them and work out the best combination, carefully sorting out colours, textures and patterns. You may find that when it comes to choosing and mixing patterns, it is more difficult to achieve a harmonious combination. It is important that the scheme has some pattern and you may find that subtle designs, those which give the appearance of a paint effect for example, may be easier to match than those with strong, large-scale designs.

Often the best way of building up a scheme is by basing it on a strongly patterned carpet, wallcovering or fabric. Not only will the pattern show you which colours work well together, but it also suggests in which proportions they work best. Usually the largest colour area in a room should be a muted restful one, with dominant shades used sparingly to avoid an overpowering end result. Use the background colour of the design as the room's background colour for the walls and curtains for example, then pick out another colour for the carpet, also using it in small doses as an accent colour on cushions and tablecloths. Any remaining colours can be used as accents for cushions, lampshades and other accessories.

If you are having difficulty mixing colours and designs, consider building your scheme around one of the many fabulous co-ordinated fabric, wallpaper and border collections. In recent years wallpaper and fabric manufacturers have been producing a wealth of stunning co-ordinated ranges which enable any amateur to redecorate a room successfully with style and individuality. The secret of these ranges is the careful use of the same colours across a whole range of different designs, so although the designs are often different, they can be mixed and matched to great effect because they all use colours from the same palette. Look out for the unusual designs and gorgeous colours used in the collections from Skopos Designs, whilst Jane Churchill has co-ordinated collections which can be mixed and matched within their own product ranges as well as with ranges from other companies.

GUIDELINES

Now you understand the basics, you are ready to start having a go yourself, although it may help if you follow these guidelines:

- Start by selecting a background colour for the walls, ceiling and carpet.

- Introduce other colours in smaller quantities. (Equal quantities of different colours will only result in an unbalanced scheme.)

- Introduce accent colours – small touches of strong colour – into contrasting or harmonising schemes.

- Avoid a totally monochromatic scheme which can look dull.

- Avoid using too many strong patterns for the carpet, upholstery, curtains and wallcoverings for example, they will fight with one another and look messy. A wall of books or pictures forms a 'pattern' which can be just as overpowering as a patterned fabric.

- Different patterns and prints will work together provided they are colour-related.

Finally, if you are ever unsure about your choice of colours, try to find an equivalent in nature as reassurance. Flowers, in particular, offer many stunning colour combinations which you may not consider would work together. Violet and dark green with a touch of yellow may seem a strange mixture until you think of clematis; fresh bright yellow and green may seem rather vivid until you see a mass of daffodils; shades of orange combined with clear bright blue may seem odd until you look at autumn leaves against a clear blue sky.

A colour scheme should reflect your taste and individuality, so don't be scared, just have a go.

A GUIDE TO DECORATING

Although planning a new decor scheme can be fun, the actual job of decorating can be equally rewarding provided you follow some basic guidelines. Decorating is mostly a matter of common sense, following the rules and taking your time. Don't fool yourself into thinking it is a job which can be rushed, because the key to good results is careful preparation. After all there's no point in planning a new decor scheme, painstakingly searching out colours and patterns, if you then spoil the end result by bad preparation. A new coat of paint will not hide a bumpy surface or conceal cracks, whether they are on woodwork or a plain wall, whilst bumps can still show through a papered surface. So make sure the surface is thoroughly prepared and absolutely clean before you start.

DECORATING OPTIONS

The kind of surface finish you choose will depend largely on your budget, the finished effect you would like to achieve and the condition of the existing surface. For example, you may prefer a simple paint treatment, but if the wall is uneven, its imperfections may be emphasised. For internal walls the choice is between paint, wallpaper, tiles and some kind of cladding (a textured treatment such as Artex or timber cladding). With woodwork you can choose a painted or varnished finish or a natural stripped wood look, although if you opt for the latter you will need to make sure the base timber is in good condition.

Another important consideration is the suitability of the chosen finish for the room. In a living room or bedroom you will want the finish to be decorative, but in a kitchen or bathroom practicality is more important.

When it comes to cost, painted walls are probably the cheapest of all forms of decor, offering a wide range of colours. If the wall is not particularly even or if you would like some pattern, try one of the many paint effects described in this book. Next up the price scale comes wallpaper, although costs will vary depending on whether you opt for one of the cheaper plain papers or a more expensive vinyl or decorative hessian. An embossed relief wallcovering such as Anaglypta is worth considering as you can change its appearance simply by painting with a different colour, making redecorating a simpler job. Textured wallcoverings are worth considering if your walls are in a bad state of repair as it saves the cost of having them replastered. The one drawback is that you will need to like the finished effect because once on the walls they are not easily removed. Ceramic tiles and timber cladding are the two most expensive options, although they will give a harder wearing and longer-lasting surface finish.

PREPARATION

Before you start to decorate you will need to make very careful preparations. Whatever the job try and work out how long you think it will take before you start. Be realistic allowing plenty of time for meal breaks and rests, particularly if you are not used to the physical hard labour redecorating involves – believe me painting a ceiling is very tiring on both the neck and the arms! There's no virtue in rushing through the whole job if you're not going to be happy with the finished result; much better to work steadily and take your time.

Be prepared for the house to be in chaos for days as you will need to clear the room to be decorated of all movable items. Large pieces of furniture can be moved to the centre of the room and covered (old sheets will do). Take up rugs and, if possible, any carpets, spraying water on the floor and sweeping it to collect loose dust. Tiled or polished wood floors will need to be protected. Remove all fittings, such as lights, curtains, curtain rails, pictures and picture hooks. Unscrew and remove all door furniture – keeping the door knob with you at all times just in case you get shut into the room accidentally. Once the room has been cleared, carry out any necessary repairs and alterations. Scrape away old or loose putty from around the window panes and, if you have a chimney, get it cleaned, as soot can ruin new decorations.

When it comes to preparing yourself, wear old comfortable clothing, although you should avoid woollens as the fibres may adhere to new paintwork. It may be worth investing in a special pair of lightweight decorating dungarees. If you're going to be working on a ceiling, some form of headgear will protect your hair and it may be sensible to wear protective goggles to prevent paint dripping into your eyes. Whatever shoes you wear, always leave them in the room whenever you leave, to avoid spreading paint, wallpaper paste and other debris around the rest of the house. Finally, always keep some clean rags or cloths about you to wipe your hands clean as you work.

No matter what kind of decorating you will be doing, at some time you will almost certainly need some means of reaching the more inaccessible areas of the room or stairwell. For safety never use makeshift devices which can be unstable and therefore potentially dangerous. Always use a proper ladder, a pair of steps or some form of purpose-built tower. If you don't own any you should be able to hire them.

Stepladders are essential and although the traditional wooden ones are still available, they have been mostly superseded by lightweight, aluminium alloy ones. You will need at least one pair standing about 2 m (6' 6") high to reach a ceiling. A shorter pair may be more convenient for other jobs. If you plan to buy a pair of steps, choose one with a platform at the top so that you can put down cans and trays. Make sure the treads are comfortable to stand on — wide flat treads are the best — and look for one with an extended stile to give you a handhold at the top. Finally, make sure there is a locking device which holds the two halves in the open position.

SAFETY

More accidents occur because of stupidity in using ladders than as a result of faulty equipment. So make sure you follow these safety rules:

- Erect the ladder safely before you ascend and move it when the work is out of reach — never lean out to the side or you could overbalance.

- For inaccessible areas, two stepladders with a plank between them will make a more secure platform than a single stepladder. But first check the manufacturer's instructions to ensure the ladder is suitable for this purpose.

- Any plank used as a platform spanning more than 1.5 m (5') will 'bow' and flex. Strengthen it by putting another plank on top of it, tying the two together securely, and to the supporting ladders, with rope.

- For awkward areas, like stairwells, hire purpose-made systems or use an arrangement of long ladder, stepladder and planks. (See diagram.)

- Any ladder placed on stairs or at the top of stairs should be held in place by nailing a batten behind it to prevent it slipping. (See diagram.)

- Always tie planks securely to their ladder supports.

- Tie padding to the tops of a ladder to protect the walls.

- Always nail together any planks crossing over at right-angles.

- Never stand too high on a ladder as you will not be able to balance properly; keep your waist below the top rung.

WALLS

You can now get down to the nitty-gritty of preparing the surfaces for redecoration. If you have a wall which is just painted, all you need to do is wash it down with a detergent solution, rinse with clean water and leave to dry. You're then ready to paint over the top. If you are dealing with a wall which is already papered, it's advisable to remove the old paper completely. *Always* remove the old paper if there are:

- Already several layers of paper on the wall.

- If the paper is peeling.

- If it has an impermeable surface.

- If the wall is showing signs of damp.

Washable wallcoverings and vinyls *must* be removed, although with easy-strip vinyl all you need to do is remove the vinyl to reveal the paper backing. Just carefully peel away the top layer of vinyl, starting with a corner at skirting board level. If the backing is reasonably clean, in good condition and still firmly stuck to the wall you can use it as a basis for paint or as a lining for another wallcovering. However, ensure that the vertical joins in old and new papers do not line up as the finish could be weakened.

You can paint over a papered surface although you may face the following problems:

- Water-based paints, such as emulsion, can soften the wallpaper paste and the paper may peel off. The older the paste the more likely this is to happen.

- The inks in the paper may bleed through the new painted surface, resulting in unsightly blotches.

- Any dirt or grease embedded in the paper's surface could prevent the paint adhering, resulting in an uneven finish.

- Joins and irregularities in the surface will show through the paint.

Before you start to strip off old paper, turn off the electricity at the mains for safety – you could inadvertently soak the light sockets and switches. Ordinary wallpapers should be thoroughly soaked with plenty of water applied with a wall brush, sponge or a small hand-held spray. Adding a proprietary wallpaper stripper or a few drops of washing-up liquid will help the water to penetrate the paper. Allow the water about 10 or 15 minutes to soak through the paper then strip off using a stiff broad-bladed scraper, starting from a seam and being careful not to chip the plaster underneath.
   Wallpapers which have been painted with emulsion, or which have a washable finish, will not respond to simple soaking and scraping as they are designed to keep moisture out. You will need to score the surface with the edge of the scraper, a wire brush or with a special serrated tool known as a Scarsten scraper. Be careful not to damage the plaster underneath. Once the surface has been scored it should be

soaked with water, then stripped as above.

If the paper won't scrape off easily or if you are left with small patches which refuse to budge, just repeat the soaking process and they will eventually respond. Continue working in this way, soaking and stripping, until the wall surface is bare. Once the bulk of the paper has been removed, wash the surface thoroughly using a solution of household bleach. Rinse with clean water and allow to dry.

For large rooms or if you are removing several layers of paper, it would be worth hiring a steam wallpaper stripper to make the job easier and quicker. (Look in Yellow Pages for your nearest hire shop.)

Once the old paper has been removed you can see what condition the wall is in. If the walls are powdery and dusty, apply a coat of stabilising solution before redecorating. If the surface is flaking or cracked, has efflorescence or mould, remedial work will need to be carried out.

Cracks and **holes** are common faults in plaster walls. If they're fairly small they are easily filled with a cellulose filler. Open out hairline cracks with the tip of a screwdriver or putty knife (filler will not be effective on cracks less than 1 mm wide). Dust clean then dampen the area with water before applying the filler with a flexible filling knife. Sand smooth when dry.

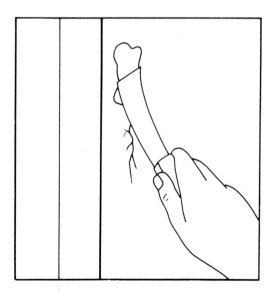

Large holes in solid walls can be filled with plaster. Finish with a layer of proprietary filler to give a smooth surface. Level off by passing a timber batten over the top using a 'sawing' action. If you are in any doubt about achieving a smooth surface, call in a professional plasterer.

Large cracks and holes under 75 mm (3″) diameter in plasterboard can be filled with an adhesive mesh repair tape like Fibatape. Cover the crack or hole with tape, then spread patching compound over the top using a filling knife, leaving a level surface. Leave to dry then sand smooth. Larger holes or damaged areas will need to be patched.

The only cracks and holes that are not easily filled are those found between masonry and woodwork such as door and window frames. Ordinary plaster fillers fall out as the wood expands and contracts. Instead use a permanently flexible filler such as acrylic-based caulk which is sold ready to apply in cartridges, and is extruded into the gap like toothpaste. Alternatively, Solvite's Expanding Filler, an expanding foam filler which works on an aerosol principle, would do the job.

Crazing happens when one type of paint is applied over another which is completely different. As the original paint expands and contracts at a different rate from the new paint it causes cracking. If the fault is extensive the entire surface must be stripped down. Small areas can be completely rubbed down with wet and dry paper.

Efflorescence usually occurs in new plaster, although it can appear in old plaster. As the walls dry out, the salts in the plaster work their way to the surface leaving a white deposit. Brush away these salts with a clean cloth or brush until they no longer appear. If you are painting the walls use emulsion paint. Don't wallpaper or use oil-based paints on new plaster for at least 12 months.

Flaking paint is usually caused by insufficient surface preparation before painting. Remove the flakes by scraping the affected area and then sanding smooth. Prime the exposed plaster before redecorating.

Mould, identified by a black fungus growing on the walls, is normally caused by damp and can be caused by condensation, penetrating damp or rising damp. You will have to establish the cause and cure it before you can redecorate. To do this, dry out a damp patch with a hair dryer and stick aluminium foil over the area with adhesive tape, making sure the edges are completely sealed. Leave for a week then check. If there are water droplets on the exterior surface it is condensation; if the foil is dry outside but damp inside, it's rising or penetrating damp.

Condensation is the result of too much moisture in the house and inadequate ventilation. To cure it you will need to improve the ventilation. Fit extractor fans in the kitchen and bathroom; check that all exterior airbricks are clear; if you have a blocked-in fireplace, ensure it is fitted with a ventilation grille. If the mould is caused by rising or penetrating damp, seek professional advice from a builder, surveyor or organisation, such as Rentokil, to establish the cause and recommend a cure.

Once the problem has been cured, wash away the mould using a fungicidal wash such as the one from Castle Products' Mould Busters range, following the manufacturer's instructions. Or make up a solution of one part of bleach to four parts' water, leave for 48 hours and wash off with clean water. Repeat the process if necessary. If you will be wallpapering, use an adhesive containing fungicide. In rooms where condensation may be difficult to avoid — the kitchen or bathroom — use eggshell paint.

New plaster needs to be wiped with a damp cloth, to remove any dust particles, and then primed. If the wall is to be painted do this with a 'mist' of emulsion paint thinned down with water.

Painted walls which are in good condition should just be washed down with a detergent solution, rinsed clean and left to dry before decorating over the top.

Despite all these preparations some walls may still be rough and uneven and not really suitable for a painted finish. Consider the following:

■ Use a paint effect or consider a textured coating.

■ If you can afford to lose a little space, dry line the walls using plasterboard mounted on battens. This will give an even surface and provide additional insulation. Alternatively, give the wall a decorative wood cladding.

■ Have the walls skimmed with a layer of plaster to level them out — a job for a professional.

■ Wallpaper using a small random design or use a woodchip paper or an embossed relief covering, such as Anaglypta, and use this as a paint base.

WOODWORK

Wherever possible try to avoid stripping off old paint from woodwork, it's a tiring, time-consuming and often unnecessary chore. If the surface is in a good condition it makes a perfect base for the new coat. All you need to do is sand down to produce a 'key' for the new paint, wipe over with a clean damp cloth to remove all traces of dust, allow to dry, then start painting. Alternatively, wipe over the surface with Liquid Sander from International Paints. This product softens the top paint layer to provide good adhesion for the new coat. It takes literally seconds to wipe on and wipe off and eliminates the need to remove any dust.

If the woodwork is damaged, if there are bubbles or blisters for example, the paint will need to be stripped off and the damage repaired. Wherever possible just strip the affected area.

Blisters and **bubbles** are caused by moisture or resin trapped in the wood underneath the paint. This usually happens where there is a knot in the wood. Cut out the blistered area with a knife and clean underneath. Apply knotting to the area if necessary, fill with topping, then sand the area smooth. Leave to dry then prime and paint.

Chips and **dents** are easily repaired. Remove the loose paint, prime any bare batches, then fill with stopping or filler. Small dents or holes and chips in protruding corners may need to be treated with several layers. Build up until the area stands slightly proud of the surface, then sand level. Prime when dry and paint.

If you have an older property or the woodwork has been sadly neglected it is likely that you will have to strip off all the old paint completely.

There are three ways to do this:

Burning off is the quickest way to strip large areas of paintwork, but it needs a certain amount of skill so be careful. Use a blow torch or hot air gun to soften the paint, playing it over the surface. As the paint shrivels, scrape it off, being careful not to let it fall on your hands. Use a scraper on flat surfaces and shave hooks on mouldings and in corners. Always turn the heat source away from the surface as you scrape to prevent burning the wood and be extremely carefully when working close to plaster walls. Keep any heat away from glass.

Chemical strippers can be used right up to the edge of glass without the risk of cracking and are also very useful for stripping paint from intricate woodwork and mouldings. Although they are relatively easy to use, they are the most costly method of stripping paintwork and need to be handled with care. There are several types available, suitable for different jobs, so ask the advice of your retailer and always follow the instructions on the can carefully.

Dry scraping literally means scraping off the paint using a paint scraper. It is really only suitable for very small areas or where the paint is lifting off the surface.

CEILINGS

Ceilings are prepared for redecoration in much the same way as walls — they're just more awkward to work on. Many ceilings have a **textured finish** created with a plaster-like compound; Artex is probably the best-known brand name although there are others with different properties. Artex and similar products need to be protected with paint, others are waterproof; some are essentially thickened emulsion paint.

They're all relatively easy to redecorate. Just wash the surface with a warm detergent solution then rinse off. Test a small area first just to make sure you won't wash off the texture! If the surface is water-soluble, just brush it to remove any dust before painting.

It's more than likely that your ceiling will be full of cracks, which is due to natural movement of the ceiling joists flexing as people walk on the floor above; as the joists flex so does the ceiling. Fill in all cracks as you would cracks in a wall, but avoid standing directly underneath the area you're working on — you'll get plaster and dust in your eyes. Seal cracks between sheets of plasterboard, or in the angle where the ceiling meets the walls, using a flexible mastic which is applied like toothpaste. Once applied, just pass a moistened finger over the surface to give a neat finish.

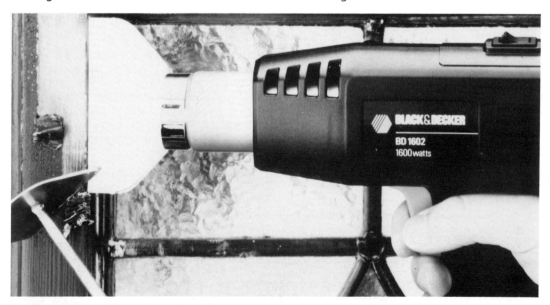

The Black & Decker Heatgun is a safe and fast way of stripping large areas of paintwork

Uncover and conserve the natural beauty of wood

Our NON-CAUSTIC process removes paint and varnish from doors and furniture without damaging joints or surfaces like other methods.

Full restoration service also available.

Collection and delivery service.

The Furniture Care People

PAINTS AND PAINTING

If you're looking for a quick way to change a room's decor, the natural choice has got to be paint. Painting is one of easiest DIY jobs and, with the wealth of excellent DIY products available, all designed to make the job as quick and easy as possible, you can almost guarantee good results no matter how inexperienced you are. What's more, because painting is relatively inexpensive, if you don't like the finished result, you can always just paint over the top.

There are three golden rules to successful results:

1. Always choose the right paint for the job.

2. Always read the manufacturer's instructions carefully before you start and follow what they say.

3. Always thoroughly prepare the surface to be painted; this may be tedious, but it is well worth while.

PAINT TYPES

There is such a bewildering variety of paint types and brands on the market that it can be confusing knowing what to buy; if you are ever in doubt ask the retailer. Basically there are only two main categories: gloss or oil-based paints, and emulsion or water-based paints.

Oil-based paints, also known as solvent-based, include liquid and non-drip gloss, undercoat, mid-sheen paints (like eggshell or Dulux Satinwood) and finishes like enamel and lacquer. They are usually used on wood and metal, although mid-sheen paints can be used on walls. They need to be applied with care and will take time to dry. On bare surfaces it is essential to use both a primer and undercoat first. Most require thinning and cleaning with white spirit, although some can be cleaned with strong detergent and water immediately after use; check with the manufacturer's instructions on the tin. This group gives a hardwearing surface finish which is scrubbable and will stand up to moisture and condensation, making them suitable for use in kitchens and bathrooms.

Water-based paints are all water-soluble and include emulsion, solid emulsion, acrylic and vinyl. They are designed to be used on walls and ceilings and are simple to apply, fast-drying and require no undercoat. All brushes can be cleaned with warm water and detergent. The term satin, silk or matt refers to the shine of the painted surface. A satin finish is shiny and easier to clean than a matt one, although it will also magnify any surface irregularities. A silk finish gives a slight sheen, so is ideal for use over papers. A matt finish gives a velvety, non-reflective coat ideal for uneven surfaces. Non-drip solid emulsion comes in its own paint tray and has the texture of cream cheese. It is designed to be used with a roller and will not run or drip so it is very easy to apply, making it ideal for ceilings.

GUIDE TO PAINTS

To help you understand the jargon here is a brief guide to some of the terms used:

Eggshell is a solvent-based paint recommended for walls, it can also be used on wood and metal. It dries to give a hard-wearing, soft sheen surface. If painting on bare plaster, use over an all-purpose primer. Suitable for kitchens and bathrooms where condensation may be a problem as it effectively seals the wall. Avoid using on papered surfaces.

Emulsion is a water-based paint for interior and exterior surfaces, which allows surfaces to breathe. Will wash out of brushes and clothes. Usually requires two coats and acts as its own undercoat. Available as either a liquid or as a solid block, with a texture like cream cheese, which comes in its own tray designed to be used with a roller. This is particularly suitable for ceilings as it is less likely to splash or run. (See also Vinyl.)

Gloss is the most common solvent-based paint for wood and metal, which dries to give a durable, mirror-like finish. Easy to clean. If applied too thickly, it may chip.

Knotting is applied to knots in wood before the primer or paint, to prevent resin from the knots 'bleeding' through. Proprietary products are available or use shellac (a liquid varnish and sealant made from natural resin).

Microporous versions of both solvent- and water-based paints allow wood surfaces to breathe. The finish is highly flexible, so cracking

Subtle combinations of colour and finish from Crown Paints

and blistering should not occur. They give a gloss finish and should be applied to a freshly primed surface.

Primer is a coating specially formulated to protect new or exposed wood or metal surfaces and is applied before an undercoat or topcoat.

Shellac see Knotting.

Textured paints are water-based and very thick, suitable for covering flawed surfaces, as well as providing a decorative finish for both walls and ceilings. Once applied they can be difficult to remove.

Thinner is the name given to the appropriate solvents for each type of paint. If a paint is too thick, it cannot be applied properly and must be thinned before use. For most solvent-based paints, use white spirit; for water-based paints use water. Check with the instructions on the can which will say what thinner should be used and what to use for cleaning the brushes.

Thixotropic paints are thick, non-drip, solvent- or water-based paints which can be applied directly onto sound surfaces. Normally one coat is sufficient, although with non-drip gloss you are likely to see brush marks and the quality of finish will not be as good as a liquid gloss. Water-based types dry quickly.

Undercoats are specially formulated to be used with solvent-based top-coat paints. They dry to an opaque colour and provide a good base surface on woodwork and metal.

Vinyl is found in most modern emulsion paints, making them easy to clean and more resistant to wear. Vinyl paint will wash out of brushes and clothes when wet, but is almost impossible to shift when dry. They come in a matt finish, giving a velvety, non-reflective finish, ideal for uneven surfaces; silk finish, giving a slight sheen, so ideal over papered surfaces; and satin finish, giving a shiny surface resistant to steam, so suitable for kitchens and bathrooms.

CHOOSING THE RIGHT PAINT

Type	Uses	+/– Points
WATER-BASED		
Matt vinyl emulsion *liquid* *solid emulsion*	Walls and ceilings. Can be used on new plaster or porous surfaces like brick.	+ Covers well. Reflects little light so will not highlight surface imperfections. Easy to apply. Fast drying. Washable. – Will show scuff marks and develop a sheen with washing, so use in light-wear areas.
Silk vinyl emulsion *liquid* *solid emulsion*	Walls and ceilings.	+ Tougher and more washable than matt vinyl. Effective on relief papers and textured wallcoverings. Easy to apply. Fast drying. – Will highlight imperfect surfaces.
Textured paint	Walls and ceilings.	+ Gives rough-stone finish which will diguise imperfect surfaces. – Difficult to wash. Very dificult to remove.
OIL-BASED		
Eggshell Mid-sheen	All-purpose paint. Walls and ceilings. Wood and metal.	+ Tougher than emulsion, more subtle than gloss. Wears well. Washable. Normally needs no undercoat (bare surfaces should be primed). – Takes 12–16 hours to dry. Needs more careful application than emulsion.
Gloss *liquid* *non-drip*	Woodwork requiring maximum protection.	+ Easy to clean. Hardwearing. Liquid flows on evenly. Non-drip needs no mixing and is less likely to splash and run. – Takes 12–16 hours to dry. Highlights any surface imperfections. Liquid can be difficult for beginners to use and needs an undercoat.
Primer	Essential on bare wood and metal. All-purpose primer suitable for all surfaces.	+ Seals surface and provides key for next coat. Cover with undercoat and topcoat as soon as possible.
Undercoat	Use after primer on bare wood or metal. Use on old paintwork when changing colour.	+ Good covering power. Easily rubbed smooth ready for top coat. – Must be painted over as quickly as possible.

EQUIPMENT

The next thing to consider is the equipment. Consider the options available and always take your time choosing what you'll need. Run brushes over your hand and discard any which moult a lot. Assess the weight of the rollers and wall brushes until you find ones which feel comfortable to use. Don't be tempted to select the largest available to speed up the job; it may be cumbersome to use. Always clean equipment immediately after use.

Brushes are the traditional form of painting equipment and will give a smooth, even finish. They come in a range of sizes as you'll need a different size depending on the job you're going to do. For wood and metal 75, 50 and 25 mm (3, 2 and 1") are a good choice plus a narrow cutting-in brush; for walls use a 100 mm (4") brush. If you are likely to do a lot of decorating it's worth investing in natural hog's hair brushes which, though expensive, will give the best results. Bristles should be tapered at the top so that you can smooth the surface for a fine finish, a process called 'laying off'. New brushes should be washed in warm soapy water before use, to soften the bristles and to remove any loose ones.

To use, hold a wide brush by its stock (the part between the bristles and handle) and a small brush like a pencil; this will give maximum control. Dip the brush into the paint until the bristles are half- covered, then remove any excess before you start painting. Keep brushes moist when you stop work (to have a cup of tea for example) by standing them in a pot of water or use BrushWraps from Castle Products, a non-toxic fluid which comes in individual sachets designed specially for this purpose. When you have finished working, always clean the brushes with the appropriate solvent and hang them up to dry.

Rollers provide a quick way to cover walls and ceilings, particularly if used with an extension handle, and are one of the most popular ways of painting a wall. Widths vary from 175 to 300 mm (7" to 12"). A variety of sleeves is available and what you use will affect the finished results. **Foam** is cheap but is likely to make the paint splash – always wear protective clothing. **Lamb's wool, sheepskin and their synthetic equivalents** are good all-round materials, particularly suited for use with vinyl matt emulsion and textured paints, but use a short pile on a smooth surface and a long pile on textured surfaces, such as Artex. **Mohair** is the most expensive sleeve, but gives the best result with vinyl silk, eggshell and solid emulsion.

Rollers are used with a paint tray. Pour the paint into the base of the tray and roll the sleeve back and forth in the paint until it is coated. Remove any surplus by running the roller over the ribs of the tray. When you have finished work always clean the sleeve in the appropriate solvent and leave to dry. Store in a clean polythene bag.

Paint pads are easy to handle and, because they won't splash or leave brush marks, are ideal for the complete novice. However, the finished result may not be as good as the one achieved with a roller. Pads comprise an absorbent head fixed to a handle and they come in a number of sizes from 25 mm (1") sash pads up to 200 mm (8") wide pads; some are hinged at the handle to make it easier to paint round obstacles. Like rollers, paint pads are used with a paint tray.

PREPARATION

Although painting itself is a relatively speedy job, you will always achieve better results if you take the time to prepare the surfaces properly, filling in cracks and holes in both walls and woodwork.

- In rooms with a polished floor, clean the skirtings carefully. Any wax on them will prevent the paint from adhering.

- After clearing the room and preparing all the surfaces, but before you start painting, vacuum thoroughly to remove all traces of dust and fluff to prevent them sticking to the new paintwork.

- When using oil-based paints, always work in a well-ventilated room to disperse fumes.

- When you have worked out the number of coats of paint and the amount of paint required for a room, write it down and keep it for reference.

Follow the correct order of painting to ensure that any slips or mistakes are erased by the next stage. Before you paint the ceiling or walls,

awkward areas which will be inaccessible to a large brush, pad or roller – such as corners, the area above the skirting board and around doors and windows – should be painted with a small brush or pad. This is called 'cutting in'.

1. Start at the highest point of a room – the ceiling. Give any decorations (ceiling rose, etc.) an initial coat first, then paint the ceiling. Apply the second coat of paint to any ceiling decorations last.

2. Next paint the walls, starting from the lightest point of the room, for example by a window, and work from the top downwards in blocks about 750mm (30") square. Unless you are left-handed, start in the right-hand corner.

3. The woodwork is last, window frames, picture rail (if applicable) doors and skirting board in that order. If you are papering the walls, the woodwork should be painted after the ceiling.

PAINTING A CEILING
Equipment

- Paint – solid emulsion is the most popular choice for ceilings

- Roller and paint tray

- Stepladder(s) and scaffold board

- Cutting-in brush

- Clean lint-free cloth

Method

1. Clean the lid of the paint can (to stop debris falling into the paint) and lever off the lid.

2. Decant paint into a paint tray, to fill the lower third only. Alternatively, use solid emulsion.

3. Set up the stepladders and scaffold board to provide a safe, secure painting platform. (See diagram overleaf.)

4. With a cutting-in brush, paint a narrow strip around the edge where the ceiling meets the wall.

5. Dip the roller into the paint and run it over the slope of the tray to remove any surplus. Don't overload the roller, otherwise it will drip.

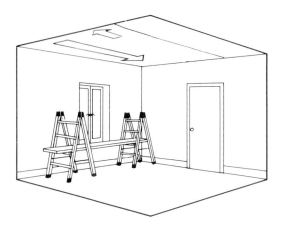

6. Starting at one end of the ceiling, paint a strip parallel to the brush-painted strip, but leaving a gap between the two.

7. When you reach the other end, go back in the opposite direction joining the first two strips.

8. Start a new strip parallel to the previous one, leaving a gap between the two.

9. Go back in the opposite direction joining the two strips.

10. Continue in this way until the ceiling has been completed.

PAINTING WALLS

The way you paint a wall will depend on the type of paint you use.

Gloss or **semi-gloss** paint should be applied in sections about 500 mm (20") square, starting at the top right-hand corner of a wall (unless you are left-handed).

Emulsion should be applied in bands about 200 mm (8") wide, working across the wall from top to bottom. (See diagrams.)

Equipment

- Paint
- Paint tray and roller, or paint pads, or wall brush and paint kettle
- Stepladder(s) and scaffold board
- Cutting-in brush
- Radiator brush (if required)

Method

1. Clean the paint lid and lever it off. Decant paint into a paint kettle if using a brush, or a paint tray if you're using a roller or pads. 'Flick' the bristles of the brush through your fingers to remove any dust.

2. With a cutting-in brush, paint around the edges of the walls, door and window frames, light switches, power sockets and the skirting board.

3. Dip the wall brush into the paint, to a depth of no more than half the bristle length, scrape the excess off by drawing the bristles across a piece of string or wire fixed across the kettle. Follow step 5 (painting a ceiling), if using a roller or pad.

4. Using the sequence outlined above, apply the paint.

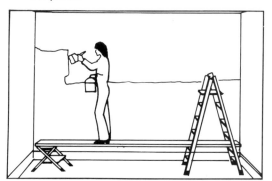

Paint emulsion in horizontal bands

Apply oil-based paints in vertical strips

With a brush: hold the brush as you would a pencil, as it will enable you to move your wrist freely in any direction. Put the handle between thumb and forefinger with your fingers on the metal ferrule and your thumb supporting it from the other side. Use horizontal strokes, followed by vertical strokes if using an emulsion paint; use vertical strokes followed by horizontal strokes if it's a solvent- based paint. When the brush glides smoothly over the surface, indicating an even covering, 'lay off' the paint with light vertical strokes.

With a roller: follow the same sequence, but apply the paint in a criss-cross direction trying to keep the roller on the surface at all times. With solvent-based paints, finish in one direction, preferably towards the light.

With a pad: follow the same sequence, but keep the pad flat to the wall, sweeping it evenly up and down. With solvent-based paints finish with vertical strokes.

5. Continue working until the wall is completely covered.

PAINTING WOOD

Gloss and eggshell are more difficult to use than emulsion because their reflective finishes emphasise any mistakes. Ensure the surface to be painted is properly prepared and thoroughly cleaned.

- Never overload the brush when working.

- Never wipe the bristles against the rim of the can, debris may fall into the paint.

- Doors and windows must be painted in strict sequence.

- Hold the paint brush like a pencil and always paint along the wood grain, applying the paint in parallel stripes.

- Do the job in one session because any pauses will result in hard edges which are impossible to remove.

Equipment

- Paint shield or masking tape

- Paint and paint kettle

- Stick for stirring paint

- Cutting-in brush or sash paint pad (for glazing bars and mouldings)

- 25 mm (1") brush (for window and door frames)

- 50 mm (2") and 75 mm (3") brushes for skirtings and doors

- Lint-free cloth moistened with white spirit

Method

1. Mask the edges of any windows with masking tape, or use a paint shield.

2. Flick the bristles of the brush through your fingers to remove any dirt.

3. Clean the lid of the paint can and carefully lever it off.

4. If a skin has formed over the paint, cut around the edge with a knife and lift it off. Pick out any bits of dried paint adhering to the rim, then stir the paint thoroughly with a stick.

5. Decant the paint into a paint kettle then dip the brush or pad into the paint, being careful not to overload it. Remove any excess by drawing it across a piece of string or wire fixed across the kettle.

6. Hold the brush by its metal ferrule as you would hold a pencil, then apply the paint to the surface in long parallel strokes, following the direction of the grain and working lightly back and forth. Don't attempt to cover the surface completely but produce a series of parallel stripes; this is called 'laying on'.

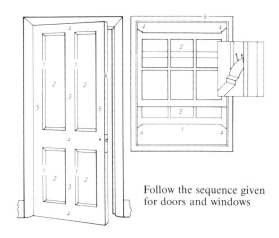

Follow the sequence given for doors and windows

7. When the brush starts to run dry, start 'brushing out', working the brush at right-angles to the stripes, to spread the paint over the surface.

8. Now follow the direction of the wood grain, to remove any obvious brush marks and leave a perfect finish.

9. Follow the sequence given for doors and windows (see diagram) when one area is completed, recharge the brush and move on to the next. Overlap areas whilst the paint is still wet, otherwise a join line will be left.

GUIDELINES

■ Always clean the lid of the paint can before opening it to stop any dust or debris falling into the paint.

■ Don't stir non-drip gloss or solid emulsion, they will liquefy.

■ Solvent-based paints may form a surface skin in the can. Cut around the edge with a sharp knife and lift out. Remove bits of dried paint adhering to the rim. Stir paint with a clean stick, using a beating motion, until any sediment or oil is mixed in and the paint is smooth.

■ Always flick the bristles of the brush through your fingers to remove any dirt before you start work.

■ Always decant paint into a paint kettle if you are using a brush. Tie a string or wire across the top of the kettle so you can use it for wiping off excess paint from the brush. Decant paint into a tray if you are using a roller or pads.

■ Never wipe the bristles of a brush against the edge of the paint can, debris may fall into it.

■ When painting ceilings or walls always work from a safe platform made from stepladders and scaffold boards, a chair or stool could easily overbalance if you overstretch.

■ The way you paint a wall depends on the type of paint used. With gloss or semi-gloss paint work in sections about 500 mm (20") square, starting at the top right-hand corner of a wall (unless you are left-handed).

Emulsion should be applied in bands about 200 mm (8") wide, working across the wall from top to bottom.

■ When painting a wall with a brush and emulsion paint, use horizontal strokes first followed by vertical strokes. With a solvent-based paint, use vertical strokes followed by horizontal strokes. When the brush glides smoothly over the surface, indicating an even covering, lay off the paint with light vertical strokes.

■ When painting a wall with a roller, apply the paint in a criss-cross direction trying to keep the roller on the surface at all times. With solvent-based paints, finish in one direction, ideally towards the light.

■ When painting a wall with a pad, keep the pad flat to the wall, sweeping it evenly up and down. With solvent-based paints, finish with vertical strokes.

■ When painting doors and windows, do so in strict sequence (see diagrams on page 59).

■ When painting woodwork, mask adjacent surfaces such as the glass in windows, with masking tape. Alternatively use a protective paint shield.

■ When using solvent-based paints, always do the job in one session, overlapping areas whilst the paint is still wet. Any pauses are likely to result in hard edges in the finish which are impossible to remove.

■ Oil-based paints take several days to harden completely. Don't put books and ornaments on to newly painted shelves or window sills.

As soon as you've finished painting, clean your equipment immediately, to ensure it keeps in good condition and lasts.

■ Wipe the rim of the can of paint before you replace the lid. Tap the lid in place by holding a piece of softwood over it and gently tapping down with a hammer.

■ Remove emulsion paint from brushes, rollers and pads by first dabbing any excess on to absorbent paper, then washing in a detergent solution.

- Remove solvent-based paints with white spirit or a proprietary brush cleaner, wash in a detergent solution then rinse in clean water.

- If a brush is badly clogged up, drill a hole through the handle and push a long nail through it. Use this to suspend the bristles of the brush in a jar of cleaning solution. Rinse clean.

- Wrap brushes in clean absorbent paper, held in place with a rubber band, and leave to dry.

- Roller sleeves and paint pads should be allowed to dry completely before being wrapped in clean paper or stored in a polythene bag.

PAINT COVERAGE

Paint type	Coverage (m^2 per litre)	Recoatable (in hours)
Eggshell	15–16	12–16
Emulsion:		
matt vinyl	12–14	2–6
silk vinyl	10–11	2–6
textured	2–2½	2
Liquid gloss	17	12–16
Non-drip gloss	12–14	12–16
All-purpose		
primer	7 (wood)	16
	11 (metal)	16
Undercoat	15	16

DECORATIVE PAINT EFFECTS

Paint can be used in a number of creative ways to give a surface pattern and colour, while some paint effects are particularly useful for disguising imperfections such as an uneven surface. Far from being difficult to do, most are relatively simple to master, sponging, ragging and colour washing, for example, are all quickly learnt techniques. Once you've mastered how to do them you can move on to the more complex treatments such as dragging, marbling, stippling and stencilling.

DIY sponging kit from Dulux

Because of the great interest in paint effects over the past years most of the equipment required to carry them out is easily found. Dulux, for example, have produced kits containing all the equipment (minus paint) you need to sponge, stipple or stencil; whilst there are several companies offering a wide range of pre-cut stencils, fast-drying paints and specialist stencil brushes – Carolyn Warrender, Stencil-itis and Stencil Decor.

When you first try any paint effect, practise on a small item of furniture or a piece of wood first to master the technique. But don't worry about achieving a perfect finish, remember that most of these effects are meant to look irregular.

COLOUR WASHING

This is probably the softest form of broken colour, giving an uneven but translucent colour with a faded appearance. It is particularly suited where a country-cottage look is required. For the most natural look choose a soft, delicate colour for the wash, applied over a white base.

Method

1. Paint your wall with the chosen emulsion base colour and leave to dry.

2. Thin the colour emulsion you have chosen for the wash with water following the manufacturer's instructions on the can – the paint should be neither too runny, as it will drip, nor too thick, as you will lose the soft translucent effect.

3. Paint on the first coat of colour wash with criss-cross strokes (cross hatching) using a 100 mm (4″) wide paintbrush and avoiding any paint runs – don't try to apply the paint evenly and do leave some of the background exposed.

4. Leave to dry then apply a second coat, brushing the whole wall using the same random criss-cross movements.

COMBING

Combing is a way of adding surface interest to a large area and is achieved by passing a comb over a wet paint surface to form a variety of different patterns. You need a wide-toothed comb (an Afro comb works well or you can buy a special steel graining comb) to comb the paint in straight lines, curves, diagonals or wavy lines, the choice is yours. For the best effect the top colour should provide a contrast to the base colour.

This treatment can be very effective on floors, but remember to apply at least three layers of heavy-duty polyurethane varnish over the surface once the paint has dried, to protect the finish.

Method

1. Paint the surface with eggshell and leave to dry.

2. Brush on the top colour – emulsion, eggshell or gloss – then, with a wide-toothed comb, carefully pull it over the surface to create a line effect.

DRAGGING

This gives a textured, finely striped effect, the result of 'dragging' a brush through a wet glaze, although you do need a steady hand to achieve the look. Its slightly formal appearance makes it suitable for high-ceilinged rooms or traditional settings.

This technique is not simple as it's important that the strokes producing the 'dragged' effect are kept as straight as possible. Don't stop working between bands, as this will allow the glaze to harden forming visible lines.

Method

1. Paint the wall with eggshell in a light tone and leave to dry.

2. Mix up the glaze from scumble (this is a special transparent oil available from specialist decorators' shops), eggshell and white spirit in a 7:2:1 mix, using a dark-coloured but toning eggshell.

3. Starting at the top of the wall and using a wide brush, apply the glaze in bands about 500 mm (20″) wide, going carefully from top to bottom in one stroke where possible.

4. If it helps, mark a faint guideline down the wall with a plumb bob near the corner where you intend to start and at intervals across the wall.

5. Using a special dragging brush (although a paper-hanging brush will do) 'drag' it through the glaze with a light steady movement, creating the striped effect.

MARBLING

As the name suggests, marbling is used to simulate the appearance of real marble. It is particularly suited on small items such as tables and fireplace surrounds, as well as areas where real marble might be used. It is one of the more difficult paint treatments to achieve, so have a piece of real marble to use as a guide and try out the technique on a piece of wood before tackling large areas.

Method

1. Marble is perfectly smooth so, for the best results, ensure your base layer is as smooth as possible. Fill in all the cracks, then sand, clean, prime and undercoat before applying two coats of eggshell.

2. For a white marble finish, apply an ivory or light grey glaze, made from scumble (see Dragging), eggshell and white spirit in a 3:5:2 mix, over the surface.

3. Before it dries, dab over the glaze with a clean rag to soften the appearance.

4. Apply grey paint veins diagonally across the surface with a fine brush while the glaze is still tacky, remembering to vary the thickness of the veins and to make them irregular, just like real marble. Don't make the mistake of painting too many veins.

5. Carefully soften and smudge the veins to give a delicate, misty result.

6. Allow to dry and protect with a polyurethane varnish.

RAGGING

This is a very simple and effective paint technique and one of the easiest to achieve, giving a broken colour effect. With ragging, or ragging-on, you simply dab paint on to the surface using a bunch of clean, dry, crumpled-up rags. The effect achieved can vary quite considerably, depending on the type of cloth you use; hessian, cheesecloth, net, chamois or muslin all give interesting results. Experiment to find which effect you like best, but do ensure that the cloth is lint-free and semi-permeable.

For the best results ensure that the cloth outline does not become blurred. When it does replace the rag with a new one. To further enhance the effect you can apply a second, contrasting, colour over the first, but always finish with a lighter colour to give a muted effect.

Method

1. Paint the wall with emulsion and leave to dry.

2. Pour your emulsion top colour into a paint tray. Take a clean rag and crumple it up into a ball, then dip it into the paint. Remove all excess paint by dabbing the rag on to a piece of paper.

3. When you are happy with the effect, dab the rag over the wall, working from top to bottom with a random movement.

4. The success of this finish is its irregularity, so stop frequently to keep crumpling the rag to produce a different design.

Ragging is simple but effective

5. Once the outline becomes blurred, replace the rag with a new one; place the old cloth in an airtight container.

6. Stop and look at the result every so often, filling in any areas you may have missed while the paint is still wet.

7. Once the first colour has dried, apply the second colour if used.

RAG-ROLLING

Very similar to ragging, in that you use a cloth to apply the colour, rag-rolling, or ragging-off, requires a little more expertise to achieve. The difference is that you first paint the wall with a base colour, apply a glaze and then roll a 'sausage' of cloth over the surface, literally taking off the top colour to expose the base coat. When you first try this effect, you may find that it will help if there are two of you working on it: one applying the glaze as the other rags it off This way you will avoid hard edges forming, which could spoil the finish.

Method

1. Paint the wall with eggshell and leave to dry.

2. Make a glaze from scumble (see Dragging), eggshell and white spirit in a 7:2:1 mix and apply a strip of glaze, about 500 mm (20") wide, to the wall with a paintbrush.

3. Take your rags, loosely rolling them up into a 'sausage', and roll or dab them over the wet surface, working from the top downwards, changing the direction as you go to vary the pattern.

4. When you reach the skirting start again, overlapping the edges slightly.

5. Continue until the room is complete, but don't stop half-way along a wall as this will allow the glaze to dry, forming a hard edge.

6. A second lighter coat can be applied once the first is dry.

SPONGING

Sponging is probably the quickest and easiest way of creating a soft, patterned surface. All you need is a natural sponge – a synthetic one is too regular and will not give an attractive random finish. For the best results ensure that the sponge is never overloaded with too much paint, this will give a solid appearance, and keep turning the sponge as you work, to avoid a regular pattern.

Method

1. Paint the wall with an emulsion base coat and leave to dry.

2. Pour a little of the pattern colour (use emulsion) into a paint tray.

3. Soak the sponge in water and wring out well to ensure it's soft and pliable, then dip it into the paint, being careful not to take up too much paint. Squeeze out any excess paint and dab the sponge on a piece of paper until you are happy with the result.

4. Start sponging the wall, working from top to bottom, dabbing at random over the surface. Vary the direction as you work, turning the sponge to avoid a regular pattern.

5. Continue working over the wall, being careful to avoid any build up of colour and taking care around door and window frames.

6. Once you've finished, leave the wall to dry before sponging on a second colour, overlapping the areas so that the colours merge.

STENCILLING

This effect gives a definite pattern which is particularly useful for forming borders and friezes along a skirting or below a window ledge, for example. It is also a useful way of brightening up pieces of plain furniture. The design can feature several different colours, or you can overlay several different designs, but don't be too ambitious with your first attempt, keep to a simple one-colour design until you've mastered the technique.

You can either buy pre-cut stencils or make your own from stencil card or clear acetate, the paint can be applied with brushes or sponges depending on the effect you want. The secret is to be sparing with the paint. Apply two thin coats rather than one thick one, always remove any excess paint from the brush or sponge on to scrap paper before applying, and dab on the colour rather than paint it. If you are creating a border, make sure the stencil is straight by drawing small guideline marks on the wall beforehand.

If you are going to try stencilling for the first time, look out for the products offered by Stencil Decor. Instead of paints, they use solid oil-based paints in crayon form, which eliminate the danger of paint runs and smudges, which can ruin the finished effect.

Method

1. Fix the stencil in place with masking or double-sided tape, having first checked that the tape will not damage the base surface when it is removed.

2. Put your paint into a saucer and dip in the end of the brush (a stubby, flat-ended pencil brush is the best). Remove excess paint on a piece of scrap paper.

3. Holding your hand upright, apply the paint in stabbing motions to the relevant areas of the design – the end of the brush must not be applied at an angle.

4. If using a second colour, leave the first to dry completely before applying in the same way.

5. When the paint is dry, carefully remove the stencil and clean thoroughly.

6. For a border pattern, repeat the process, being careful to marry up the design.

STIPPLING

This gives a fine dotted effect caused by removing wet glaze with a special stipple brush, a square-shaped pad of soft thick bristles, although initially you could use a new shoe brush, dusting brush or even a hairbrush providing the bristles are an even length.

Method

1. Paint the wall with an eggshell base coat and leave to dry.

2. Make up the glaze with scumble (see Dragging on page 62), eggshell and white spirit in a 7:2:1 mix and apply to the wall with a paintbrush in strips about 500 mm (20″) wide.

3. Working from the top of the wall downwards, apply the stippling brush to the glaze using a firm, stabbing action so that all the bristles come into contact with the glaze at the same time. This will gradually reveal tiny dots of the base colour.

4. Continue until the entire strip is stippled.

5. Repeat this process until the wall is finished, cleaning the brush frequently to avoid a build-up of paint.

6. Don't stop in the middle of a wall, leaving the glaze to dry, as the join will show. Also don't work round a room. Once you've completed a wall, go to the opposite wall (not the adjacent one) to avoid smearing the wall you've just completed.

A combination of decorative effects using Crown Paints

WALLCOVERINGS & PAPERING

I f you want to put pattern, texture or colour onto your walls, there is a wallcovering suitable for the purpose, from hardwearing vinyls to delicate silks and grasscloths. But there are so many different wallcoverings available nowadays that making the right choice can be very difficult. With so many patterns and colours to choose from in such a wide range of materials and finishes, it's not surprising if you get confused. Perhaps the first thing to understand is that you will be covering a large area and so need to consider the impact the design will have.

Large, boldly patterned designs which are busy and detailed will make the room look smaller, whilst small designs on light backgrounds will make a room appear larger because they give the effect of looking through the design. Obviously striped designs can visually heighten a room, but should only be used with a cornice, coving or picture rail to balance the overall appearance. Small random designs are a good choice for walls with an uneven surface, or if the walls are out of true, and borders offer a multitude of decorative options, from creating the impression of a dado rail or coving, to emphasising a doorway.

If you've never tackled wallpapering before, don't choose either a very expensive paper or one which is cheap and thin and so liable to stretch and tear. Instead pick an inexpensive medium-weight paper with a free-match, all-over design and decorate a room which is not likely to be on show – a guest bedroom for example.

WALLCOVERING TYPES

Before you go out to buy any wallcovering, it would help if you know the differences between the many types. First come the wallcoverings which can be painted, often known as **whites**.

Embossed papers are made from wood pulp and have a textured design created by pressure from a metal roller. The uncoloured off-white papers are intended to be used as a base for paint only. Duplex papers, such as Anaglypta Original, are made from layers of paper bonded together before the design is embossed, to give greater strength and resistance to stretching.

A striking effect created using Anaglypta Original

High relief wallcoverings, like Anaglypta SupaDurable, have a more pronounced design than embossed papers. They are made from mixing wood pulp with cotton and clay, laying it down as a paper web then, while it's still damp, passing it through embossing rollers. Another type of relief wallcovering is made from blown vinyl; chemicals are deposited onto a base paper through a patterned screen to create the design and then baked so that the design rises (Anaglypta Luxury Vinyl).

Lincrusta is the most luxurious relief wallcovering available, containing linseed oil, paraffin wax, whiting and resin, which is first mixed then fused onto a heavy paper backing and embossed by steel rollers. It has a very pronounced design which gives a rich opulent look, but it may be a bit heavy and difficult to hang.

Woodchip, made from sandwiching chips of wood or sawdust between two layers of paper, is available in light, medium and heavy grades. It is designed to cover imperfect wall surfaces.

Vinyl relief wallcoverings are inherently washable. They have a paper backing bonded to a raised vinyl design. Choose a vinyl silk or satin paint to highlight the design to the best effect.

Available in thousands of designs and colours, most printed wallcoverings are made by machine. Hand-printed papers, where the design is created by blocks or machines, are available but are very expensive, will probably need to be trimmed and can be difficult to hang.

Borders and **friezes** are designed to co-ordinate with wallcoverings and fabrics, although they can be used to great effect on their own. Borders are used to highlight door frames, skirtings, dados and picture rails, or they can be used as a pattern in their own right. Friezes, which are usually wider than borders, are normally hung at picture-rail height.

Foamed polyethylene (Novamura) is a lightweight covering which has a matt finish and is warm to the touch. Made from polyethylene foam, it does not have a paper backing, so is easy to strip. Because you paste the wall rather than the wallcovering, it is fairly easy to hang, although it does have a tendency to stretch so should be handled with care. It is not suitable for difficult areas like ceilings.

Ready-pasted wallcoverings are given a coat of adhesive during the manufacturing process, so that instead of having to paste the covering you emerse it in a trough of water prior to hanging. They are easy for first-timers to use, but always leave them to soak in water for the recommended time, otherwise the paste may not be fully activated.

Standard printed papers have designs which are printed directly onto the surface by machine. There are several different weights and some may be fairly flimsy to handle, so always choose a medium-weight paper which is less likely to tear when wet.

Vinyl wallcoverings are water-resistant, washable and scrubbable. The pattern is printed directly onto the plastic (vinyl) surface which is then backed with paper. Because of their construction, vinyls can be dry stripped; you just peel the vinyl surface off the wall leaving the paper backing as a lining paper. Some vinyls are pre-pasted, others will need to be hung with a fungicidal paste. If overlapping is unavoidable, use a special adhesive.

Washable papers are printed papers finished with a protective thin clear film of plastic. This gives the paper a surface which can be wiped or sponged clean.

Cork-faced papers have a paper base with slivers of cork mounted on the surface. Soft to the touch and attractive to look at, they can be difficult to cut and trim and the cork may tear when it's being handled.

Flock papers usually have a paper backing with a raised pattern, which has a velvety texture, picked out in synthetic or natural fibres on the surface. Standard flock papers with cotton, silk or wool designs are difficult to hang as the paste may ruin the fibres. Vinyl/nylon flock is more robust.

Grasscloth has natural grasses woven with cotton onto a paper backing. Although it is very attractive, it is expensive, very fragile to handle, difficult to hang and clean and may fade in sunlight.

Hessian can be bought unbacked or with a paper backing. The paper-backed varieties are much easier to hang. Unbacked hessian should be either fixed to a pasted wall or fixed to the wall on battens. Deep colours may fade in strong light and there is a danger of the edges fraying.

Metallic foils usually have a paper backing with a metallised plastic film surface, making them easy to wipe clean. They are suitable for feature walls, although they should only be used on a completely smooth, even base as they will emphasise any wall imperfections. They crease easily and so are not easy to handle, and they may conduct electricity and should never be tucked behind a light switch or socket.

Before you fix any type of wallcovering, you should ensure that the wall surface is clean, smooth and sound. Some wallcoverings may cover up minor wall blemishes, but if you have a poor surface you will achieve better results if you line the wall beforehand.

Lining papers are cheap, buff-coloured papers available in three weights: light, suitable as a paint base; medium, suitable for most wallcoverings; and heavy, designed for relief and vinyl wallcoverings. Hang the paper horizontally so that the joins don't overlap.

An alternative is expanded polystyrene which comes in thin sheets. It will cover cracks and small holes and act as a wall insulator as well as a base for conventional wallpaper. Because it dents easily it should not be used in heavy-wear areas, such as hallways. Although not a lining paper, woodchip can be used to cover up an imperfect wall and also provides an attractive textured base for painting.

EQUIPMENT

In theory wallpapering is relatively simple, you just cut the paper to size, apply the adhesive — or soak the paper in water — and then hang it on the wall — simple. But in practice there's a lot more to it. As with any job, if you have the right equipment, the task will be much easier.

You will need:

- Plumb bob and chalk, to mark vertical guidelines on the walls.

- Plastic bucket, wallpaper paste and stick for stirring (for unpasted papers), or a trough for soaking ready-pasted wallcoverings.

- Paste table and string for holding the paper in position as you paste.

- Pencil and ruler for measuring and marking lengths.

- Small scissors and/or trimming knife for cutting round light switches, etc.

- Pair of shears to cut the lengths.

- Paste brush with synthetic bristles, which are easier to clean than natural ones.

- Smoothing or paperhanger's brush.

- Damp sponge to wipe paste from the surface of the paper.

- Clean sponge for smoothing down embossed wallcoverings.

- Seam roller for pressing joins on all but the embossed wallcoverings.

- Stepladder for access.

PREPARATION

With any papering job the secret is to make sure you have everything you need before you start and then to work carefully and methodically. Buy all the paper at the same time, making sure the batch numbers are the same. If they're not, you may find some slight colour variations. Never try to economise by under-estimating the required quantity.

Ensure all the walls have been properly stripped and prepared. This can be quite a time-consuming chore, so don't be tempted to rush; allow yourself plenty of time. Use the correct equipment and always work by good light — natural daylight is best.

Once all the preparatory work has been completed, paint the ceiling and all the woodwork before you start papering. Now work out in which order you will work. Always try to work away from the light, such as a window, towards the darkest corner, so that the joins are less obvious, although, depending on the room itself, where you actually start will vary.

- If the room has a chimney, position the first roll in the centre of the chimney breast and then work outwards in both directions, treating each half of the room separately, until you reach the door.

- In a simple room without alcoves and just one window, start at the corner nearest the door and work right round in the same direction until you come back to your starting point.

- In a room with a large picture window, or several windows on one wall, position the first roll against the right-hand window and continue to the end of the adjacent wall. Next paper the window wall, then the left-hand wall and finally the wall opposite the window(s).

METHOD

1. Walls are rarely straight so you need to mark a vertical line on the wall at your starting point as a guide — you will need help to do this. Coat the string of the plumb bob with chalk. Hold the top of the line at ceiling level and allow the line to steady. Hold the line against the wall near the skirting with one finger. Pull the string

away from the wall and let it 'snap' back. The first roll of paper should line up exactly to this chalk line. Mark a vertical line every time you turn a corner.

2. Make up the paste in the bucket according to the manufacturer's instructions, stirring with a clean stick, and leave to stand. Tie a length of string across the bucket, fixed to the handles, to use for wiping off excess paste from the brush.

3. Using a pencil and extendable metal rule, mark a scale on the edge of the pasting table to make measuring and cutting easier. Tie a length of string loosely round the table legs at one end to stop the paper rolling up as you work.

4. If you are using a free-match design, cut the paper to length by measuring the height of the wall at the starting point, using the expandable metal rule, and adding an extra 100 mm (4") for trimmings at the top and bottom. Always double check this measurement before you cut any wallcovering. Roll out the paper on the table and use a straightedge and a sharp knife to cut several lengths.

5. Place the lengths face side down on the table, so they overlap one long edge slightly; this will prevent paste getting on to the table. With a pencil, indicate which is the top edge of each of the rolls on the wrong side.

6. Dip the paste brush into the paste, wiping any excess on the string. Start pasting, working from the centre of the roll away from you towards the overlapping edge. Completely paste one edge. It will be necessary to fold one end of the pasted paper over and slide the length along the table to gain access to the other end.

7. Once the first edge has been pasted, carefully pull the paper towards you and repeat the process along the second edge (see diagram).

8. Fold the pasted length over so the top cut edges meet in the centre and leave to 'soak' according to the manufacturer's instructions. Any long lengths should be carefully folded concertina-fashion.

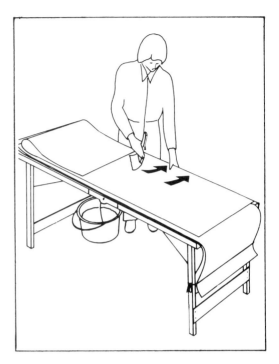

9. Pick up the folded length and carefully drape it over your arm. Climb the stepladder and open out the top half of the paper. Slide it into position at the top of the wall against the chalked plumb line. Allow about a 75 mm (3") overlap at the top for trimming.

10. Use the paperhanging brush and brush diagonally from the centre outwards in all directions to remove air bubbles and creases.

11. When you are sure the paper is correctly positioned, crease the ceiling line in the angle made by the wall and ceiling using the outer edge of your scissors. Carefully peel the top edge away from the wall and cut along the crease.

12. Smooth the paper back into position and 'stipple' carefully with the brush, using a firm stabbing action.

13. Open out the bottom half and smooth it onto the wall, using the brush to gently tap the paper along the edge of the skirting board. Crease the skirting board line , peel back the paper, cut and reposition as before.

14. Hang the next length in the same way, sliding it with your fingertips so that it butts up tightly to the first drop, making sure any pattern fits. Wipe away excess paste with a clean, damp cloth. After about five minutes, press along the join with a seam roller.

15. It is quite normal for small bubbles to appear underneath the paper, they should all disappear as the paper dries out. However, you may find that some remain. Roll it flat, or if this doesn't work, carefully cut across the blister, forming an X, peel back the flaps, paste and then reposition.

CORNERS

Never try to paper round a corner in one piece; they are rarely square and the edges of the paper will simply move out of line, causing it to crease. Instead, make the join as unobtrusive as possible by overlapping the edges in the corner. Internal corners should have an overlap of about 15-20 mm (½-¾"), external corners about 25 mm (1").

Use the plumb bob to establish the verticals. Then measure from the edge of the last length right into the corner, taking at least three measurements (top, centre and bottom). Add the necessary overlap allowance to the largest measurement. Cut this from the next length and hang in the normal way so that it turns the

corner. Use the remaining piece on the adjacent wall, hanging it so that it covers the overlap.

WINDOW RECESSES

Hang the length next to your window opening, joining one vertical edge to align, but leaving the other vertical edge so that it overhangs the opening. On this piece of paper make a horizontal cut just above the window recess opening and a similar cut at the bottom, so that you can fold the paper round to cover the side of the recess.

Cut a strip of paper which matches the overhang above the window. Paste and slip this in under the overhang, folding it round the top of the recess. Hang short lengths on the wall above and below the window, wrapping the top lengths into the recess as described.

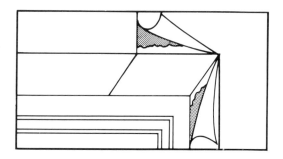

LIGHT SWITCHES AND SOCKETS

These are not difficult to paper around, but you should always remember to turn the electricity supply off at the mains first. Allow the pasted paper to hang over the switch or socket then press lightly to establish a rough outline. Make diagonal cuts from the centre of the fitting to

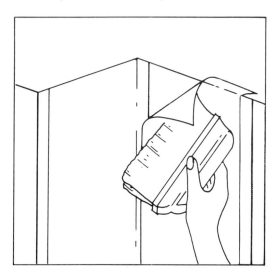

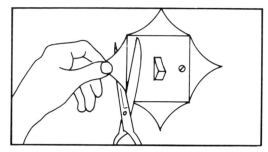

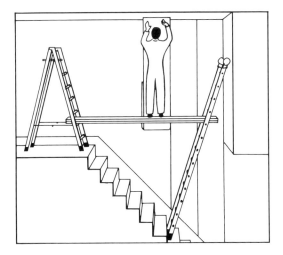

each corner and trim away the waste, leaving a 6mm (¼") margin.

Slightly unscrew the cover of the switch or socket and tuck the waste behind, then screw the cover back in position. Allow the paste to dry before switching the power back on.

STAIRWELLS

A stairwell is probably one of the most difficult areas to paper, not only because of the difficulty of access but also because of the very long drops required. Always make sure you set up a secure platform, using a stepladder and ladder and get someone to help you. Always start with the longest drop first, making sure you allow for the angled skirting in your measurements. Work away from the first drop in both directions, papering the head wall above the stairs last. Because it will inevitably take some time to hang even one length, paste the paper liberally so that it doesn't dry out while you work.

ESTIMATING QUANTITIES

Most standard sized wallcoverings are 10.05 metres (11 yd) long and 530 mm (21") wide. To estimate how many rolls you will need for a room, measure the height of the walls from skirting to ceiling. Divide the length of the roll by this figure to find out the number of lengths you can get from one roll. Now measure round the room, excluding windows and doors, to work out how many widths are required. Divide this number by the number of wall lengths you can get from one roll to find out how many rolls are needed, remembering to make allowances for short lengths caused by doors and windows. As a rough guide use this chart:

Height from skirting		Measurement round walls, including doors and windows – the figures in the columns below give the number of rolls required.									
Feet		28'0"	32'0"	36'0"	40'0"	44'0"	48'0"	52'0"	56'0"	60'0"	64'0"
	Metres	8.53m	9.75m	10.97m	12.19m	13.41m	14.63m	15.85m	17.07m	18.29m	19.51m
7'0" to 7'6" 2.13 to 2.29		4	4	5	5	6	6	7	7	8	8
7'7" to 8'0" 2.30 to 2.44		4	4	5	5	6	6	7	8	8	9
8'1" to 8'6" 2.45 to 2.59		4	5	5	6	6	7	7	8	8	9
8'7" to 9'0" 2.60 to 2.74		4	5	5	6	6	7	8	8	9	9
9'1" to 9'6" 2.75 to 2.90		4	5	6	6	7	7	8	9	9	10
9'7" to 10'0" 2.91 to 3.05		5	5	6	7	7	8	9	9	10	10
10'1" to 10'6" 3.06 to 3.20		5	5	6	7	8	8	9	10	10	11
10'7" to 11'0" 3.21 to 3.35		5	6	7	7	8	9	9	10	11	11
11'1" to 11'6" 3.36 to 3.50		5	6	7	8	8	9	10	10	11	12

FLOORCOVERINGS

Floorings represent a considerable financial outlay and for this reason you should be careful to make the right choice. Durability should be your main concern, so before choosing any flooring think about where it is to be fitted and what kind of treatment it is likely to receive. For example:

- Will it be subjected to a lot of punishment from people walking on it — in, say, an entrance hall?

- Will it come into contact with dirt from the garden — in a utility room?

- Will heavy items of furniture or equipment be stood on it — in a dining room or kitchen?

- Will it come into contact with water - in a bathroom or cloakroom?

- Will children be playing on it — in a playroom?

Next think of the comfort and aesthetic appeal. Some types of flooring are soft underfoot and also provide heat and sound insulation, others just look attractive. The colour and texture of the flooring will have a great influence on the overall look of a room, so take care to choose something which harmonises with the decor and enhances the room's character. Large patterns, borders and dark colours will make a room look smaller, whereas small patterns and plain, light surfaces create an illusion of space.

SUB-FLOOR

Before any type of flooring can be laid, you must check that the existing floor, or sub-floor, is smooth, clean, dry and sound. Any defects in the sub-floor could permanently damage and undermine the appearance of any flooring placed on top. Basically there are two main types of construction:

Suspended timber floors Most British homes have suspended timber sub-floors upstairs and many of the houses built before the 40s have them on the ground floor as well. They consist of floorboards — often tongued and grooved — or flooring-grade chipboard, nailed to the supporting timber joists; these joists are either connected to the walls of the house or, on the ground floor, held up by a network of open brickwork walls laid over a concrete foundation. If you are planning to lay a heavy flooring, such as quarry tiles or marble, check that the joists and floor are strong enough.

Floorboards can warp, curl, split and wear; nails can work loose, tacks can protrude and woodworm can set in; they may also contain grease from spillages over the years. For these reasons it is unwise to lay certain types of flooring (sheet vinyl, for example) directly onto them, as you could experience problems in the future. Instead, lay tempered hardboard over the boards to create a clean, smooth, level and draughtproof surface: tempered hardboard has been impregnated with oil to make it hard and water-resistant. Store the boards in the room they are to be laid for 72 hours before fixing, so they can adjust themselves to the moisture conditions of the house. Before laying, punch down all nail heads, then lay the hardboard, rough side uppermost, and nail to the floorboards. Plywood can be used instead, but should be screwed in place.

Solid concrete floors are usually found on the ground floor of houses built after 1939 and are laid direct-to-earth. They should have a damp-proof membrane built into them. If a solid concrete floor is uneven, it should be treated with a screed, a self-levelling compound. Small cracks and hollows need less drastic treatment and can be filled with a mortar mix (three parts sand to one part cement).

A damp sub-floor must always be corrected before any new flooring is laid, otherwise the problem will spread further. For example, damp can attack flooring adhesives and cause some types of flooring to rot. If you are experiencing problems, check that the damp-proof course is not damaged.

When it comes to choosing a new flooring, there are many different types available:

HARD FLOORINGS

- Brick
- Ceramic tiles
- Marble

Traditional hand made terracotta floor tiles by Elon Tiles

- ■ Mosaic
- ■ Quarry tiles
- ■ Slate
- ■ Stone
- ■ Terrazzo

Brick comes in a range of rustic tones, in paving bricks, thin brick tiles or slips. They can be used in a variety of attractive patterns, but are hard and inflexible underfoot, so are really only suited to conservatories. Bricks must be laid into a mortar bed on a concrete sub-floor with a damp-proof course. Brick tiles may be fixed with adhesive, but check first with the manufacturer.

Care: Brick is porous so a seal must be applied to the surface to make it water-and stain-resistant. Once sealed, wash gently with mild detergent.

Ceramic tiles are made of clay, by hand or machine, fired at high temperatures, then glazed. Available in a vast range of shapes, colours and designs, they are hardwearing and waterproof and ideal for use with underfloor heating. However, they are cold underfoot, tiring to walk on, can crack if heavy objects are dropped on them and can be slippery. If you want to use ceramic tiles upstairs, check that

the joists are strong enough to take the weight. They should be laid on a concrete sub-floor with a sand and cement screed or, alternatively, on a smooth sub-floor with a latex screed.

Care: Keep clean by sweeping, wiping with a damp mop and soapy water, then rinsing.

Marble is elegant, but expensive, a natural, hardwearing material which comes in many beautiful colours and variations, in blocks, thin sheets and as tiles. Impervious to water, it is cold, hard and noisy underfoot. Marble should be laid on a cement bed on a concrete sub-floor, but first check that the sub-floor will be able to bear the weight – marble is heavy. Because it is a difficult material to handle, marble should be laid professionally.

Care: Sweep, wash or scrub clean, but avoid abrasive or acid cleaners.

Mosaic is an ancient style of flooring made from glass silica, marble or clay (glazed or unglazed). It offers endless design possibilities, but can be expensive. Hardwearing, it can be rather tough underfoot. Mosaics should be laid on a screed sub-floor and those which are sold for DIY use come in sheets with peel-off paper backings.

Care: Sweep, wipe with a damp mop and a mild detergent. Do not polish glazed types. Seal or polish porous types.

Quarry tiles are made from unrefined alumina clay and have a rich, earthy colour and finish, giving a warm, rustic look. They are usually sold as rectangular, square or Provencîal-shape tiles and are very durable and impervious to water, but can be cold, hard and noisy underfoot, and almost anything dropped on them will break. In time they can become pitted or worn. Lay on a concrete sub-floor with a sand and cement screed, or on exterior-grade plywood sheets at least 12 mm (½") thick.

Care: Wash with mild detergent and rinse with clean water. Polish with a special polish if required.

Slate is a natural material which comes in shades of grey, grey/green and grey/blue. It has a characteristic rippled surface and is available as tiles with either a ridged or polished finish. Slate is expensive and rather cold and hard to walk on; it can also be rather slippery underfoot. Because it is heavy and rather brittle to handle, professional laying is recommended. It should be laid on a cement bed on a concrete sub-floor.

Care: Sweep and wash with warm water and a scrubbing brush. Some types of slate can be sealed and polished.

Stone is rarely used in modern homes, although it can be found in many older houses. It comes in slabs in many varieties, like sandstone, York stone, granite or limestone. Costs vary, although a cheap option is stone chippings cast into cement slabs. Stone is hardwearing, but cold, hard and noisy. Some types are waterproof, but porous stones must be sealed to prevent crumbling and staining. Because of its weight, stone is only suitable for ground floors and a strong floor is essential. It should be laid on a concrete sub-floor with a damp-proof course.

Care: Ask your supplier for advice on sealing. Sweep and wash, polish if desired.

Terrazzo is a tough, smooth flooring which consists of marble chips set in a cement base and ground smooth. It comes in tiles or slabs in varying colours and patterns. Terrazzo, like marble, is cold and hard underfoot, although it is not quite so expensive. It should be laid professionally on a screed sub-floor with joints sealed with silicone. Once laid it will require

professional polishing.

Care: Sweep and wash with a mop and mild detergent. Do not use acid or abrasive cleaners.

SEMI-HARD FLOORINGS

- Coir or Sisal
- Cork
- Linoleum
- Plastic or PVC
- Rubber and synthetic rubber
- Rush and Seagrass
- Vinyl
- Wood

Coir or **Sisal** is a fibrous material matting which comes from coconuts. Available in rolls, it makes an ideal flooring for anyone on a tight budget. It is tough and hardwearing, although it is rather prickly underfoot; more expensive versions have a vinyl or latex backing. Available in a variety of natural colours and different weaves. Easy to cut and lay, coir lengths can be stitched together and the edges bound with jute tape to achieve a wall-to-wall effect.

Care: Vacuum regularly. Scrub dirty matting with warm water and detergent, sponge with clean water and leave to dry.

Cork is quiet, warm and bouncy underfoot. It comes in tile form in many different shades, tones and finishes. Some types are pre-sealed with a polyurethane varnish or a protective PVC layer. Cork must be sealed to make it impervious to water and stains, otherwise it will swell and lift off the floor. Cork is easy to lay and can be cut to size with a craft knife. Follow the manufacturer's instructions with regards to adhesive and lay on an even sub-floor.

Care: If unsealed, seal with a polyurethane or special cork sealer. Wash with mild detergent and rise with warm water. Do not saturate.

Linoleum is made from natural materials, can be patterned or marbled in appearance and is usually bought in sheet or tile form. Comfortable, durable and flexible, it is no longer the brittle material of post-war years. Lay, following the manufacturer's instructions, on a dry, even sub-floor. Tiles are easier to handle for beginners.

Care: Wash with mild detergent and rinse with warm water.

Plastic or **PVC** flooring usually comes in strong, plain colours, those with a high PVC content are water-resistant, tough and comfortable to walk on. Available as either woven matting or small snap-together tiles, or more expensive PVC tiles and sheeting which imitate wood and brick designs. The matting types can be cut to fit, whilst plastic tiles can be cut with a sharp knife. Both types should be laid on an even surface.

Care: Wash with mild detergent and rinse with warm water. Vacuum matting regularly.

Rubber and **synthetic rubber** is a tough, stylish, warm choice of flooring. Available in sheet or tile form, in a range of plain, marble or studded designs, it is quiet underfoot, stain- and water-resistant and non-slip. Some types will react to spirit-based liquids, whilst exposure to excessive water or sunlight can cause others to perish. Lay on a screed concrete or smooth sub-floor. Take care when cutting the edges.

Care: Watch out for a build-up of dirt on studded floorings. Otherwise clean with a mild detergent and rinse with warm water. Some manufacturers may recommend a special dressing.

Rush and **Seagrass** are usually sold in squares which can be sewn together with twine to form mats. They offer a rich variety in weave and texture and provide a cheap, temporary flooring. Rush or seagrass matting is usually laid loose over concrete or hard floors.

Care: They tend to create dust, so should be misted occasionally with fine plant spray to prevent them from drying out. Lift and sweep underneath regularly.

Vinyl makes a practical and versatile flooring which comes in a number of forms, ranging from inexpensive to medium-priced. Most popular is cushioned vinyl, which is quiet, warm and bouncy underfoot and comes in sheet form. Less expensive are the thinner non-cushioned vinyls which come in either sheet or tile form; they are less durable, harder to lay and do not have the insulating properties of cushioned vinyls. All vinyls have the advantage of being water- and slip-proof, although they can be damaged by hot objects and heavy weights. They come in a vast range of colours, textures and designs with many good simulations of natural materials. Sheet vinyls come in various widths which allow for a seamless finish. Follow the manufacturer's instruction for laying. Most vinyls are lightweight and easy to cut, but large rolls can be difficult to handle. Always allow vinyl to acclimatise to the room temperature before laying.

Cushioned vinyl is usually laid flat and requires minimum fixing; other types will need to be stuck down with adhesive. Tiles must be laid accurately to prevent water seeping between the cracks.

Care: Wash with a mild detergent and rinse with warm water. Follow manufacturer's instruction on cleaning products.

Wood flooring comes in many types, including blocks, mosaics, hardwood strips and parquet. They are generally warm and resilient, although they can be noisy underfoot. Wood will stand up to heavy traffic and, provided it is sealed or polished, will be fairly impervious to stains. Price varies greatly, but the appearance of a good quality wood floor will improve with age. Laying varies according to the type; some can be laid onto floorboards or chipboard, but with all types the sub-floor must be free of damp and level.

Care: Sweep and/or mop occasionally if the floor is sealed. In time resealing/polishing may be necessary. If the floor becomes stained or pitted, it may be possible to strip and sand it smooth.

HOW TO SAND WOODEN FLOORS

Wooden floorboards can be found in most older properties. They are both hardwearing and easy to care for and can be easily transformed into an attractive flooring in their own right by sanding and sealing.

First examine the boards to ensure they're in good condition. There's no point spending time and money sanding down the floor if the result won't be worth while. If the floor is badly warped, there are large gaps between the boards, if it's badly stained or damaged or shows signs of woodworm, weigh up the options and decide whether or not you want to carry on. If you do detect woodworm, seek the advice of a specialist contractor or treat the floor with a proprietary woodworm fluid immediately.

The only sensible way to sand a floor is to hire an industrial sanding machine; look in Yellow Pages for your nearest hire shop. The staff will be able to advise you on what you'll need and how to use the equipment properly. For the best results you'll need to use three grades of abrasive paper, coarse, medium and fine — don't be tempted to reduce costs by skimping on quantity!

Sanding will be very dusty and noisy. Empty the room of everything before you start, including pictures, curtains and lampshades. Seal round the door with masking tape, and stuff folded newspapers under it. Open all windows. Wear old clothes to work in and always wear a protective face mask and goggles, it's also advisable to wear ear protectors.

■ Hammer

■ Nail punch

■ Pincers

■ Papier mâché (made from white paper and wallpaper paste, coloured with a water-based dye as necessary)

■ Filling knife

■ Wooden fillets (for filling gaps)

■ PVA adhesive

■ Broom and vacuum cleaner

■ Goggles — to protect your eyes

■ Mask — sanding is very dusty, so you need to protect your nose and mouth

■ Ear protectors (optional) — to protect your ears from the noise

■ Electric belt sander

■ Orbital disc sander

■ Abrasive paper — coarse, medium and fine

■ Glasspaper and sanding block

■ Shave hook

■ White spirit

■ Lint-free cloth

■ Polyurethane varnish

■ Paintbrush — to apply varnish

■ Fine-grade wire wool

1. Remove any existing floorcovering and inspect the floorboards. Nail down loose or squeaking boards. Nail heads should be punched about 3 mm (⅛″) below the surface, using a hammer and nail punch. If this is not possible, nip off the nail head with a pair of pincers and punch the shaft into the wood. It is important to do this because a raised nail head will damage the abrasive paper.

2. Fill in small gaps using a thick papier mâché paste (add some water-based dye to colour it to match the sanded floor if necessary). Press down firmly with a filling knife. Larger gaps can be filled with tailor-made wooden fillets. Apply some PVA adhesive to the gap and carefully tap in the fillet with a hammer. Plane smooth if necessary.

3. Once all the gaps have been filled, sweep the floor thoroughly, ready for sanding.

4. Fit the coarse abrasive paper to the belt sander, following the instructions supplied. Put on the goggles, mask and ear protectors. Plug in the sander, loop the cable over one shoulder so it doesn't get caught in the machine, tilt the sander back so that the drum is clear of the floor and switch on. Tilt the sander forwards gently so that the drum makes contact with the floor and start moving immediately . It is important that the sander is never stationary while the moving belt is in contact with the floor or it could make a deep hollow in the floor which will be impossible to remove.

5. Work diagonally across the boards at about a 45° angle. The machine will move under its own power; just keep it in check so that it moves steadily in a straight line.

6. When you reach the other side of the room, tilt the sander onto its back castors and switch off, waiting for the drum to stop revolving before you place it back in contact with the floor. Sweep up all the sawdust before turning the machine round and going back in the opposite direction. Continue in this way, overlapping each line

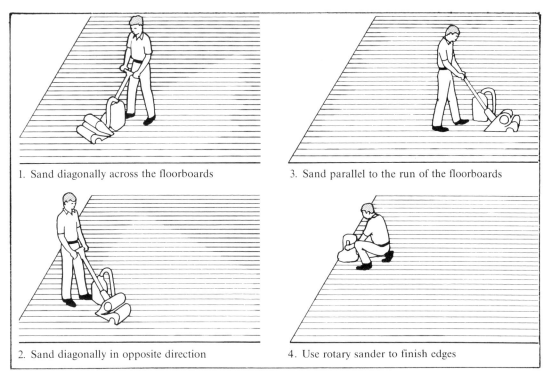

1. Sand diagonally across the floorboards

3. Sand parallel to the run of the floorboards

2. Sand diagonally in opposite direction

4. Use rotary sander to finish edges

of sanding by about 75 mm (3″), until the floor has been completed.

7. Fit new abrasive paper as the old one becomes worn or if it rips. Do this by tilting the machine onto its back castors, switching off and waiting until the drum has stopped revolving. Disconnect the power and then change the paper.

8. Change to a medium-grade abrasive paper and sand the floor again, this time working parallel to the boards, working down one strip then moving back along it in the opposite direction to sand it a second time. Once again, switch off the machine at the end of each strip and sweep up the sawdust after every run has been completed.

9. Change to fine-grade abrasive paper and, working parallel with the boards, sand again to give a smooth, finished surface.

10. The belt sander will have left an unsanded strip around the walls which you will need to tackle with the hand-held orbital sander. Progress through the various grades of abrasive as before, working in the direction of the grain, simply stroking the sander over the surface.

11. Corners and other inaccessible areas will have to be sanded by hand. Use a shave hook to get right into tight corners.

12. Once you've finished sanding, sweep and/or vacuum the floor several times, allowing the dust to settle between cleaning sessions. Once all traces of dust have been removed you are now ready to finish the floor.

13. First wipe over the floor with a clean, damp, lint-free cloth and leave to dry. Then, using another clean, lint-free cloth, apply a priming coat of varnish diluted with white spirit.

14. For a hardwearing, easy-care finish, apply a polyurethane varnish. Ensure the room is well ventilated and apply the first coat with a brush, being careful to follow the grain of the wood. Allow to dry completely, rub down with a fine-grade wire wool, remove all traces of dust and apply the second coat.

15. Apply at least three coats for a good protective finish and leave for at least 48 hours before you start walking on the floor.

LAYING SHEET VINYL

Sheet vinyl is versatile, tough, easy to clean and available in a vast range of colours and designs. It is relatively easy to lay, although if you are a complete novice, confine your first attempt to a small room and use one of the cheaper vinyls.

Vinyl is sold in sheets 2, 3 and 4 m (approx 2, 3 and 4 yd) wide, which means all but the largest rooms can be fitted with a seam-free finish. To calculate how much you'll need, measure up the floor of the room with an expandable metal rule, then draw up a scale plan of the room on graph paper, taking care to mark in all obstacles and door openings. Take these measurements to your retailer who should be able to advise on the most economical cuts. Allow an extra 75 mm (3″) on each length. Check the manufacturer's instructions on laying and buy the correct adhesive.

- Sheet vinyl
- Soft broom
- Sharp knife
- Pair of sharp scissors
- Profile or contour gauge
- Block of wood
- Straightedge/metal rule
- Adhesive or double-sided tape - according to manufacturer's Instructions

1. First ensure that the sub-floor is smooth, even and free from damp.

2. Lay the roll of vinyl in a warm room for 24 to 48 hours to help it 'relax' and make it more supple. Do not stand it on its end or rest anything on it.

3. Assuming there are no seams, roll the vinyl sheet across the floor, so that it laps up all the walls by about 50mm (2″). Use a soft broom to remove any air pockets. Check that the pattern is square and centralised in the doorway, lining up with the longest wall in the room.

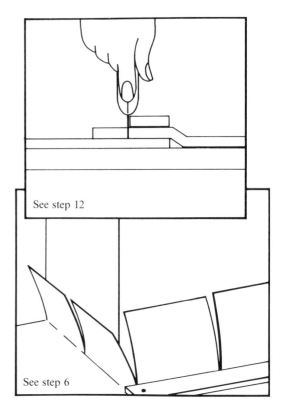

See step 12

See step 6

4. With a sharp pair of scissors or a knife, make a series of freeing cuts around the edges, cutting down from the edge of the vinyl to near the floor join, so that the sheet lies more or less flat on the floor.

5. Mark the approximate positions of any internal corners on the back of the vinyl, cut a triangular notch, then trim out the waste. The important thing is that you don't cut off too much, so err on the side of caution, cutting a little at a time until the vinyl fits snug into the corner.

6. At external or protruding corners, allow the vinyl to lap up the wall. Make a freeing cut downwards from the edge of the sheet to the point where the wall meets the floor, so that the vinyl laps up to the skirting board on both sides of the corner. Roughly cut away the excess, then press the vinyl into the angles and trim carefully to fit. By this stage the vinyl should be flat and smooth.

7. Make a series of freeing cuts around any door frames, cutting down from the edge of the vinyl to the point where it meets the floor. A profile or contour gauge will provide you with a very accurate outline of the door architrave and will enable you to make a much neater trim.

8. Once the preliminary fitting has taken place, prepare for final cutting. Use a small block of wood and press the vinyl firmly into the base of the skirting board all round the room. The block should leave a crease where the two surfaces meet.

9. Now trim along this line with a sharp knife, using a metal straightedge for guidance. (This will only work successfully on the thinner, more flexible vinyls.)

10. Stop to remove any waste occasionally, checking that a good fit has been achieved.

11. Once the vinyl fits, you will need to follow the manufacturer's instructions for fixing. 'Lay flat' floorings will need to be fixed at doorways and seams using double-sided tape. Other vinyls will have to be stuck down with adhesive around the edges and along any seams.

12. If you need to lay more than one sheet of vinyl, it will be necessary to 'join' the sheets. Overlap the sheets, making sure the pattern on both is running in the same direction and that it matches. With a sharp knife and a metal straightedge, cut through both sheets parallel to the overlap. Remove the trimmings and you should have a perfect fit.

13. Awkwardly shaped obstacles or alcoves can be dealt with in a number of ways. The easiest way is to make a paper template to mark and cut the vinyl. Cut out the shape roughly from paper and fit it around the obstacle. Then make scissor cuts all round so that tongues can be bent up for a more accurate fit.

14. Snip off the tongues along the pencil line, tape the template to the back of the vinyl and transfer the outline of the obstacle. Use a sharp knife to cut carefully around this line, making sure the vinyl is resting on a piece of board and not on any vinyl which has already been laid.

15. Fit the cut sheet to the obstacle and trim to fit.

16. If your edge trimming is not quite perfect, don't worry, you can always cover up the joins around the skirting, using quadrant moulding.

CARPETS

Carpets usually represent the largest single outlay in an interior design scheme and for this reason it is vital to make the right choice. Consider the quality of carpet needed for the room in which it will be laid and how much wear it is likely to receive. Generally speaking, natural fibres are more expensive than manmade ones.

Carpet is sold in various widths, according to your needs. A carpet referred to as **broadloom** is most commonly used for room size widths. **Bodywidth** refers to narrower carpets, suitable for halls and passages. Carpet **squares**, like room-size rugs and carpet **tiles**, are usually 500mm (20") square and widely available, they are popular for kitchens.

The finish on a carpet depends on the way the pile has been treated and you can get an idea of how durable a carpet will be by assessing the weight, density and durability of its pile. Short, dense-fibre carpets are usually the most hardwearing. Press your thumb into the pile – the quicker it returns to normal, the longer it will last. Most carpets will have a label indicating its construction and usage. The British Carpet Performance Rating Scheme uses the following categories:

A - Extra heavy wear. Suitable for contract use.

B - Very heavy wear. Suitable for heavy domestic use in family homes; halls, stairs and living rooms.

C - Heavy wear. Suitable for busy domestic areas; halls, stairs and living rooms.

D - General wear. Suitable for dining rooms and living rooms in small family or adult-only homes.

E - Medium wear. Suitable for rooms not subjected to concentrated use, such as dining rooms and bedrooms.

F - Light wear. Suitable for occasional use rooms, such as bedrooms and guest rooms.

An all wool velvet pile carpet from Tintawn

Unfortunately, not all manufacturers and retailers follow this grading. More and more firms are now using small sketches indicating which rooms the carpet is suitable for, so seek the advice of a good retailer.

If there are young children or pets in your family, it's inevitable that your carpet will have to withstand a great deal of wear and tear. In these instances it would be worth buying a carpet which has been specially treated to withstand stains. Any carpet bearing a label indicating that is has been treated with Scotchgard, Scotchgard Stain Release (found on carpets made from Tibrelle) or Antron Stainmaster will be particularly resilient to stains caused by foods and drinks, although foods with natural dyes, such as curries or mustard, may cause permanent staining. Once again, a good carpet retailer will be able to advise you about what's available.

Carpets come in a number of different finishes. These include:

Berber - originally woven from undyed Karakul wool, a coarse hairy fibre in natural shades of cream and brown, Berbers are now made from synthetic fibres as well and are called Berber-style. They usually have a nubbly loop pile and a flecked appearance.

Brussels weave - a tightly looped pile which is uncut.

Flat weave - a smooth, woven appearance which has no pile.

Loop pile - continuous run of uncut loops which give a closely curled boucle-type appearance.

Plush pile - fairly long, smooth pile, not as dense as a velvet pile.

Sculptured pile - a combination of cut and looped pile. The pile is cut to different lengths to form an interesting pattern.

Shag or **long pile** - made from long cut strands. Needs good care, with regular raking and vacuuming. Do not lay on stairs as it can catch on heels and could be dangerous.

Twist pile - the pile yarn is tightly twisted to give a sturdy, hardwearing finish, textured in appearance.

Velvet pile - a short-cut, dense pile which is smooth in appearance. It can become patchy and marks fairly easily.

As well as the different finishes, there are a number of carpet types which relate to the actual method of manufacture.

Axminsters are woven carpets where the pile threads are inserted individually into a jute or hessian backing. They are usually highly patterned, although plain and mottled varieties are available. The pile can be cut short or long, and they come in a variety of widths.

Bonded carpets are made just like a sandwich. The filling is the carpet pile with the outer layers being the specially woven backing. The pile is sliced in the centre to give two bonded carpets. They are made from natural and synthetic fibres and are available in a range of colours and widths.

Tufted carpets are non-woven, made by stitching the pile threads into a woven hessian or polypropylene backing which is coated with adhesive to anchor the tufts; a second backing of foam, jute or polypropylene is then added. The pile can be cut, looped or sculpted. Comes in a variety of widths.

Wiltons are close textured with a surface pile which is either smooth and velvety, close looped or a combination of the two to give a sculptured effect. Any yarn not used on the surface is woven into the backing, adding thickness and strength. Patterned Wiltons are available, but the majority are plain.

Carpets are made in a variety of different fibres both natural and synthetic, on their own or blended. They include:

Acrylic a synthetic fibre with characteristics closely resembling wool, although it is not as hardwearing. Dyes well. Trade names include Acrilan and Dralon.

Animal hairs such as goat, horse or pig hairs, are often combined with synthetic fibres to produce a hardwearing, fibre-resistant carpet which does not attract dirt.

Cotton is hardwearing and easy to clean and usually used for dhurries, rubber-backed bathroom carpets and some velvet pile broadlooms.

Nylon is used on its own or mixed with other fibres, particularly wool. It is durable and has good resistance to abrasion. However, it is not fire-resistant. Early nylon carpets were not popular because they soiled easily and were prone to static, but both these problems have been overcome with the new generation of nylon fibres. Trade names include Enkalon, Timbrelle, Antron and Anso IV.

Polyester is soft, pretty, waterproof and easy to clean, but it flattens easily. Mainly used for bedroom carpets, it is sometimes blended with polypropylene to make it more hardwearing. Trade names include Acron and Trevira.

Polypropylene is widely used as a backing material as well as for carpet pile. Durable and dirt-resistant, it is highly moisture-resistant, so won't absorb stains, but it is not fire-resistant. Used on its own or blended with wool. Trade names include Duron and Meraklon.

Viscose rayon is a cheap fibre which is easy to dye and inherently non-static. Not particularly hardwearing, it is usually blended with other fibres to provide bulk. Trade name, Evlan.

Wool is the premier carpet fibre, hardwearing, good-looking, soft, warm and resilient to fire and dirt. However, it is the most expensive fibre. It takes colour well, so comes in a wide choice of colours. Wool is used on its own or mixed with nylon, acrylic, viscose and polypropylene. An 80/20 wool/nylon mix is the most familiar.

UNDERLAYS

If you are going to pay out a lot of money for a good carpet, it's worth investing in a good underlay which will help it wear better and last longer. It will also add comfort and provide sound- and draught-proofing. **Never, ever** be tempted to use an old underlay with a new carpet, or even an old carpet; it's false economy. They will damage the new carpet. Your carpet supplier will be able to advise you on the best choice of carpet underlay, but briefly the types are:

Crumb rubber is the most hardwearing and resilient of the rubber underlays, although it is not particularly soft to walk on. Because it wears well, it is ideal for areas which are subjected to a heavy usage, such as halls, stairs and landings.

Felt comes in various thicknesses and the thicker the better. Suitable for use on stairs as it provides good sound insulation. A good choice for seamed carpets.

Felt paper can be used in conjunction with other underlays, to prevent dust penetrating the floorboards, or on its own with foam-backed carpets to prevent them sticking to the floor.

Felt/rubber combinations may not be as hardwearing as felt or the better rubber underlays, but they can combine the advantages of both.

Latex rubber usually has a ribbed profile which offers a high degree of comfort. A value for money underlay, which is unlikely to wear as well as the more expensive crumb rubber underlays.

Pads are designed for use under stair carpets.

Sponge rubber is usually contoured or has a waffle finish. It is particularly soft and very resilient, although it may not recover well from marks made by heavy furniture.

Hearth-rug from Tintawns Irish Collection

If you want a fitted carpet, leave the job to a professional. If you are paying out several hundred pounds for a new carpet, it would be silly to economise on carpet fitting. For the best results, a carpet should be stretched. For details of professional carpet fitters in your area contact the National Institute of Carpet Fitters, 17-21 George Street, Croydon, Surrey CR9 1TQ. Lightweight carpets, however, particularly those with a bonded foam backing, can be successfully laid by an amateur. But do make sure the sub-floor is sound, even and damp-free.

New carpets will tend to show a certain amount of 'fluffing' as lengths of loose fibre work their way to the surface. Just vacuum sparingly. If single tufts or loose ends stand proud of the pile, don't pull them out but use a pair of sharp scissors to cut them level.

To preserve their good looks and increase their life, carpets need to be vacuumed regularly to remove dust and dirt, try and follow the principle of little and often – aim for once a day in high traffic areas. Long and shag pile carpets should be raked regularly with a special shag rake. Although you won't be able to see the build up of dirt and grit, if it's allowed to accumulate at the base of the carpet fibres, it will wear down the pile shortening the carpet's life. When your carpet needs a more thorough cleaning, a professional company will

be able to clean it for you in situ or hire the necessary equipment and do it yourself.

Always deal with any spills immediately to prevent a permanent stain.

RUGS

Rugs can be used in many ways. They offer an alternative to wall-to-wall carpeting, look particularly good on wood floors and can also be used effectively with carpets. Not only do they provide a comfortable surface, but they can also introduce colour and texture to a room, often providing an interesting focal point. Some oriental rugs are bought as an investment, others provide a simple and cheap type of floorcovering.

Caucasian - brightly coloured rugs with distinctive stylised figures and an elaborately decorated border.

Chinese - often in soft yellow, pink, peach, apricot, blue or black colourways. They are thick and rich in texture, displaying Chinese motifs.

Dhurries - hand-woven cotton mats, usually from India. Reasonably priced they come in a wide choice of colours and designs. Do not place directly onto light-coloured carpets, as the colours may bleed.

Flokati - a fleecy woollen rug, usually white or off-white, made in Greece.

Kelim - a tapestry made in thick, harsh wool, usually from Turkey or Iran. Some types are very brightly coloured.

Numdah - an inexpensive Indian rug, usually in soft colours depicting native images.

Persian - a high quality rug from Central Asia. Many varieties are available, usually rectulangular with stylised motifs. Made from knotted wool, commonly in shades of red and blue.

Serape - coarsely woven rugs from Mexico, with fringed edges.

Turkish - styles vary from region to region, but common motifs are a pointed prayer arch at one end flanked by two pillars of wisdom.

Rugs can generally be cleaned with a vacuum; turn them now and again and vacuum the back

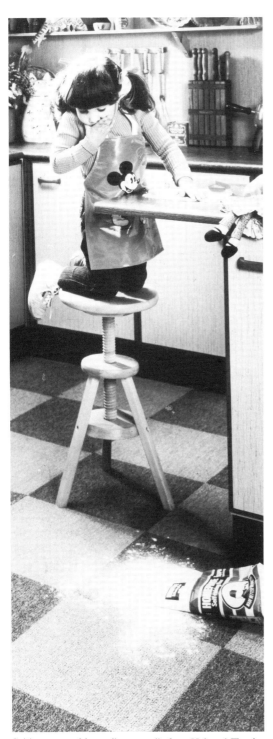

Cuisine — a real loop pile carpet tile from Halstead Flooring

as well. When you buy a rug, make sure you ask for care instructions. Most cotton and wool rugs are washable and can be washed in warm water with a mild detergent; spin dry if possible. Rugs which are similar in character to carpets, can be shampooed. Valued, oriental rugs should always be taken to a specialist cleaner. Dhurries can be dry cleaned.

LAYING FLOOR TILES

Soft floor tiles are available in a variety of different materials: vinyl, rubber, cork and carpet. They are all relatively large so you can cover a floor fairly quickly. Obviously the method of fixing the tiles will vary depending on the material chosen. For example, vinyl tiles are usually self-adhesive, rubber and cork tiles need to be bedded on an adhesive base, whilst carpet tiles are usually loose laid.

Whatever tiles you use, most are laid out using the same basic process, but for the best results ensure that the existing floor or sub-floor is smooth, clean, dry and sound.

MARKING THE FLOOR

1. You first need to find the centre of the room. To do this find the centre of two opposite walls and snap a chalked string line between them to mark a line across the floor *(pic A)*.

2. Loose lay the tiles at right-angles to this line up to one wall. If there is a gap of less than half a tile width, move the line sideways by half a tile width to give a wider margin. Remove tiles.

3. Now draw a line at right-angles to the first. To do this attach a pencil to one end of a length of string and a drawing pin to the other to make an improvised compass.

4. Fix the drawing pin at the centre point of the first line, then scribe an arc at equal distances either side of it. From each point scribe arcs on both sides of the line which bisect each other.

5. Join these points to form a line across the floor *(pic B)*. The centre point of the room is where these two lines cross.

6. Loose lay the tiles at right-angles to the new line to ensure that the border tiles are at least half a tile width, as before.

7. Once you have established the two guidelines, nail a guide batten against one line to align the first row of tiles.

8. If the room is oddly shaped, centre the first line on the fireplace or a door opening.

9. If you want to arrange the tiles diagonally, just draw the lines from corner to corner.

LAYING THE TILES

For the best result always stack tiles in the room they are to be laid for 24 hours before work starts. If the tiles have a directional pattern, make sure you lay them correctly, some will have arrows printed on the back.

1. The first tile should be placed in the angle of the intersecting lines. *(pic C)*.

2. **If using self-adhesive tiles**, remove protective paper backing from tile, then press the edge against the guide batten. Align one corner with the centre line. Gradually lower tile on to floor and press down.

3. **If you are laying an adhesive bed**, only cover a small area at a time and open all the windows for good ventilation. Read the instructions supplied with the adhesive as you may have to wait for it to become tacky before the tiles are laid. Always lay the tiles in position, do not slide them in place. Use a block of wood to tap down edges of tiles and a damp cloth to remove surplus adhesive as you work.

4. Lay second tile on the other side of the centre line butting it up against the first.

5. Form a square with two more tiles then lay tiles around the square to form a pyramid *(pic C)*.

6. Proceed in this way to fill one half of the room.

7. **Fitting along the wall**. Walls are rarely straight, so you will need to cut the border tile to the skirting profile. Lay a tile on top of the last full tile matching it completely. Place another tile on top of this with its edge touching the wall. Draw along the edge of the top tile with a pencil to mark

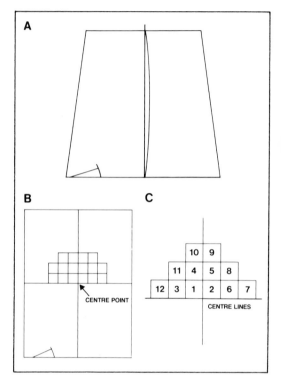

the tile below. Remove marked tile and cut along the line with a sharp knife. Place cut tile in position.

8. **Fitting around awkward shapes**. To tile around awkwardly shaped obstacles and curves you will need to make a paper template. Cut out a paper tile and fit it round the obstacle, cut 'fingers' in the template which can be pressed against the object to reproduce the shape exactly. Transfer template to tile and cut out shape. For complex curves use a profile gauge.

9. **Fitting around pipes**. Mark position of pipe on tile using a compass. Draw parallel lines from this point to the tile edge. Measure halfway between line and cut a straight slit to the edge of the tile and a hole for the pipe. Fold back slit and slide tile in place.

10. Once you have completely tiled one half of the room, remove the guide batten and complete the second half in the same way.

11. When you are finished, vinyl tiles should be wiped over with a damp cloth to remove any fingermarks.

PART 3

HOW TO IMPROVE YOUR HOME

KITCHEN IDEAS

We all have our own ideas of what the 'dream' kitchen should look like. For some it's the rustic appeal of solid wood units set off with terracotta floor tiles and plenty of blue and white accessories, while others prefer the sleek modernity of white, high gloss polyester units combined with plenty of chrome accessories. Maybe your ideal kitchen is fitted with colourful, easy-care laminate units or one of the individualised hand-painted ranges which have become increasingly popular.

Whatever your preference, there's such a staggering selection of ranges and styles to choose from that, when you do decide you want to change your kitchen, you must be prepared to spend a great deal of time looking round.

WHERE TO BUY

Fitting a new kitchen can be an expensive business, so if you have a limited budget, self-assembly ranges are probably the least expensive option available. They come in a wide range of styles and materials with plenty of extras which will enable you to create a stylish and individual layout. However, if you choose a flat-pack range you may not be able to achieve a fully fitted look because many ranges only come in standard sizes. Another potential problem is that the assembly instructions may not be very clear and you may experience some problems putting the various components together. If you do have any trouble, most retailers will be willing to offer advice; some may even assemble the units for you (for a charge of course). Another DIY option is a rigid range, where the units come pre-assembled and you just have to fit them into the room.

Whatever you choose, remember that with a self-assembly range you will need time and patience to put it all together and if anything goes wrong you've got to sort it out yourself. Uneven floors and bulging walls are typical problems which you might be faced with. If DIY fitting does not appeal, remember you could still buy the units and ask a builder to take care of the fitting.

Self-assembly kitchens are available from most builders' merchants and home improvement stores like Texas, Magnet, Wickes and B & Q.

Kitchen specialists should take all the worry out of fitting a new kitchen. You just choose what you want and they will take care of everything else from planning the layout to arranging the installation and decorating work. Because of the high degree of service these outlets offer, they can be quite expensive,

The Craftsman range of kitchen units from B & Q

so it makes sense to go to one which has been recommended to you or to deal with one which has a good reputation. Most of the well-known kitchen companies, such as Wrighton, Bosch, SieMatic and Wellmann, are available through specialist outlets.

Any company belonging to the Kitchen Specialists Association (KSA) should be totally reliable as they must take full responsibility for planning, ordering, supply and installation and adhere to the association's high standards. The KSA operates a consumer protection scheme so that if a member goes bankrupt, the association will complete the work at no extra charge to the customer. For a list of members in your area write to the Kitchen Specialists Association, Information Office, 8 St Bernard's Crescent, Edinburgh EH4 1NP. ☎ 031-332 8884.

The epitome of the ideal kitchen is one which is tailor-made to your own specific requirements with units specially designed to suit the room. Of course this type of kitchen is not cheap; they work out as expensive as top-quality rigid ranges from specialist outlets. Always check to find out what you get for your money before placing an order. Smallbone, Woodstock and Keith Gray are just some of the companies offering a custom-made service.

An increasingly popular method of buying a kitchen is through one of the many direct sell companies which advertise in newspapers and magazines. Theoretically they should be one of the cheapest ways of getting a kitchen because they cut out the middle man. Unfortunately, the quality of units supplied and level of service offered vary, and you may not be getting the bargain you thought you were. For example, it's not usually possible to inspect the quality of the units before you buy — a sample door is not sufficient to check the construction, hinges, drawers, etc. Furthermore, some direct sell companies employ very skilful sales staff who may pressurise you into buying a kitchen or offer 'free' extras.

If you do buy a kitchen through direct sell,

When you're good – the word gets around . . .

›rational‹
DIE KÜCHE

INFORMATION

WHATEVER YOU ARE COOKING YOU'LL HAVE. EVERLASTING FUN WITH

CONSULTATION

MEASURING-UP

DESIGN/OFFER

DELIVERY

FITTING

CUSTOMER SERVICE

Range 95

There are many good reasons for ›rational‹ being "Britains's best selling European kitchen".

›rational‹, with over 25 years experience in the kitchen industry and 15 years established experience in Great Britain, not just offer their extensive collection of door fronts and design varieties but a built-in kitchen of high quality and design that you will enjoy day after day and long into the future.

Our specialist partners are carefully chosen for the ›rational‹ network in Great Britain for their comprehensive service and advice which they extend to you, the customer.

›rational‹ Built-in Kitchens (U.K.) Ltd.
468 Malton Ave, Trading Estate Slough SL 14 QU
Tel: 07 53 / 69 35 53 · Fax: 07 53 / 69 22 62

›rational‹
PARTNER TO THE SPECIALIST

German quality at its best with over 25 years experience.

NEW

Enhance the clean lines of modern living . . . with co-ordinated themes and styles to make your kitchen individual.

We at the English Kitchen Company derive great pleasure for ourselves as well as our many friends in producing many designs from the past epochs of design and excellence, reproducing with a great love for detail, improving the techniques employed by past craftsmen by utilising modern methods previously denied.

THE ENGLISH KITCHEN COMPANY

Manufacturers and Purveyors of Quality Fitted Kitchens and Bedrooms.

FREEFONE

0800 269766

OR FREE POST TODAY
NO STAMP NEEDED

NAME _____

ADDRESS _____

POSTCODE _____ TEL. No. _____

POST TO: THE ENGLISH KITCHEN COMPANY
 FREEPOST
 OLDHAM
 OL1 3BR

DISTINCTIVE

Based in Toronto, Canac Kitchens is one of the world's largest manufacturers of high quality kitchen furniture.

We strive to provide quality kitchens to suit any need, taste and budget.

The designs are European in concept, crafted to the highest standards using only the finest quality materials and offering an extensive range of laminate, traditional Canadian timbers, including Cherry, Oak, Mahogany

KITCHENS

& Pine, through to lacquer and baked polyester finishes in various colourways.

Compare your free estimate from Canac to any other kitchen manufacturer... and smile!
We will not be undersold!

Main Agents for WESTINGHOUSE.
Free Planning & Design service.
Fast efficient delivery and fitting.
Complete design, fitting & ancillary services available.
Trade/Retail enquiries welcome.

BY *Canac*

Elm Grove,
Wimbledon SW19 4HE
Telephone: 01-946 0338
9am - 5.30pm Mon to
Sat or by appointment

the law allows you to change your mind within five days of signing an order and paying the deposit and if you cancel you are entitled to a full refund. This only applies to certain types of credit agreement, so check with your local Citizens' Advice Bureau.

UNIT CONSTRUCTION

No matter where you buy your kitchen, you will need to check that the construction matches the kitchen's appearance. Although price is usually a good indication of quality, it's always worth visually checking the construction and fittings.

The **carcass**, or open-fronted box, forming the shell of the units, is usually made from melamine-faced chipboard and should have a fixed back to provide rigidity and stability. Although some manufacturers offer solid wood carcasses, manmade materials are more stable and less expensive. Look carefully at the construction, at the materials used and how the pieces are joined. Cheaper units may use thin chipboard and be inadequately held together.

Hinges, usually concealed within the units will provide a 90° or 170° opening. Most are spring-loaded to prevent the door staying open. Period-style ranges may be fitted with ornate exterior hinges. Keep opening and shutting the doors to see how well the hinges work and check to see if they can be adjusted.

Drawers are a good way of telling the quality of a kitchen. Many modern drawers are made from knockdown plastic kits with just a flimsy hardboard base which will provide little support. A drawer should be well constructed, with a base strong enough to withstand any accidental knocks. Look at the corner joints to see how they're made; they may be just snapped together or glued. check the drawer front and handle which should be securely fixed, and make sure the drawer runs smoothly as you open and close it. It should not stick when fully loaded.

When it comes to the choice of finish, there is an extensive range to choose from:

Solid wood is very attractive and long-lasting, but also one of the most expensive finishes. Wood may become scratched and marked but the damage is less noticeable than with manmade finishes and, as the wood mellows, it develops its own character. Oak and pine are popular at the moment, although you can get ash, beech, cherry, sycamore, chestnut, walnut and mahogany. The finish may be left natural, stained, antiqued, lacquered or painted.

Wood veneers give the appearance of solid wood, but are generally less expensive. Because the veneer is fixed to a stable base material, such as chipboard, it is less likely to warp than solid wood. Wood veneers will not wear as well as solid wood and any deep scratches are likely to reveal the base material. Available in an extensive range of wood finishes which are sometimes painted or lacquered.

Laminate-faced chipboard is the standard kitchen door finish and relatively inexpensive. It is extremely tough, withstanding scratches, and comes in a wide range of colours, textures and designs with a choice of finishes from high gloss to matt. Laminate is frequently combined with solid wood, used for frames, trims and handles, offering practicality with a softer, more luxurious look. Formica is the best-known brand name.

Melamine is a plastic-impregnated paper which is sometimes used as an inexpensive alternative to laminate. It is susceptible to chips and scratches and is not suitable for worktops.

Polyester is a factory-applied paint widely used in good quality ranges. Cheaper than laminate and more durable than melamine, it comes in a good choice of colours.

Lacquer either a clear varnish-like finish applied as a protective coating or a top-quality paint, which gives a hardwearing, gloss surface.

Special finishes, such as bamboo and hessian are usually found at the top-end of the price scale. In recent years hand-painted finishes such as rag-rolling, sponging and stencilling, have also been offered and are becoming increasingly popular.

The one part of the kitchen which needs to be extremely hardwearing is the worktop, so make your choice with care.

- Most worktops are made from a chipboard core about 25 to 40 mm (1-1½″) thick. Generally the thicker the core the better.

- The surface should be scratch-, stain- and heat-resistant, easy to keep clean, yet firm and cool to the touch.

- A post-formed or curved front edge will make the worktop easier to keep clean, more comfortable to use and less susceptible to damage than a square-edge finish.

- An upstand at the back of the worktop will make it easier to keep clean and more hygienic as no crumbs can get trapped in the gap.

When it comes to choosing a finish there are several options:

Laminate is durable and stain-resistant, capable of withstanding heat for short periods. Although it is reasonably scratch-resistant, do not use a laminate worktop as a chopping board.

Hardwood makes a very expensive but attractive worktop. Provided it has been sealed with teak or linseed oil, it will be hardwearing and resistant to stains and heat. Although it can be used as a chopping board, in time the surface will become very scratched.

Ceramic tiles must be laid on wood-edged baseboard and grouted with waterproof grouting, epoxy resin grout is ideal. They make a durable, attractive worktop easy to clean and stain-, scratch- and heat-resistant, although the glaze of some tiles may crack under a very hot pan. The grout may also become stained in time.

Solid stone, granite and **marble** make durable but expensive worktops. Granite is particulary attractive, but marble is porous and likely to stain. As an alternative to marble consider **Corian**, a solid, durable, non-porous material, which can be cut to any shape or size. It is particularly hygienic as a special adhesive is used to weld the material together eliminating the cracks and crevices which attract dirt. Its one drawback is its cost.

PLANNING

Before you start thinking too much about colour and finish, you should give some thought to your requirements so that you can plan a suitable layout. A well-planned layout is

The beautifully finished 'Synchro' kitchen from Bosch

essential if your kitchen is going to work successfully. After all it is primarily a workroom, so its basic functions of food preparation, cooking and washing-up need to be satisfied. Of course, if you go to a kitchen specialist or a company offering a kitchen planning service, they will be able to advise you on all these aspects, but they will still need to know something about your lifestyle. To help sort out your priorities, ask yourself the following:

■ How many people are there in your family? Do they tend to use the kitchen at the same time?

■ If you have young children, would you like an area for them to play in safely as you work?

■ What kind of meals do you cook? For how many? How often? The more complicated cooking you do, the more space you'll need.

■ Is your kitchen used just for preparing food and cleaning up or do/would you eat there sometimes/always if possible?

■ Do you shop several times a week or more irregularly? The more frequently you shop, the less storage space you need.

■ What type of food do you tend to buy: fresh, frozen, packets, cans? This will affect the type of storage space required.

■ Do you keep crockery and glass in the kitchen? If so you'll need extra cupboards.

■ Is your kitchen used for hobbies, as a laundry, for homework, etc?

■ What kind of appliances would you like to fit into the kitchen? If you can't afford them all in one go, you can leave space for them to be fitted later.

■ Do you like utensils and equipment to be on display on open shelves and hanging up, or do you prefer everything concealed behind closed doors, or a mixture of the two?

■ What style of kitchen do you prefer: a country look with natural textures or something sleek and modern?

When all these questions have been answered you'll have a much better idea of the kind of kitchen you'd like and the things you consider to be important.

LAYOUT

The essence of a well-planned kitchen is a sensible and safe arrangement of units and appliances, although, because kitchens come in

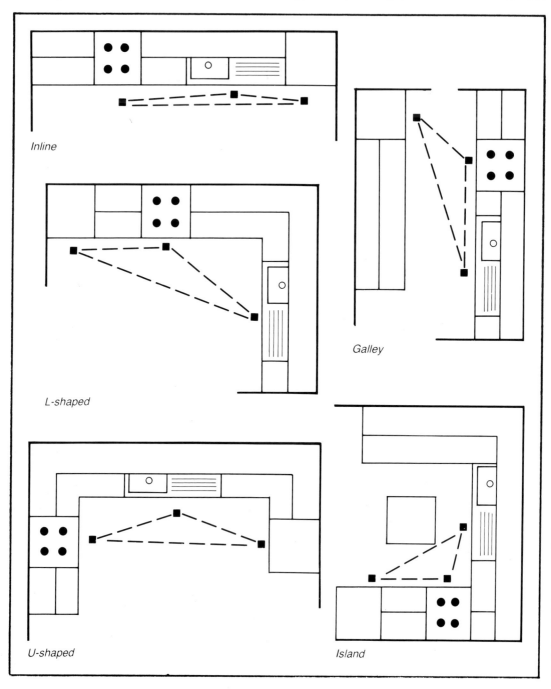

Inline

L-shaped

Galley

U-shaped

Island

all sorts of shapes and sizes, there's no such thing as a 'right' layout. As a general guide however there are five basic kitchen layouts which will provide the maximum working efficiency.

The simplest is the **inline** arrangement, where all the units and appliances are set out along one wall. It is particularly suited to long, narrow rooms and is less expensive than other layouts simply because fewer units are required.

Next comes the **galley** kitchen where two rows of units are arranged parallel to one another. It can be a less tiring layout to work in than the others, but it can become congested if the central aisle is also a throughway between two access doors.

An **L-shaped** layout is where the units and appliances are arranged along two adjacent walls. This is a good choice for awkwardly shaped rooms or where space is limited as the two legs of the 'L' can be of different lengths to suit the available space.

Probably the most flexible layout is the **U-shaped** kitchen where units and appliances are arranged on three adjacent walls. It is also the most practical choice for a kitchen/diner as a peninsular unit can be turned into a breakfast bar or make a useful serving area.

Finally there's the **island** layout, which is usually an L-or U-shaped kitchen with an island of units placed in the centre. To work successfully you really need plenty of space for this type of layout.

Using one of these layouts, most professional kitchen planners start by working out the work triangle – the path you take between food storage area (refrigerator), preparation area (sink), cooking area (cooker) and back to the storage area. This divides the kitchen into zones, so all related equipment can be grouped within it. For example, pots and pans near the cooker, rubbish bin near the sink and so on. Although there are no hard and fast rules, the total length of the three sides of the triangle should be between 3 m (12') and 6 m (22'). Any less and the kitchen will be cramped; any more and it will be tiring to work in.

Obviously the layout you choose will depend on your existing kitchen and it may be possible that the work triangle per se is not possible. If this is the case, try to avoid an arrangement

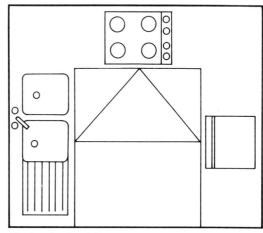

The 'work triangle'

that allows people to enter the room or cut across the route between sink and cooker. Whatever else, the layout should be safe to work in, so once you've come up with a suitable plan, look at it from a safety point of view.

APPLIANCES

When it comes to choosing the appliances, there's just as wide a range of makes to choose from as there are unit ranges, all offering a whole host of clever features. Depending on your preference, you can opt for built-in appliances to give a streamlined appearance, as well as slot-in and freestanding appliances.

Built-in appliances are designed to fit flush with the kitchen units and go in under the standard-height work surface, or be built in at a suitable height above the work surface in a special housing unit. To give a totally uniform appearance, most manufacturers offer a complete range of co-ordinating appliances from built-in hobs and ovens, through to dishwashers and freezers. Many can be fitted with a decor panel to disguise their appearance totally. (A decor panel is a thin piece of wood, laminate or veneer, usually made by the unit manufacturers, which slots into a frame at the front of the appliance to cover everything but the controls.)

Because of the popularity of streamlined kitchens, many manufacturers have produced freestanding appliances which have a built-in look – slip-in cookers for example. They are made to the same dimensions as standard fitted units so that the hob is at the same height as the work surface, and they can be sited anywhere within a run of units, even into a corner. Because they fit snugly against the units, they eliminate the unsightly gaps at either side which are a common feature of freestanding appliances.

If money is an important consideration, you can't beat freestanding appliances, which are a lot cheaper to buy than their built-in counterparts. You don't have to buy costly housing units and when you move you can

easily take the appliances with you. Modern freestanding appliances also offer greater flexibility when it comes to kitchen planning.

There's no doubt that having a new kitchen will involve a great deal of inconvenience and upheaval: you may be without cooking and washing-up facilities and the house will be full of dust. Be prepared for the worst and you may be pleasantly surprised. If you have young children it may be a good idea if they can stay with relatives or friends for a few days whilst the work is completed.

The exclusive Castell range from Tielsa in yew and maple

GLOSSARY

Antiqued - *hand-rubbed finish giving a two-tone effect on solid wood fronts or bronze fittings.*

Baffle - *also called a light pelmet or light rail, a continuous strip of wood or laminate fixed to the bottom edge of a wall unit to cut out glare from the strip light.*

Butterfly - *handle in shape of a butterfly.*

Cassette panel - *square-edged door or drawer panel.*

Carousel - *revolving shelf fitting for corner units to use otherwise inaccessible space.*

Cathedral arch - *traditional arched panelling found on door and drawer fronts.*

Cornice - *decorative edging with a pronounced profile which gives a finished look to the top of wall units.*

CP - *chrome-plated handle.*

Decor panel - *a thin panel of wood, laminate or veneer attached to the front of kitchen appliances with a decor frame to co-ordinate them with the rest of the units.*

Distressed - *old worn look achieved by rubbing or beating solid wood fronts.*

Dowel - *a rounded wooden peg tapped into correspondingly-sized holes in two pieces of wood to form a very rigid joint.*

Drawer-line - *base unit with combined door-fronted cupboard and a top drawer.*

Drop - *decorative hinged handle or fingergrip.*

D-shaped - *handle which looks like a letter D.*

Escutcheon - *ornate keyhole plate usually of brass or bronze.*

Fielded panel - *panelled wood or veneer front with pronounced carved edge.*

Finial hinge - *long exposed hinge with decorative ends.*

Finger pull - *finger-sized drop handle.*

Full height - *a base unit with a single door only.*

Gallery ends - *or rails, miniature balustrade fittings found along the front edge of open shelf units.*

High-line - *same as full height.*

Inset - *built-in hobs and sinks which are set into a hole specially cut for them in the worktop.*

Integrated - *method of concealing built-in appliances by connecting the appliance door to a door which matches the units.*

MDF - *medium density fibreboard.*

MFC - *melamine faced chipboard.*

Mid-way unit - *shallow, storage unit or shelves which make use of the space between the base and wall units.*

Mitred joint - *joint made by fixing the ends of two pieces of wood cut at 45° angle.*

Moulding - *decorative features usually referring to raised panel edging.*

Nosing - *worktop which has a veneered or wood front edging. Also called lip/lipping.*

Peninsular unit - *an arrangement of units with access from three sides.*

Plinth - *base unit support set back from front edge to allow foot space. Sometimes adjustable.*

Post-formed - *rounded edging on laminate surfaces.*

Raised and fielded - *panelled wood or veneered front with grooves carved around the centre panel to create a raised appearance.*

Soft formed - *melamine door panel with a shaped edge.*

Square framed - *a plain raised frame holding a flat central panel.*

Stile - *vertical edging on or adjacent to doors sometimes finished in contrasting colour or materials.*

Stirrup grip - *see D-shaped.*

Upright - *raised back part of a worktop set at right-angles to the work surface to prevent dirt and crumbs slipping down the back.*

BATHROOM IDEAS

When it comes to fitting out a new bathroom, there's no shortage of sizes to choose from ranging in design from the traditional to the modern. But despite the fact that a bathroom is very much a work room, you're likely to be faced with a problem of trying to fit a bath, toilet and wash basin all into the space just 2 × 3 m (7' × 10') – the size of the average British bathroom. If you want to add a separate shower or bidet, as well as some cupboards and a heated towel rail in your bathroom, you could have some problems.

BATHS AND WHIRLPOOLS

The standard bath measures 1700 mm long × 700 mm wide (67" × 28"), although other sizes are available. Armitage Shanks, for example, offer a compact Moritz bath 1394 mm long × 797 mm wide (55" × 31") . If you have the space, longer and wider baths are available, but remember that large baths will need more hot water to fill them up – will your hot water tank be able to cope with the demand? Corner baths can make good use of space and will fit into a relatively small area; the Lisbon corner bath by Heatons, for example, only needs a 1300 mm (51") corner. Circular baths are large, deep and luxurious.

In the past few years whirlpool baths have become an increasingly popular luxury addition for many bathrooms – luxury because they will set you back at least £1,000 – and are available in a wide range of single and double bath sizes. Whirlpool baths are a pleasant way to relax aching limbs, although some enthusiasts claim more specific benefits, such as relief from rheumatic and arthritic pain. Always take medical advice before you use one if you have any kidney ailments, if you are pregnant or simply if you bruise easily.

Two types of system are used in domestic whirlpool baths. Firstly, the true **whirlpool jet system**. This uses a pump to extract water

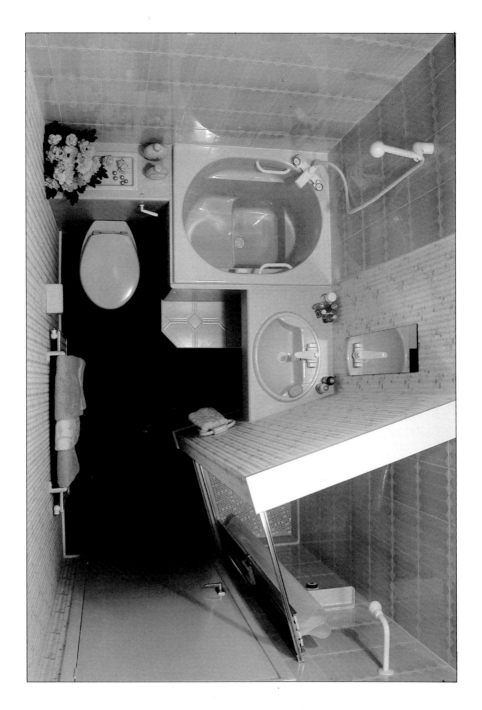

MANTALEDA BATHROOMS
Unique Solutions to Problem Areas.

Leeming Bar Industrial Estate, Northallerton,
North Yorkshire, DL7 9DH
Telephone: Bedale (0677) 24451 Fax: (0677) 24616

Relax in the Mira whirlpool bath from Jacuzzi

from the bath, which is mixed with air and recirculated into the bath via outlets ranged along the sides. These outlets have adjustable nozzles which enable you to control the direction of the jets. In some systems the pressure at which the water is pumped from the nozzles can also be adjusted. Jacuzzi is the brand name given for the original whirlpool system and is not a generic term.

Airbaths or **spa baths** have an air compressor which forces air into the water via tiny holes in the base of the bath and sometimes in the back rest as well. The effect is not as specific as a whirlpool system.

Some baths incorporate both whirlpool jet and airbath systems, which can be operated together or separately.

Activity space needed is 1100 mm (43″) along the bath with a 700 mm (28″) width at the tap end.

BASINS

There are three types of wash hand basins:

Pedestals are supplied in two pieces with a bowl and pedestal, their main disadvantage is they give a fixed height which may not be suitable for all members of the family. A standard pedestal basin height is 780-800 mm (31-32″), although other sizes are available. The bowl width will be between 500-700 mm (20-28″), projecting 400-700 mm (16-28″) from the wall.

Wall-hung basins offer the same range of basin sizes as pedestals, but can be fixed at any convenient height. They are less expensive and occupy less space than pedestals, but most leave their plumbing exposed, so it may be an idea to fit a false wall to conceal this. Small hand-wash basins designed specifically for cloakrooms are available and can be fitted into a corner or even recessed into the wall.

Vanity basins are designed to fit in or on a countertop. These will take up more space than the other types, although they do provide useful storage space. Whether you choose an over-mounted bowl with a raised lip or an under-mounted bowl set flush with the top, make sure the edges are well sealed to avoid any water leakage. Vanity tops should be between 500-800 mm (20-32″) wide and project 440-550 mm (17-22″) from the wall.

The activity space required for all basins is 700 mm (28″) depth from the rim and 1000 mm (39″) along the width.

TOILETS

Toilets have either a high-level cistern with a **feed-pipe** attached to the pan (this is the more traditional old-fashioned type, suitable if you want a period-style bathroom), or are **close-coupled** where the pan and cistern are one unit and therefore will take up less space. Close-coupled units measure 760-790 mm (30-31″) high by 410-520 mm (16-20″) wide and project 650-790 mm (26-31″) from the wall.

Wall-hung or **back-to-wall** toilets, where the cistern is hidden behind the wall, take up as much total space as close-coupled models, but less floor space and offer a neater profile.

The activity space required for all types is 800 mm (32″) width by 600 mm (24″) depth.

There are two types of flush systems to choose from. The traditional wash-down system which flushes out water from under the rim, creating a downwards pressure to wash away the waste. Then there's the syphonic system which sucks the waste away as the water is flushed; this is the quieter of the two, but not always as efficient.

BIDETS

Bidets are now available to match most sanitaryware ranges, complementing the design of the toilet. They will either be back-to-the-wall styles, fitting flush against the wall, or wall-fixed suspended on wall brackets. Basic models have a simple over-rim water supply,

The quiet elegance of the Cottage suite from Armitage Shanks

whilst the more sophisticated styles come with a spray fitted in the base of the bowl. They measure 400 mm (16") high by 340-400 mm (14-16") wide and project 530-700 mm (21-28") from the wall. They require the same activity area as a toilet.

SHOWERS

For a refreshing and versatile alternative to having a bath, you can't beat a shower. A shower is a quick, convenient way to wash and more economical than having a bath — it uses just one-fifth of the water a bath takes and proportionally less energy for heating. What's more a shower can be fitted virtually anywhere, provided you have enough space and the plumbing requirements are met.

Probably the simplest place to fit a shower is over the bath, although a separate enclosure in a bedroom, downstairs cloakroom or convenient alcove may actually prove to be more practical if you have a large family. Showers occupy very little space and the majority of trays are between 700 and 900 mm (28 and 36") square although larger designs are available. A separate cubicle occupies less than one square metre; for comfort you will also need a clear area of at least 400mm (16") in front for access 700mm [28"] if there is an outward-opening door).

Wherever you decide to site your shower you will need to ensure that the surrounding area is adequately heated and ventilated so that you avoid excessive condensation; fit a specially designed extractor fan if necessary.

Installing a shower will inevitably mean making alterations and additions to your domestic water supply. You will need to make sure long pipe runs are avoided as they can be expensive, affect the efficiency of the shower and result in drainage problems. Any alterations must comply with the local water authority by-laws administered by your local water authority who will require a minimum of seven days' notice before work can start. If you fail to install the fitting correctly and your water authority subsequently inspects your work, you may be prosecuted and the authority can insist on the fitting being removed. Clearly the authority will not need to inspect all installations when they are notified of any changes, so approval is often given without an inspection. If you are in any doubt about what

is possible call in a qualified plumber who will be able to advise you.

If you plan to make any alterations to the drainage system or structure of the house, you will need Building Regulations approval from your local authority. All electrical work must conform to the Institution of Electrical Engineer's (IEE) regulations, so must be carried out by a qualified electrician. Gas installation must be carried out by either British Gas or an installer registered with the Confederation for the Registration of Gas Installers (CORGI).

The type of shower you choose will depend on your domestic plumbing system, the distance between the base of the cold water tank and the shower head and whether you have a continual source of hot water available.

A fully **direct system** is where all the cold water in the house is supplied direct from the rising main and hot water is supplied by an instantaneous heater, combi-boiler or high pressure hot water cylinder. If you have this type of system a thermostatic or non-thermostatic mixer valve is the best arrangement. Showers on these systems give around nine litres (two gallons) of water per minute and accept variable spray heads.

An **indirect system** is where all of the water in the home - except for the drinking water in the kitchen — is supplied from a cold water storage cistern tank in the loft or airing cupboard. This feeds a separate hot water cylinder below by gravity.

The most common system found in this country is a **mixed system,** part directly fed (the cold water) and part indirectly fed (the hot tank).

If you have hot water on an indirect system and it is not available at times when you wish to shower, fit an electric instantaneous shower. However, if you have available hot water on an indirect system you can install a thermostatic or non-thermostatic mixer valve, gravity fed, providing that you have at least a 600mm (24") head of water. (The head of water means the vertical distance between the shower rose and the bottom of the cold water cistern. Obviously the higher the cistern the better.) If the head of water is not high enough, you can raise the tank in the loft by putting it on blocks; fit an electric pump to increase the force of the spray or install an instantaneous shower. It is important that the cold water is drawn from

"People often comment on our imaginative bathroom showrooms".

While you could well leave your Rucksack at home, the lure of our invigorating Pumped Showers will soon have you reaching for your Hiking Boots to discover Bathrooms that can be Antique, Contemporary or Futuristic.

On a tour of our Showrooms you'll find the centuries celebrated in Porcelain, Pottery and plumbed perfection. The Bathroom Warehouse has the Practical as well as the Pretty, the Best Quality as well as the Best Value.

Whatever your wont – be it to wallow in Victoriana or soak in designer splendour, the Bathroom Warehouse have the Bathroom you've always dreamed of owning – and at the right price.

WAREHOUSE AND MAIN SHOWROOMS
at

4 Chapel Street,	Unit 3, Wykeham Estate,	37 Queen Street,
Guildford, Surrey	Moorside Road, Winnall,	Maidenhead, Berkshire
(0483) 573434	Winchester (0962) 62554	(0628) 32622
Tuesday - Saturday	*Monday - Saturday*	Tuesday - Saturday
Town Centre Bathroom Shop		Town Centre Bathroom Shop

The Bathroom Warehouse

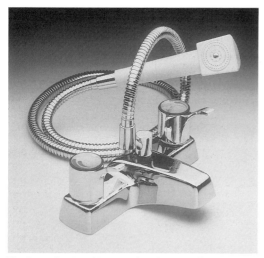

The Superdisc bath/shower mixer from Armitage Shanks

the same supply cistern as the hot water cylinder and in the same size pipework. Obviously these types of shower can be fitted to indirect or direct plumbing systems but should not be fixed to a mixed system.

There are various types of shower. The simplest being the **bath/shower mixers** which are designed to replace existing bath taps. They comprise a standard monobloc tap with an additional outlet fitted to a flexible hose and handspray, plus a knob or lever which diverts the water from the tap to the handspray as required.

Although it is an easy way of providing a shower, it does not always give satisfactory results, as you may have to fiddle with the taps to find the right water temperature and spray force. Sophisticated designs, such as those by Berglen, are now fitted with a thermostatic mixing valve which allows you to adjust the water temperature without altering the water flow. Where a non-thermostatic bath/shower mixer is fitted an anti-scald device, such as Truflow Brassware's Showersafe, fitted to the shower outlet for around £15 is a useful safety measure, especially where the temperature is affected by the use of water in other parts of the house.

Shower-only mixers can be fitted over a bath or in a separate shower cubicle and can be either surface mounted or fitted flush into the wall. The supply pipes can be left exposed, although most people prefer to conceal them

neatly behind the wall so that all you see is the shower head and water controls. With this type of shower the head may be fixed − which can be a disadvantage − or the spray head may be a handset on a flexible hose with fixed or variable 'parking' places. As they need both a hot and cold water supply they can be fitted to a full direct or indirect system, but in the latter the cold water must also be run indirectly.

Showers mixers are available with or without a flow control and with or without thermostatic controls. The most convenient and safest are those which offer independent control over the water flow and temperature. If plumbed correctly a shower mixer is unlikely to give any problems on an indirect supply. However, if a direct supply is being used or if the shower will be regularly used by young children, the elderly or the infirm, it is advisable that a thermostatic mixer, correctly set, is always fitted, alternatively consider fitting a Showersafe anti-scald device unit.

Some showers may have a temperature limiter to prevent anyone selecting too hot a water temperature, however, temperature limiters are *not* thermostatic controls and will *not* eliminate the danger of scalding.

Instantaneous electric showers are the perfect choice for homes where no hot water is normally available on tap as they heat water only when it is required. Basically they comprise a water heater housed in a splashproof case, which is fitted with a supply inlet and handspray outlet with a flexible hose, usually fitted to a slider rail. The water/temperature controls are mounted on the case.

When the shower is turned on, the cold water from the rising main passes through the casing and is heated up to the pre-set showering temperature by an electric element. Adjusting the water temperature alters the actual water flow, so that the hotter the temperature the lower the flow. A pressure sensor will turn the heater off if the water pressure is too low, whilst a temperature-sensitive switch does the same if the water gets too hot. Make sure the shower is fitted with a temperature stabilising device, which will maintain the shower temperature if the water pressure varies.

The disadvantages of instantaneous showers are that the best result in summer from an 8 kW electric shower will only give about three litres

(¾ gallon) per minute, even less for a 7 kW shower, and the over temperature (anti-scald) switches will operate at about 50°C, which is usually higher than would normally be safe for use by young children, the elderly and the infirm. So consider these aspects before buying a shower and ideally choose a model designed for added safety. Alternatively provide additional safety by fitting an anti-scald unit.

Gas instantaneous heaters are basically gas water heaters designed to provide hot water to various points at mains pressure. They are known as combi-boilers or multi-point heaters and are direct systems. They work in a very similar way to electric instantaneous showers as they are connected to the rising main and only heat up water as required. Normally available as flued or balanced flue versions, they should be used with thermostatic mixers to avoid any fluctuations in the water pressure which may occur through simultaneous use of water elsewhere in the house.

Similar in some ways are high pressure indirect heating systems which use an unvented storage tank and water heated by a central heating system through indirect coils in a cylinder.

Becoming more and more popular in this country are **power showers** which give a much more forceful spray than any other shower type. They also offer hot and cold water at mains pressure, that is a direct system. There are two ways of connecting them. Outlet pumps pump mixed water *out* of the shower/mixer to the shower head, whilst inlet pumps pump hot and cold water *into* the shower/mixer then to the shower head. These pumps may boost the water power to an equivalent of a 20m (60') head of water and will give from 5-13 litres (1-3 gallons) per minute.

One disadvantage is that the pump can be noisy, so try and install it in a loft or in a cupboard to deaden the sound. Another disadvantage is that it will use more water than

A quick and convenient way to shower — the Ambassador cubicle from Armitage Shanks

a conventional shower, although it should still be less than the amount of water required for a bath.

One of the major advantages of this type and directly plumbed types of shower is that the water spray can be controlled and, by using a multi - function shower head, you can choose the type of shower you want, for example a soft spray, invigorating needle jet or torrent spray with either a narrow or wide angle spray. Even a special 'massage' spray head can be found with some models. Manufacturers such as Tapmate, Caradon Mira, Truflow and Ideal-Standard all have power showers in their ranges.

For real luxury, consider a **steam shower** made by companies such as Nordic and Majestic. Not just a shower, they are designed to be installed in a shower cubicle so that you can have the option of either taking a shower or creating a healthy steam environment. Most are sold complete with a folding seat.

Wherever you decide to site your shower, you will need to make sure the area around it is completely waterproof. If internal walls form part of the shower area cover them completely with ceramic tiles or laminate and finish with waterproof grouting and sealants at the joins.

To prevent water splashing into the room you will need some form of enclosure. **Curtains** in either nylon or pvc, make the simplest, cheapest and easiest screen. Hung on a rail system, they can be either door width for a separate cubicle, bath length or angled. Always make sure the curtain hangs inside the bath or tray when the shower is in use so that water does not drip on the floor. **Shower roller blinds** are another inexpensive option, and the ranges offered by Croydex fully co-ordinate with other bathroom accessories such as bathmats, roller blinds and bathroom clocks!

A rigid enclosure offers more efficient protection against splashes. Consider a **screen** made of safety glass (complying to BS 6262) or reinforced plastic fixed in a rust-proof frame. If you are providing a bath screen it can be either permanently fixed in place; hinged to allow 180° movement so it can be folded back when not in use; or can consist of several panels hinged together which can be folded away against the wall when not in use.

Sliding doors are available for both baths and cubicles. Made from plastic or safety glass set into rust-proof panels they either slide or fold-back concertina-fashion to enclose the bath or cubicle completely when the shower is in use. Shower cubicles set into a corner can be fitted with a curved frame.

Fixed doors are often used for separate cubicles. Made of safety glass or plastic they can open in a number of ways: hinged at one side like a conventional door; two half-width doors hinged at both sides or joined together to form a bi-fold; a central or off-centre 'pivot' door, which requires less space to open; internally gliding doors which open back into the shower.

If you are planning a separate shower cubicle allow plenty of room for movement, bear in mind that even one row of tiles around the smallest shower tray will restrict the actual showering space. **Purpose built cubicles** can be expensive but are probably the easiest way of fitting a shower outside a bathroom. They come supplied with the tray, walls and screen, whilst some, such as the Leisure Lifestyle, also include the shower fittings.

MATERIALS

Most bathroom fittings come in a wide range of materials, except for bidets and toilet pans which are always ceramic. Choosing the right material will be just as important as choosing the right size.

Acrylic and **glass-reinforced plastic (grp)** have similar qualities, both are light and warm and will retain the water temperature. They can be moulded into virtually any shape although cost and durability depends on the thickness of the sheet and the strength of the frame. Cheap models may 'give' slightly when filled with hot water making it difficult to keep a watertight seal between a bath rim and the adjacent wall. Sharp implements, nail varnish remover, lighted cigarettes and abrasive cleaning powders will all damage the surface.

Ceramic is heavy, non-porous, durable and easy to clean making it ideal for toilet pans and bidets. It is more likely to chip than enamelled steel or cast iron and large ceramic baths are expensive. Hand basins are usually made in vitreous china although a few are made from glazed fireclay. Both are heavy, durable materials with a glossy surface but may craze or crack if roughly treated.

The 'Windsor' slipper bath from Exclusive Bathrooms

Porcelain-enamelled cast-iron is heavy and expensive and usually only available in a limited range of plain designs, the old-fashioned roll-top design bath is probably the best example. They have a solid feel, are very attractive with a glossy finish and are extremely hardwearing. If you opt for this material make sure your floor is strong enough to support a bath full of water, and check that you will actually be able to get the bath into the bathroom itself – measure the hall, stairs and landing before making the purchase!

PLANNING

Your next step is to look at the size and shape of the room to ensure you make best use of the space; this will only be achieved by careful planning. Make an accurate scaled floor plan of the room drawing in all the fixed features such as doors, windows, water supply and waste. Where possible make use of the existing plumbing runs as any alterations – or additions – must comply with the local water by-laws

and changes to the waste with Building Regulations. A qualified plumber will be able to advise you.

Now make scaled cut-outs of all the fittings you would like to fit in the room and play about until you find the best arrangement.

A bathroom will constantly suffer from warm, humid air so give careful thought to the lighting, heating and ventilation.

The best combination is a centre light giving general lighting with a fitting(s) around the mirror(s). If space permits you may want to fit a downlighter or spotlight to light up a specific area such as the basin or bath. For safety, all lighting must be completely wired in and operated by a pull-cord inside the room. You can have a conventional switch if it's sited outside.

There's no fun in being in a cold bathroom so provide background heating with a radiator or heated towel rail linked to the central heating/hot water system. Alternatively consider a separate heater such as an oil-filled radiator or towel rail, wall-mounted convector

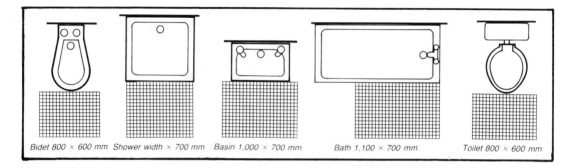

Bidet 800 × 600 mm   Shower width × 700 mm   Basin 1,000 × 700 mm   Bath 1,100 × 700 mm   Toilet 800 × 600 mm

or high level radiant heater. You must never bring a portable fire in a bathroom, it's potentially lethal.

Condensation is inevitable in a bathroom so ensure it's well ventilated. This can be done with an opening window (which will cause draughts) or with an electric extractor fan fitted to an exterior wall or window.

DECOR

When it comes to the overall decor of the bathroom choose practical coverings for the walls and floor.

Flooring should be comfortable and hardwearing and, if you have a habit of padding around in bare feet, warm. Cushioned sheet vinyl and vinyl tiles are a practical choice, so are well-sealed cork tiles. If you choose a carpet ensure it's suitable for a bathroom. Try and avoid dark colours, they will show up every speck of talcum powder and dust making cleaning a nightmare.

Walls must be able to withstand exposure to steam and splashes. Ceramic tiles finished with waterproof grout are ideal, if you prefer a wallcovering choose one with a vinyl finish, whilst paints should be matt or silk vinyl emulsion. Alternatively you could consider mirror tiles or well-sealed timber panelling.

If you have a particularly small bathroom consider the following:

■ Ideally, site the bath as close as possible to the waste soil stack. Preferably not against a wall with a window – bathing could be draughty and you may have to stand in the bath to clean the window or pull the blind or curtains.

■ The toilet should be against or adjacent to an outside wall close to the soil stack. Consider fitting a toilet with a slimline cistern or a wall-mounted wash basin and toilet to create an illusion of space. They will also make cleaning the floor much easier.

■ Ducted plumbing, where the pipes and cistern are hidden behind false panels, decorated to match the walls, will give an impression of space. Remember to leave access for the plumbing.

■ A wall-mounted basin or one set into a vanity unit will give useful storage space.

■ If there's no room for a separate shower fit one over the bath with a screen or shower curtain. If the room is really tiny make all the wall and floor surfaces waterproof - using ceramic tiles for example – and forget a shower curtain or screen, you can then splash around without causing any damage.

If you have a large bathroom consider the following:

■ Create a separate dressing area with twin wash basins and use fitted cupboards as a room divider.

■ Make the bath a focal point. Choose an eye-catching corner bath or place a rectangular one centrally in the room – water supply and soil stack permitting!

■ Utilise wall space to fit plenty of cupboards and storage. Consider one of the many purpose-designed fitted bathroom units.

■ Create a work-out area with your exercise bike, rowing machine, etc.

■ Make the room a place to linger in by adding a comfortable chair or small table.

■ Instead of a cabinet leave out your pretty toiletries on a washstand (in a traditional style bathroom) or a trolley (in a modern room).

For all bathrooms consider the following:

■ A bathroom will need a well-lit mirror for shaving and making-up.

■ If you have young children, medicines should be kept in a lockable cabinet, make sure one is fitted.

■ You can hang prints on the walls and have other soft furnishings such as curtains and cushions, but remember that in time they are likely to be affected by damp.

■ Plants can add considerably to the overall decor in a bathroom and many varieties will thrive in the humid conditions. A leafy green fern suspended from the ceiling in a hanging container in one corner of the room can considerably soften the most clinical of rooms.

■ Dripping taps will cause stains, so change the washers when necessary – or consider replacing the taps for ones fitted with ceramic discs.

HOW TO TILE

Ceramic tiles provide a popular, hardwearing surface which not only looks good but is also easy to keep clean. They come in a particularly wide range of colours, textures and patterns in a variety of different sizes – although 106 mm (4") and 150 mm (6") square tiles are probably the most common.

Ceramic tiles can be used in most situations where a durable, waterproof surface is required, but do make sure you don't use wall tiles on the floor – they will not withstand the traffic; that you use special heat- and frost-resistant tiles where appropriate; and you use a waterproof adhesive and grout in areas that will be subjected to water – in a shower or around a bath for example.

Basically, the tiles available are:

Field or general purpose tiles, have four unfinished edges fitted with spacer lugs to aid spacing as they're being fixed.

Rounded edge (RE) tiles have one rounded glazed edge, which can be used as an edge finish.

Double round edge (REX) tiles have two adjacent rounded glazed edges.

Universal tiles are chamfered and glazed on all four edges, so when they are laid they automatically touch one another, but leave a space at the front for grouting. They can be used in any position.

Quadrant tiles are narrow, round edge tiles used to fill joins between the bath and the wall.

Tiling itself is not a particularly difficult job, the secret is in the preparation of the wall surface, which must always be clean, sound, grease free and dry. Fill in any cracks and dents; strip off old wallpaper; wash and rinse down painted surfaces (gloss paint must be rubbed with medium grade abrasive paper to provide a key). You must never start tiling at random, but carefully mark out the wall(s) beforehand. If you are tiling an entire room, first choose the most important wall – it is usually the one that's most prominent, such as the window wall – and start tiling there.

■ Tiles

■ Ceramic tile adhesive and adhesive spreader

■ Grout and squeegee

■ Plumb bob and line

■ Spirit level

■ Tile cutter

■ Breaking board

■ Tile file

■ Battens – lengths of softwood about 50 × 25 mm (2 × 1")

■ Masonry nails and hammer

■ Tile nibblers

■ Straightedge metal rule

■ Chinagraph pencil

■ Clean sponge

Method

1. First make a gauge stick from a piece of timber 50 × 25 × 1000 mm (2 × 1 × 39"): lay several of the tiles you will be using along the length of the stick, butting them as necessary, then mark their widths on the stick.

2. Horizontally fix a straight length of timber batten the full width of the wall, using masonry nails — don't drive them in fully. The top edge of the batten should be one tile height above the floor or skirting board. Use a spirit level to ensure it's completely level. This batten ensures that the tiling lines are level even if the floor is not.

3. At this point see how the rows of tiles will relate to existing features such as windows, sinks etc. With a sink or bath it's usually better to have a row of whole tiles along the top. With a window it is usually best to centre the row of tiles on it. If you're half tiling a wall it's best to have a whole row of tiles at the top. If necessary adjust the batten.

4. Now use the measuring gauge to plan the horizontal rows (from floor to ceiling). Check that the row of tiles at the top of the wall is not too narrow; ideally it should be no less than half a tile wide and certainly no less than 25 mm (1"). If it is too narrow, drop the position of the horizontal batten a few millimetres to leave roughly equal spacing at the top and bottom.

5. Use the gauge stick to mark the vertical rows, checking with a spirit level to ensure the lines are straight, making adjustments for windows and other features.

6. Find the centre point of the horizontal batten and use the measuring gauge to determine the position of the last whole tile, nearest to the wall. Mark this point. Drop a plumb line down the wall so that the string touches this mark and draw the line on the wall with a pencil. Check to ensure this line is truly vertical with a spirit level, then fix a vertical batten to the wall along the line.

7. Check that both battens are truly square by placing a few tiles in the corner made by them. They should sit squarely.

You are now ready to start tiling. Fix all the whole tiles first, then fill in with the cut tiles and the odd shapes.

8. Start by covering about 1 square metre of wall with adhesive in the corner where the battens meet, firmly press the teeth of the spreader against the wall so that the adhesive forms ridges. Ensure the wall is covered, but don't touch the battens.

9. Place the first tile into the angle formed by the two battens, firmly pressing it in place, now butt up the tiles to one another using the spacer lugs. If the tiles do not have spacers use matchsticks, thick card or purpose-made plastic spacers.

10. Work sideways and upwards, three rows at a time, until the area of adhesive is covered. Wipe off any adhesive which has squeezed between the tiles with a sponge.

11. Continue in this way checking occasionally along the top row of tiles with a spirit level to ensure the lines are all horizontal.

12. Finish fixing all the whole tiles and allow the adhesive to set for about 24 hours before taking down the battens and fixing the cut tiles.

All cut tiles should be fixed so that the uncut or finished edge abuts another tile and the cut edge is next to a wall or fitting.

13. The simplest way of cutting tiles is to first mark the position of the cut on the tiled surface with a chinagraph pencil. Now place the tile on a piece of wood and with the help of a straightedge, score the line using a tile cutter from edge to edge to ensure a clean break — one firm cut is better than several small ones.

14. Place the tile on a breaking board with the score line directly over the wire or ridge. If you don't have a breaking board place a matchstick under the line at each edge, then press down firmly on either side to snap the tile. Alternatively use a tile cutter

rather like a pair of pliers with two wings which hold the tile and snaps the tile in two. Once the tile has been cut, smooth the cut edge with a tile file.

15. When it comes to cutting an awkward shape, the best thing to do is to make a paper template the same size as a tile. Cut 'fingers' along one edge and press them against the curve to reproduce the shape. Transfer the outline on to the face of the tile.

16. To cut corners or curves out of tiles, first score a line freehand to remove as much of the waste as you can, then score a series of grid lines and use tile nibblers to break off small pieces until the line is reached.

17. When all the tiles have been fixed leave the adhesive to harden, usually for 24 hours.

Grouting and finishing off Grout will finish off your tiling and it is essential that you use waterproof grout for showers and around baths. However, don't use ordinary grout to fill the gap between the tiled wall and a bath, shower tray or wash basin. Any movement by these fittings will crack a rigid seal allowing water to penetrate behind. Instead use a silicone rubber caulk, which remains flexible. Alternatively, you could use quadrant tiles as an edging or could fix a specially designed plastic coving strip, such as those made by OBO, behind the bottom row of tiles.

18. Mix up the grout and spread liberally between the joins using a squeegee. Use a sponge to wipe off any excess grout from the face of the tiles before it sets. Wash out the sponge frequently in clean water (do not rinse it under the tap as the grout could clog up the drain).

19. As the grout hardens run a round-ended stick along the joints to give a neat finish.

20. When the grout has set, polish over the surface with a clean soft cloth. Do not use a tile shower cubicle for seven days to ensure the grout has thoroughly dried and hardened.

Tiles need not be just practical — 'Gardenia' from Cristal Tiles

WELCOMING HALLS

U sually the hall is the first part of your home anyone will see, so, if you want your visitors to feel relaxed the moment they step across the threshold, it should look friendly and inviting. However, the chances are that you've given scant thought to the decor because your hallway is little more than a small square with just enough space to open the front door, or is particularly long and narrow, making it impossible to fit in any furniture to help make it look more interesting. So what can you do?

As with any other room, you will first need to assess your hallway, so measure its dimensions and draw up a floor plan. Now mark all the relevant details on the plan, such as door and window positions, aspect of windows, socket positions, radiators, etc., then indicate any other relevant details, such as dark spots and bright, sunny areas. Next think about the effect you would like to create: bright and modern, classic and elegant, dark and dramatic or cool and sophisticated and, using the floor plan, determine whether this is possible. For example, if you have a small dark north-facing hall, it would be silly to try to make the decor dark and dramatic; warm, bright colours would look better.

Because you don't actually live in a hall and just use it as an area to pass through, you can choose more adventurous colours than you would for living rooms. Choose red and grey for a modern look, shades of green for a classic style, bright yellow and green for a zingy, fresh scheme or shades of blue and orange for a warm, fresh mood. Think about colour combinations and effects. Before you make a final choice you will also need to consider the decor of any rooms leading off the hall and landing. If they are quite dramatic, it may be better to choose a soft, neutral scheme, in shades of cream and peach, for example.

Walls and woodwork will need to withstand constant wear and tear, particularly if you have children. Choose a washable vinyl wallcovering or a silk vinyl emulsion or oil-based eggshell which can be easily cleaned. Light colours will show up the dirt and scuffs which are almost inevitable. An attractive idea is to fix a dado rail - either made of wood or using a wallpaper

The elegant Edwardian Dado wallcovering from Anaglypta

border to create the illusion of one — with a dark paint colour or heavily patterned wallcovering below it. This looks particularly effective when taken up the staircase. Wooden bannisters and hand rails should be painted with gloss paint for a hardwearing finish, or, if you prefer a natural look, stripped and varnished with polyurethane.

If you have a particularly small hall, consider the following decor tips:

■ Avoid bold, large patterned wallcoverings or ones with obvious stripes as they will make the room appear cluttered and fussy and even smaller than it is. Instead choose plain colours or tiny prints on a light ground to help increase the impression of space. Use the same colour/design throughout to maximise the feeling of space.

■ Use strong colours as accents only, for example, to emphasise a door frame or for the lampshades.

■ To create an impression of space use the same colour/design throughout, preferably one which is fairly light. Always use the same colour on all walls if the room is square.

■ Don't use dado rails or panels, particularly in a long, narrow hall. It will divide the area, making it look even smaller. Instead add interest at ceiling height or by the skirting board, using a frieze or wallpaper border.

■ Paint any pipes and radiators the same colour as the walls to make them less dominant.

If you have a large hall, bear in mind the following decor tips:

■ Avoid using bright, primary colours throughout as they can be overpowering, but choose rich shades, plum instead of red, for example.

■ If the ceiling is high, paint it a dark colour to bring it down. Provided there is enough natural light, this colour can be brought right down to the picture rail.

■ Utilise the wall space effectively by displaying pictures, prints or photographs. But group them together for the best effect; spread out they will get lost on a large expanse of wall.

■ Utilise 'wasted' space by fitting additional storage in the form of cupboards or shelves or turn a large corner into a study area with a desk, chair and shelving.

■ Use wallcoverings from one of the many co-ordinated ranges throughout the hall, up the stairs and through to the landing.

The flooring will need to be practical and safe. Don't pick anything which is likely to be slippery underfoot, particularly when it gets wet, ceramic tiles for example. Of the semi-hard floorings, vinyl, cork and wood are all easy

to clean and hardwearing, while if you prefer a carpet, choose a heavy-quality one in a colour and design which won't show dirt easily. Rugs are not recommended as they could cause people to trip over.

Be careful what you use on the staircase. Deep-pile carpets are not suitable as you could catch a heel in the pile and trip; nor is coir which, although hardwearing, is also slippery underfoot and therefore potentially dangerous. It's a good idea to have a door mat immediately inside the front door so that people can wipe their dirty shoes before entering the house.

Good, bright lighting is essential on the stairs where there shouldn't be any dangerous shadows. Recessed downlighters are a good choice for a long hall, while spotlights, which can be adjusted to any angle, can be used to light stairs and highlight pictures. Wall lights will provide soft mood lighting on the landing. If your staircase has a half-landing, make sure it is well lit.

Windows are usually fairly small and are needed to admit as much light as possible into what is probably a naturally dark area, particularly any which are sited on a stairwell. Ideally the window treatment should frame the window and allow as much natural light to enter as possible. Consider framing the window with some pretty frilled curtains held with tie-backs and finished with a pelmet, using a roller blind at night. Alternatively, an Austrian or festoon blind in a gauzy fabric which softly filters the light, will soften an ugly angular window.

If there is very little spare room, avoid cluttering up the hall and landing with furniture. If possible try to fit in some form of cupboard to store coats and shoes — any freestanding or open coatstand will soon look cluttered and unsightly. If space permits, add a narrow console table or chest of drawers for the telephone, with a mirror above. If this is not possible, move the telephone to another room.

On the other hand, if you have a large hall and landing consider utilising some of the extra room for storage; any type of unit with drawers and doors will look much neater than open shelving. Or think of creating a study area with a desk and chair. Alternatively, an occasional chair with a bookcase and small table and table lamp could make a quiet reading area.

LIVING ROOM COMFORT

A living room should be a place you feel comfortable in. So it needs careful planning to ensure that the decor and furnishings provide a friendly, relaxing atmosphere. It's likely to be the room you 'live' in, literally, where you watch TV, listen to music, sit and relax, read or talk or whatever, as well as being the one room in the house you entertain visitors in. So when it comes to planning the decor and choosing the furnishings, you need to consider carefully how it will be used. Will it be used mainly at night for listening to music or watching TV? Is it the family reading room? Will the children play in there during the daytime? How often will you entertain guests?

PLANNING

Once you have sorted out how it is to be used, the next step is to plan a practical and sensible room layout. First make a plan of the room and small cut-outs of all the furniture you have, or propose to buy, to the same scale. You can then move all the items around to work out the best possible arrangement. Remember that you will need to leave access to any doors leading in and out of the room, as well as sufficient space around the seating.

A well-planned room should have a focal point, so use this as a starting point to plan your arrangement. It could be the fireplace, a view from the window or a stunning arrangement of pictures, but do try to avoid making the TV the central feature. Where possible place the TV on a sideboard or in a storage unit which blends into the background. Placing it on a swivel unit so that it pushes flat against the wall when not in use is a useful ploy, or hide it away completely in a special TV cabinet.

If space permits you may be able to devise two arrangements, one for winter, centred around a fireplace, and one for summer, with the focal point around the window. If the natural focal point is the fireplace, don't forget that it can look attractive when it's not in use if it is filled with flowers or other ornaments.

SEATING

Probably the most important part of the room is the seating and if you are buying new furniture consider the options very carefully. Seating placed at right-angles and fairly close together will make conversation easy. Seating arranged on either side of an occasional table can give an intimate, friendly atmosphere. Whatever you decide, make sure the seating is arranged away from 'traffic' routes. Nothing is more irritating than someone walking across the room in front of you while you are trying to talk or watch TV.

How about size and flexibility? Do you want your seating to be easy to move around or will it remain more or less fixed in one position? Will a three/two/one seating combination fit well into the room or would two two-seater settees fit in better? When it comes to buying new seating, there's no reason why it has to be identical. A sofa and contrasting, but complementary-shaped, chairs can look just as effective as a matching suite.

It's virtually impossible to know how well made a chair or sofa is just by looking at the outside, so always buy from a reputable store or look for a well-known name. Most upholstered furniture has the same basic construction: a frame, suspension, filling or padding and a cover.

The **frame** determines how long the furniture will last and so needs to be well constructed and durable. Most have a wooden frame in either hardwood – beech is the traditional choice – or a softwood, such as pine. Traditionally made frames are joined by dowels, then glued and braced. Modern timber frames are likely to be fixed with screws, staples and glue.

The **suspension** bridges the frame, providing a base for the padding. It will comprise metal springs (coil, continuous or tension); elasticated or rubber webbing; or a woven elastic or diaphragm platform. All work well, provided they are firmly attached to the frame. Press against the seat back and underneath the cushions with your hand. The chair seat should be firmer than the back and if the seating has a spring suspension, you should not be able to feel it.

The **padding** or filling in a good quality seat should provide support combined with softness, strength and resilience. Nowadays

The Tiffany suite from Perrings lends itself well to a mixture of styles

most manufacturers tend to use different grades of foam, although some may supplement this by using a loose filling, like feathers and down, in the cushions. Foam will regain its shape faster than feather and down, and generally will always looks neater. Press the back padding and cushions with your hand; if you can feel the frame the padding is inadequate.

Covers can be either tight or loose, but whatever you choose you need to ensure that the fibre content of the covers will wear well. Generally the tighter the weave of the fabric the more hardwearing it will be, as it will not pull out of shape. Avoid a glazed finish if the seating will be subjected to a lot of wear.

When buying any seating you really need to sit in it for at least 30 minutes to test its comfort. If this is not possible you can tell a lot about a chair after sitting in it for about 10 minutes. As you sit there check for the following:

■ Move around, to ensure you can adopt several different positions.

■ How easily can you sit down and stand up? If too much effort is required there's something wrong with the design.

■ When sitting do you feel relaxed; do both your feet touch the ground?

■ Push right back into the chair against the back rest, do your feet touch the ground without any pressure being applied behind your knees?

■ Does the seat provide good lumbar support for the small of your back?

■ Do any buttons, seams or prominent features dig into you? How about the front edge of the seat cushion?

■ Does the back rest dig uncomfortably into your back or shoulder blades? Is it correctly angled so that you can sit back comfortably.

Whatever you do, take your time and don't be rushed into making a decision. Never buy any seating when you are tired or after an exhausting day's shopping when everything you try will feel comfortable!

Following a spate of fatal domestic fires, when many people were killed by the lethal carbon monoxide and hydrogen cyanide fumes given off by their burning foam-filled furniture, the Government has taken action to ban the use of certain foam furniture fillings. From March 1989, only combustion-modified high-resilience foams can be used in furniture. From March 1990 all upholstery cover materials have to be match-resistant. Check the permanent labels fixed to the furniture (all furniture must carry them) to ensure that it complies with the 1988 Fire Regulations. A square green 'RESISTANT' label indicates that it has passed both the cigarette and match ignition tests. If you are in any doubt seek the advice of the retailer.

STORAGE

Once you've decided on your seating and know where it is to be placed in the room, everything else can be fitted in around it. You will probably need somewhere for the TV, video and hi-fi, along with all the other paraphernalia of leisurely living, such as records, cassettes, tapes, books and the like. For this purpose you can choose from a wide range of adaptable storage units, both freestanding and wall-hanging, which come in a variety of finishes to suit your decor style. Make sure they will be strong enough to support the load and that any freestanding units will not topple over if overloaded.

Alternatively you could fit purpose-made shelving units to provide the appropriate storage space — shelves and cupboards fitted into alcoves on either side of a fireplace, for example, make a particularly attractive feature. Whatever you choose, ensure that it visually enhances the overall decor, to create a relaxing atmosphere.

Make sure there are plenty of low occasional tables around the seating, to provide somewhere for glasses, magazines, ashtrays, etc, but don't position them so that they divide up the room. Small circular tables, covered with floor-length cloths, will be suitable for displaying collections of family photographs, decorative china or whatever.

LIGHTING

Lighting is probably one of the most important aspects in a living room as it will help create a relaxed, pleasant atmosphere. A single ceiling pendant light is totally inadequate for this multi-purpose room, as it provides neither good general lighting nor adequate task lighting. Instead you will need several different types of lighting, each serving a different purpose.

To start with there should be good **general** lighting, which provides light that enables you to see. Consider fitting recessed downlighters or use table lamps and uplighters, these can all be fitted to a dimmer switch so that the lighting level can be adjusted as required.

Next fit **mood** lighting, which provides pockets of light in a certain area, and **accent** lighting to highlight any of the room's more attractive features, such as a picture or group of ornaments. Individual picture lights, spotlights, uplighters, table lamps and concealed cabinet lights are all suitable and will create dramatic interest in the room.

Finally, you will need some **task** or **directional** lighting, such as a spotlight, table lamp or freestanding work lamp positioned at a convenient height to enable you to read, sew or whatever.

DECOR

The overall colour scheme and decor will affect the room's atmosphere, so try to choose a scheme which is friendly and relaxing, not one which is too stimulating. Whatever colour and style you select, try to make the room appear spacious and uncluttered; a room which is cluttered causes confusion to the eye and makes it difficult to move around. Clutter can be caused by having too much furniture in the room, but it can also be a result of having too many shelves filled with ornaments, or of using too many patterned surfaces in the room.

Wall surfaces don't need to be highly practical, so you can opt for virtually any kind of wallcovering. However, if there are young children in the family it would be sensible to choose a washable finish, such as a vinyl wallcovering or paint. The floorcovering, however, needs to be reasonably hardwearing and if you have children or pets, avoid pale colours. A plain carpet or varnished floorboards with a rug over the top often looks cosier than

A gentle relaxed atmosphere is created with the Mazda Style Light range

a fitted carpet, and can be moved around to avoid the almost inevitable wear area which occurs in front of the sofa.

Because a living room is the main area in the house for entertaining and relaxing, there are many ways in which you can choose to decorate and furnish it. Just remember that, as it will be in almost constant use, it needs to be both comfortable and practical.

FIRES AND FIREPLACES

Before the introduction of central heating an open fire was just about the only way in which you could heat a room. Although they did give a room a cosy, warm appearance, they also had a lot of unwelcome side effects, dust being the most common problem. Nowadays, after years of emphasis on central heating, people are once again realising the attractions of a fire, particularly as many of the problems have been overcome and the choice available is so wide.

At its simplest, a fire is an opening fitted within a firebrick enclosure, featuring a fireplace surround finished with a decorative front panel which hides the grate and ashbox. The heat output is mainly by radiation. These traditional style open fires are still available, but they are much easier to light and look after than their predecessors, are cleaner-burning and more economical. Some use a fan or underfloor draught system so that the rate at which the fire burns can be more closely controlled, you can now turn a slumbering fire into a blazing one in seconds. Others are freestanding, where the fire is in a self-contained unit standing on the hearth in front of the surround with a flue connecting it to the chimney.

Apart from acting as a simple source of radiant heat, many open fires can also be fitted with a back boiler which will heat the domestic hot water. With the addition of a high output

Beautiful homes deserve the very best to keep them looking warm and comfortable. And in the "Special Collection", you'll find the fire, surround or suite that's just right for your home. Craftsman-made in beautiful materials with lots of solid brass for that really luxurious look, they're in all good stores and electricity board shops.

so warm to come home to

the **JR GLENLOMOND** *Special collection*

back boiler they will also power up to eight average-sized radiators.

More sophisticated is the **roomheater**, which is the name given to any appliance which has a real fire completely enclosed by heat-resistant glass doors, although they can be inset into a fireplace or be freestanding. Roomheaters are safer than open fires as there is no danger of coals falling out onto the hearth and they can be controlled more finely than most open fires, giving both radiant and convected heat. At minimum setting they will idle for hours without needing any attention. Briefly there are five types available in a wide choice of styles from imitation Victorian stoves to sleek modern designs:

- The first, sometimes known as a dryback roomheater, only heats the room it is in.
- The second heats the room it is in, plus the domestic hot water.
- The third heats the room it is in, the domestic hot water and up to nine radiators.
- The fourth is a gravity feed roomheater incorporating a container for holding fuel, called a hopper, which gradually releases the fuel onto the firebed. They can also heat the domestic hot water and up to nine radiators.
- The fifth, sometimes called a smoke reducing roomheater, burns ordinary house coal and actually burns the smoke which

Making a feature of the fireplace with a decorative fire surround from W.H.Newson

would normally pass out through the chimney, so can be used anywhere in the country including Smoke Control Areas.

In areas covered by the Clean Air legislation only smokeless fuels such as Coalite, can be burnt. The Solid Fuel Advisory Service provides details of the wide range of fuels available and will be able to advise which is most suited to the appliances available.

Remember that solid fuel fires will need regular attention and to burn efficiently the chimney must be kept clean and swept at least once a year, preferably twice. You will also need a large store for the fuel.

If you want the look of an open fire without the inconvenience consider one of the many gas fires.

Radiant heaters are the most traditional of gas heating appliances with radiant panels in front which glow. Fairly simply constructed, they feature either a simplex or duplex burner: simplex designs have a single flame across the whole width; duplex designs have any number of flames across the width, to be used in any permutation from one to six to give the heating level required. The whole unit is fitted into an outer case of pressed steel often with wooden sides and top and has a guard incorporated into the design for safety. The thermal efficiency of a typical radiant fire is about 45%.

Radiant/convectors differ from radiants in that they have a heat exchanger which transfers heat from the waste gases to the surrounding air, so that as air inside the case becomes heated it rises and disperses through the louvres in the outer case. They are 60% to 65% efficient. Some of these appliances can be combined with a back boiler or circulator unit to provide hot water and limited central heating.

Living Flame or **Live Fuel Effect fires (LFEs)** are actually mounted on the hearth. They have flames which pass up through an imitation fuel of either ceramic coals or logs to give a realistic fire. Fitted with a heat exchanger which increases their efficiency, they emit both radiant and convected heat. Generally they have two burners: the main burner, usually of duplex construction situated beneath the ceramic fuel bed, and a flicker burner positioned to send flames through spaces in the fuel to imitate the flickering of the burning fuel. Sometimes a ceramic glass panel is fitted on the front of the fire to increase the overall efficiency which ranges from 45% to 60%.

Inset LFEs are the most recently introduced variation of the gas fire. They are designed to be fully installed within a fire opening with a minimum of case projecting over the surrounding hearth and as far as possible simulate the solid fuel they often replace.

Decorative Fuel Effect Fires (DFEs) are entirely open and are really designed for visual effect to provide a focal point in a room. More commonly used in hotels and restaurants, they simulate coal or log fires without the dust problems and are up to 40% efficient. They should not be chosen as the sole means of heating a room.

When choosing a gas fire it is advisable to look for the BSI Kitemark or BSI Safety Mark to be confident that it is a quality safe gas product. All gas appliances should be installed by a qualified gas installer who is a member of the Confederation for the Registration of Gas Installers (CORGI). Your local gas showrooms should have a copy of your local CORGI register or contact them at St. Martins House, 140 Tottenham Court Road, London W1P 9LN. ☎ 01-387 9185.

Both solid fuel and gas fires will need an adequate supply of fresh air for burning and a flue or chimney to get rid of the gases. If you are opening up an old blocked-up fireplace ensure that it is in good condition and free from defects and blockages which could result in serious problems.

If your home does not have a chimney consider fitting a pre-fabricated system such as those offered by Kedddy Ltd. Alternatively a balanced flue gas appliance which uses a co-axial duct through an outside wall to draw in air for combustion and expel waste gases, makes an attractive choice. If you do not have a suitable external wall, Tower Flue Components produce a fan-assisted flue system fitted with ducting which enables a gas fire to be positioned on an internal wall.

The look of an open fire without the inconvenience — a decorative fuel effect fire from Verine

If you have no suitable storage space for solid fuel and are without a gas supply, you can still consider an electric coal or log effect fire. They give radiant heat and come in both traditional and modern designs. The most basic models have elements fixed in front of a metal reflector, usually chromium plates, which concentrates and directs the heat where required. More sophisticated heaters have illuminated burning coal or log effects which can be used on their own to give a cosy glow or combined with the radiant elements. Modern fires are fitted with automatic energy controllers which maintain comfortable warmth economically. A control knob sited on the appliance can be adjusted to give the desired temperature.

The fireplace itself, complete with surround and mantelpiece, must be made from non-combustible material, ideally with a surface that's easy to clean. They can be virtually any size, although the minimum width is usually around 1,400 mm (54"). All fires must have a hearth which extends at least 300 mm (12") in front of the fire and any combustible material, such as a wooden mantelpiece, should be no closer than 150 mm (6") from the fire opening.

To find out more about solid fuel fires, contact your nearest Solid Fuel Advisory Service office or simply dial 100 and ask for Freephone Real Fires. If you would like to see a comprehensive selection of fireplaces, write to the National Fireplace Council, PO Box 35 (Stoke), Stoke-on Trent ST4 7NU for a copy of their book *Fireplaces*. It contains fireplace designs, names and addresses of the manufacturers plus useful information and advice on selecting a fireplace for your home.

MAKING THE MOST OF SPACE

One of the more popular ways of creating more space within a home is to knock down a dividing wall and make one large room from two smaller ones. Most people tend to just think about removing the wall between a living and dining room. In fact there are number of other options available. You could remove the wall between the living room and hall; between the kitchen and dining room; between a kitchen and utility room; between two bedrooms and between a bathroom and separate toilet. Depending on the type of property you have, there are probably a number of other options available as well.

You'd be surprised at how effective the new enlarged room will look, but just bear in mind that you will be loosing valuable wall space and that, although the alteration pleases you, it might be a liability when it comes to selling the house. For example if you make one large bedroom from two smaller ones, you're effectively turning the house into a two-bedroomed property.

Before you start any work at all, go to your local authority and talk to the Building Control Officer about your proposals. He will want to make sure that the planned alteration complies with Building Regulations and neither affects the structure of your property – and any adjoining houses – nor makes it unsafe in the event of a fire.

The most important factor will be whether or not the wall you propose to remove is load-bearing or not. If it is a load-bearing wall the gap will have to be spanned by a RSJ (rolled steel joist) or in the case of a timber framed house a beam or lintel, this is a job which you might prefer to leave to a competent builder. If the wall is non-load bearing, it can be removed without any problems, although you would be advised to strengthen the ceiling joist above the wall you remove.

The job of removing the wall itself is not as difficult as you might think. Don't forget to remove all furniture from the rooms, take up any carpets and remove any wall fittings and fixtures. The work will be very messy.

1. Before you start check to ensure that the wall does not contain any electrical cables or pipes which will need to be re-routed.

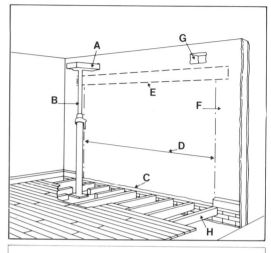

A Needle
B Acrow prop
C Floor level
D Width of new opening
E Opening for RSJ
F Wall to be retained to act as a column support for the RSJ
G Hole cut through wall for needle
H Floor joists

2. Turn off the power to any electrical outlets and, as an additional precaution, turn off the gas and water supplies before doing any work.

3. Mark the position of the opening on the wall. With a stud partition wall this should ideally be located between the existing stud positions. Prise away the skirting on both sides of the wall and any coving.

4. Before removing a loadbearing wall, you will have to put temporary supports in place above the opening. Hire adjustable steel props and scaffold boards.

5. Make holes in the wall at intervals above the proposed opening. Use a club hammer and bolster chisel on a brick wall; with plasterboard first stitch drill (a series of small holes adjacent to one another) around the opening, then cut through with a pad saw.

6. Once the holes have been made, push through heavy timber beams at least 150 mm by 100 mm by 1.8 m (6 × 4 × 72") long. These beams should be held in position on either side by the steel props, which in turn are supported by scaffold boards. These supports should be no more than 600 mm (24") from each side of the

wall, they will spread the load and prevent the floor from being damaged.

7. Carefully knock down a brick wall using a club hammer and bolster chisel. With stud partition walls, first cut through the plasterboard joints on one side of the wall with a trimming knife and remove. Repeat the process for the other side. Now cut though the studs about 75 mm (3") away from the top (these are used to provide the new supports for the beam or lintel.)

8. Once the wall has been removed the RSJ, beam or lintel can be inserted. An RSJ must be firmly supported at each end by brick piers – the remaining wall is often used. Whilst timber supports or cripple studs, are used in the case of a beam or lintel.

9. For an attractive finish which complies with Building Regulations, the RSJ, beam or lintel will need to be covered. The neatest method is to box it in with plasterboard, which can then be filled in and finished off.

Once the wall has been removed, you will need to fill in the gap in the floor, this is relatively easy using a single board, although aesthetically the finish will not be very attractive. The biggest problem may be that the floor level in the two original rooms is different, leaving you with a slight ramp. Levelling off the two floors professionally could be very expensive, so the simplest solution is to just cover it up. Choose a thick, spongy carpet underlay, topped by a good quality carpet.

STORAGE SOLUTIONS

Storage is probably the single most important requirement in any home, whether it's cupboards in a kitchen, wardrobes in a bedroom, shelves in a living room, or display cabinets in a dining room.

The problem is not so much what kind of system to have, but finding the space to fit it in. In fact there is probably some unused space free in most homes which could be utilised for

storage. It's just a question of identifying where it is.

Your first step should be to assess your home – and that means every room – very carefully and consider all the possibilities. It would help if you walked around with a notebook, jotting down the following information for every room:

■ How much free wall space is there, for fitted furniture, free-standing units or shelving systems? Is there room for a complete floor-to-ceiling arrangement or are there only corners and alcoves free?

■ Is the floor space adjacent to the walls free for floor-to-ceiling cupboards or free-standing units? Is there only enough room for shelving systems starting at waist-height.

■ Is there any space within the rooms themselves for free-standing furniture? Could a storage unit be used as a room divider, for example?

■ If the space available is very limited, would a series of wall grids be useful for hanging lightweight items?

■ Could some form of storage system be suspended from the ceiling, for example in a kitchen or a stairwell?

■ Would movable storage, in the form of a trolley, provide a solution where space is tight?

One of the biggest mistakes most people make is not thinking carefully about their storage requirements, often with disastrous consequences. What's the point of paying hundreds of pounds for a unit designed to house your hi-fi equipment and record collection, only to find it doesn't fit? So, once you've looked critically at the space, consider the sort of items you need to put away and try to calculate how much space they will occupy. At the same time, decide whether you want them to be on display or hidden away. For example:

■ Books, records, glasses, ornaments, drinks and hi-fi equipment are usually found in a living room. Do you want a decorative storage system where the items are on view, where they're hidden, or a bit of both?

■ Food – fresh, tinned and in packets – is kept in the kitchen along with a whole variety of utensils and equipment. How much of it would you like to be 'shown off' and easily accessible, on open shelves, hanging racks and the like, and how much hidden away out of sight behind closed doors?

■ Clothes, shoes, accessories and suitcases are all kept in a bedroom. How much hanging space do they require and how many drawers and shelves do you need for sweaters, bags, shoes?

■ Where do you keep towels and toiletries? Have you got space in the bathroom to fit in a storage system?

■ Do you have any 'collections' which need to be displayed? Ornaments, labels, ceramics, plates?

Try to be flexible about your needs. For example, it may be natural to store clothes in the bedroom, but if there is plenty of space for wardrobes in the hallway, why not store them there? You may like to keep your books in the living room, but they can just as easily be kept in the dining room or bedroom. When it comes to deciding the type and location of the storage the most important consideration is how often you will be using the items stored there.

Now you've assessed the space available, and what needs to be stored, you can start thinking about all the options.

Fixed shelves are probably the simplest form of storage and often the least expensive. You can buy proprietary systems available from most DIY stores, or make up your own using a variety of different shelving supports such as Cliffhanger and Spectrum. Whatever you choose, try and arrange the shelving so that it forms part of the overall decor scheme in the room, and if possible use it in quantity. A series of shelves running the whole length of a wall or fitted into an alcove, will look far more effective than just one or two small shelves on their own. Don't forget to ensure that the system will be sturdy enough for the purpose for which it's to be used and remember that it will only be as strong as its fixings.

Free-standing storage will take up more space than fixed shelves, but is more flexible, as it is easy to move around. Basically it will take one of two forms, either a single piece of furniture – such as a bookcase or cabinet -- or a modular system comprising shelves, cupboards and drawers which can be put together in whatever way you want. You can buy a system that will match the rest of the furniture in the room and, in some cases, it can also be used as a room divider.

Fitted furniture is an excellent way of creating a lot of storage in a relatively small area, floor-to-ceiling cupboards in a bedroom for example, fitted with hanging rails, shelves and racks. It can be tailored to fit, making maximum use of the available space, but it is likely to be more expensive than open shelving and unlike free- standing storage, you won't be able to take it with you if you move. Nevertheless, if you prefer a neat option, with everything hidden behind doors, it probably provides the best solution.

Plastic-coated metal grids fixed to the wall with baskets and hooks hanging from them, provide a useful way of storing small items, if you like an open display. Although they are particularly suited to a kitchen, they would look just as effective in a bathroom or bedroom for toiletries, cosmetics, towels etc.

Wire storage baskets which can be stacked on top of one another, are a useful idea for a kitchen, bathroom, bedroom and even a living room. They can be fitted into a cupboard, hidden behind wardrobes and slotted under a work surface. Some systems can even be fitted with castors so they can be moved around.

SHELVING

Putting up shelving is one of the simplest home improvement jobs as well as one of the most useful. If you put up shelves they will quickly provide extra storage space, as well as become a decorative feature in the room. However, although it is a relatively simple DIY job, it is important that you understand the basics to do the job properly, otherwise you could find your shelves depositing their load on the floor!

To help you decide on the type of shelving best suited to your needs, you need to ask yourself the following questions:

Put your collection on display using Spur Spectrum

- What kind of load will be put on the shelves?
- Do you want free-standing units, which can be moved around or wall-fixed shelving?
- Do you want the shelves to be adjustable?
- Where do you want your shelving?
- If you want wall-fixed shelving, where will they be fitted: into solid brick walls, plasterboard partitions or concrete or clay blocks?

If you have decided to have wall-fixed shelving, you will need to consider the most suitable material for the shelves. There are a number of options:

Plywood needs to be fairly thick if it is to resist bending, so is best used for displaying light objects only. If thoroughly sanded to a smooth finish, it can just be stained and varnished, or painted.

Solid timber is probably the best choice for supporting heavy weights as it is very sturdy, whilst thinner timber shelving will be most attractive for lighter loads. If you want shelves wider than 230 mm (9″) however, it will start working out quite expensive. Timber looks very attractive sanded smooth and just given a protective coat of varnish, although it can easily be stained and varnished, or painted to match the decor of the room.

Veneered blockboard is strong and will support loads similar to those supported by solid timber. Ensure the wood 'grain' runs the length of the shelf, otherwise it could bow and possibly even break if very heavy loads are put on it. The front edge will need to be covered with an iron-on wood veneer.

Veneered chipboard looks like solid wood, but will not provide such strong shelving, as it bends under weight. It is better suited to supporting light loads. Like veneered blockboard, the front edge will need to be edged with iron-on veneer.

Glass is often used for display shelving or in the bathroom. Ask the advice of a glazier on the thickness of the glass required to suit your needs and for the recommended support intervals. For safety the glass should be a minimum of 6 mm thick (¼″) and all the edges should be ground. Look in Yellow Pages for your nearest glazing specialist.

Free-standing systems are probably the best solution if the wall on which you want to have your shelving will not give a strong enough fixing – cellular core wallboard for example. They come in a variety of finishes, usually with adjustable interior fixings, allowing you to move the shelving as required. The biggest drawback is that if the unit is not deep enough you may overload the top shelves, causing the whole system to topple over.

When it comes to wall-mounted shelving there are a number of different systems to choose from.

L-shaped brackets are probably the easiest method of fixing a single shelf which doesn't have to be adjustable. Generally they are a simple L-shape, plain or ornate, steel or aluminium, big or small, available in a host of different colours. Usually they are fixed to the wall with three screws and then fixed to the shelf itself with a further three screws. They are easy to fit and relatively inexpensive.

Track and bracket systems give a strong adjustable shelving system. They comprise two or more uprights which are screwed to the wall. The shelf support brackets are then slotted into these uprights wherever they're required. This type of system is fully adjustable and, once the uprights have been fixed to the wall, extra shelves can easily be added.

Cantilever brackets are useful for single, fixed shelves, giving a neat unobtrusive finish. They comprise a single horizontal bracket (Cliffhanger) or brackets (dovil) screwed to the wall to provide the shelf support.

With any wall-fixed shelving, one of the most critical decisions is ensuring you choose a material that will best support the load you plan to put on it. As a rough guide a wooden shelf 250 mm (10″) wide and 25 mm (1″) thick can support a load of 13-18 kg (28-39 lb) per 300 mm (12″) length – providing it is securely supported.

To ensure maximum stability make sure the span between the supports or brackets follow the guidelines given below:

Shelving material	Shelf thickness	Span
Blockboard	12 mm	450 mm
Plywood	20 mm	800 mm
	25 mm	1,000 mm
Timber	15 mm	500 mm
	20 mm	900 mm
	30 mm	1,100 mm
Veneered chipboard	12 mm	400 mm
	20 mm	600 mm
	25 mm	750 mm

WALLS & WALL FIXINGS

Your next consideration will be choosing the right wall fixing to secure the supports and the first step is to identify the construction of the wall. It will either be solid or hollow.

Solid walls are either made from brick or block. The former will be dense and hard or soft and crumbly depending on the age and quality of the brick; the latter is always soft. To find out drill a few small holes into an unobtrusive part of the wall and examine the dust, if it's pinky-red it's likely to be brick; if it's grey it's block. Some interior walls may be made from hollow clay bricks, which also give a pink dust, the way to distinguish it from brick is by feeling the pressure on the drill as you go into the wall, if after 10 mm (½") there is no resistance you have entered the hollow centre of a clay brick.

Hollow walls are usually plasterboard partitions on a timber frame. Just tap the wall to establish whether it's solid or hollow.

Any wall-mounted shelving needs to be securely fixed to the wall - just putting the screws straight into the wall is simply not good enough, the shelves are likely to fall down as soon as you put something on them. To give the shelves strength and stability you should fix the screws into specially designed wall fixings. There's a whole range of fixings to choose from (made by companies such as Plasplug and Rawlplug) but the type you need will depend on what the wall is made of.

The easiest way to make holes in a brick or block wall is to use a masonry bit with an electric drill. If you make the hole too large, or it becomes distorted so that it is unable to take the fixing use a **compound filler** to fill the hole. (Rawlplug's Plugging Compound contains fibre and binder. Just soak the plug in water for about a minute, then ram the soaked plug into the hole, using the screw, leave for about 30 minutes, remove screw, position fixing and screw home firmly.)

To provide a secure fixing to a solid brick, blockwork or concrete wall you will need to use a wallplug.

Fibre plugs are made from highly compressed fibrous material to give a strong grip in most types of blockwork, brickwork and concrete.

Alternatively use a **plastic wallplug** which has a central pivotal hole and fins, barbs or jaws on the outside which expand as the screw is fixed into them, increasing their grip.

Ordinary wallplugs will not give a firm hold in block walls or soft crumbly brick, instead use **cellular block plugs**, chunky plugs with spiral fins which prevent the plug rotating as the screw is driven in.

If you have plasterboard partition walls, always try and make any fixings into the timber frame, as they will give the strongest support. The frames can be found by tapping horizontally along the wall, the hollow wall will give a ringing tone, when you reach the timber frames the sound will be much flatter. As a guide they are usually found at 400 mm (16") or 600 mm (24") intervals.

If there is no alternative and you have to make your fixing into the wall cladding, there are a number of devices you can use for a secure result, each one works on the principle that as the screw is driven in the fixing opens out and presses against the inner wall - preventing it from pulling out – spreading the load across a large area. To make a hole in plasterboard use a hand or electric drill.

Basic nylon or **plastic anchors** are simple devices. Several different types are available but they all work in the same way. The 'gripper' arms splay open against the inner wall surface as the screw is tightened. Suitable for lightweight fixings, the anchor is lost if the screw is removed.

Collapsible anchors have metal gripping 'shoulders' which fold up on themselves against the inner wall surface as the screw is tightened. They give a strong fixing and will remain in place if the screw is removed.

Expanding rubber bolts comprise a tough rubber sleeve which is placed into the hole. When the screw is inserted and tightened the rubber sleeve compresses against the inner wall surface. These give strong fixings in both hollow and solid walls and if the screw is removed the bolt can be taken out and used again.

Gravity or **spring toggles** have one or two spring-loaded gripper arms which open out

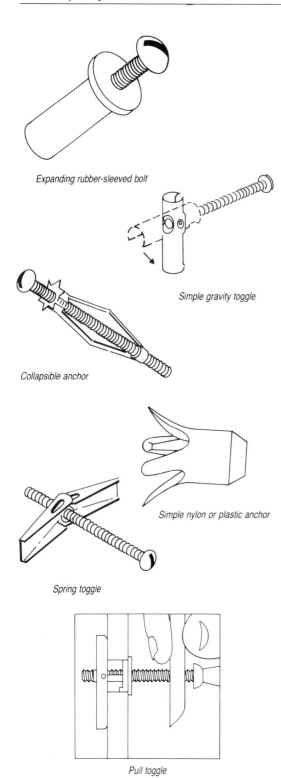

Expanding rubber-sleeved bolt

Simple gravity toggle

Collapsible anchor

Simple nylon or plastic anchor

Spring toggle

Pull toggle

once the toggle has been pushed through the hole. As the screw is tightened the gripper arms are pulled firmly against the inner wall surface. These toggles give a strong fixing but they will be lost if the screw is removed.

Pull toggles comprise a nylon collar and toggle held together by a slotted nylon strap. The toggle is placed into the wall hole and the collar slid in position along the strap so that it 'plugs' the hole and the toggle is held tight against the wall. Once the toggle is in place, the nylon strap is snapped off and the screw can then be inserted. This kind of fixing is particularly useful as the toggle will remain in place even if the screw is removed.

If you would like further information about wall fixings, contact the Rawlplug Technical Advisory Service, Rawlplug House, London Road, Kingston-upon-Thames, Surrey KT2 6NR. ☎ 01-546 2191. They offer a series of useful leaflets on the various types of fixings available and will be able to answer questions on specific fixing problems.

FIXING SHELF BRACKETS

1. With small shelves, first screw the brackets to the shelf. Hold shelf in position on the wall. Put a spirit level on the shelf and when it's completely level, mark the position of the screw holes with a pencil.

2. Depending on the construction of the wall, use the appropriate fixings and drill and plug the holes, then screw the brackets in position.

3. With long shelves, or on stud partition walls, drill, plug and screw one of the end brackets at the correct height and position on the wall.

4. Hold the other end bracket in position with the shelf resting on them both. Put a spirit level on the shelf and when it's completely level mark the position of the screw holes with a pencil. If the shelf sags place it on its edge, resting on the fixed bracket, to set the level of the second. Drill, plug and screw in position.

5. With both end brackets fixed, establish the position of any other brackets in the same way. Drill, plug and screw.

6. Place the shelf on the brackets, then measure and mark the position of any shelves which are to be placed above or below it. Drill, plug and screw all remaining brackets into position.

7. Once all the brackets have been fixed, lay the top shelf in position and hang a plumb bob over the side. Line up all the other shelves to this line and secure them all to their brackets.

FIXING TRACK SYSTEMS

1. Decide where you want the top of one track support by holding it in place and marking the top fixing hole with a pencil.

2. Drill and plug the top hole in the usual way and screw the track gently to the wall so it swings to a vertical position.

3. Hold the track and, with the aid of a spirit level, mark the position of all the other fixing holes along its length.

4. Swing the track to one side, drill and plug all the other holes and screw the track tightly into place.

5. If the track does not fit snugly against the wall, or if the wall is not truly vertical, push packing behind the upright.

6. Place a bracket into the fixed track and another in the corresponding position on a second track. Hold the second track in place against the wall and lay a shelf over the two brackets. Use a spirit level or a helper to establish when the shelf is horizontal.

7. Mark the top hole of the second bracket and fix in the same way as the first.

8. Fix other tracks in the same way.

9. When all the tracks have been fixed, slot in the brackets. Lay the top shelf in position, hang a plumb bob over the side. Line up all the other shelves to this line.

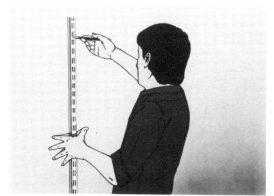

Step 1 to 2

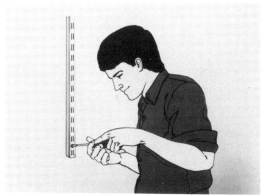

Step 3 to 5

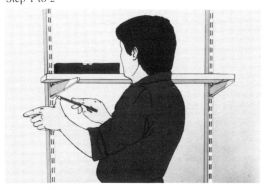

Step 6 to 8

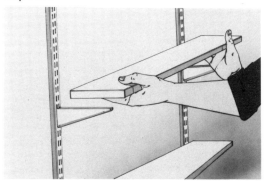

Step 9   Pictures courtesy of Spur shelving

UNDERSTANDING LIGHTING

Lighting should be one of the first things to be considered when you start thinking about redecorating, in reality it is probably one of the last. Unfortunately, when most people talk about lighting, they're really thinking about the lampshades or fittings, rather than the actual light source itself, and that is the fundamental problem. We don't really understand the implications of good lighting.

Why is it that this vitally important part of the home is so neglected? Basically for three reasons:

Safety: Lighting involves electricity and we all know that it is dangerous to start playing with wiring. We therefore tend to retain the light sources and socket outlets which are already fitted.

Jargon: Lighting seems to involve a completely different vocabulary, which the average person – that's you and me - finds both confusing and bewildering. (For starters, look through the guide below.)

Cost: Quite simply, when we start looking at some of the 'fancy' fittings, we are horrified by how much they cost, let alone the cost of consulting a lighting design expert.

It's so much easier to play safe, stick to what we know and understand and forget what can be achieved. But frankly that's a shame. If you are willing to spend a lot of time and money choosing new furnishings for a room, it could be wasted if you've neglected the lighting. Different light sources can create totally different effects so whereas one source will produce a light which will complement your furnishings, another could completely change it.

It would be well worth your while trying to understand what lighting does and how it can be used. If possible, go to a good lighting retailer where you can view all the installations, experiment with the light sources and talk about the effects you would like. If you're in doubt about the installation, consult a qualified electrician.

When it comes to changing the lighting in a room, just look upon it in the way you would any other form of decoration. Begin by carefully assessing the room, working out how it is used and what kind of lighting is needed. The types of lighting can be divided into different groups:

General lighting which does no more than provide the room with light that enables you to see. Ceiling-mounted lights are the most popular way of providing general lighting, although in some rooms wall lights perform the same function. The overall effect can be rather boring. Consider fitting recessed downlighters, wall uplighters and using table lamps.

Task lighting relates to the directional light required to enable you to do a specific job: a reading light in the living room or bedroom, a work light on a desk, a light which enables you to work in the kitchen. Usually task lighting is provided by spotlights or tungsten strip lights.

Accent lighting is used to pick out specific objects in a room, to create interest. Picture lights are the best example, although any object can be treated in this way, such as a flower arrangement, ornaments or a plant. Use spotlights, uplighters and table lamps.

Mood lighting performs a similar function to accent lighting, except it provides pockets of light in certain areas rather than illuminating a particular object. Concealed fluorescent strip lights in a glass display cabinet are a good example. Spotlights, table lamps, uplighters and downlighters can all be used for this purpose.

Once you've assessed the room and the kind of lighting you need, look at the position of the existing lighting points and socket outlets. It may be that all you need to do is change the position of a few sockets – or maybe just add a few more – and buy some more appropriate fittings to achieve the desired effect. Here's a brief guide to the types of fittings available and how they can be used.

Pendant lights hang from the ceiling and are unlikely to adequately illuminate the corners or edges of a room. Fitting a larger wattage bulb will not give any more light, it will only result in more 'glare'.

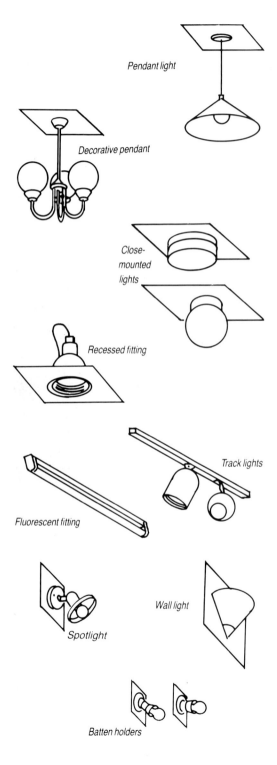

Pendant light

Decorative pendant

Close-mounted lights

Recessed fitting

Track lights

Fluorescent fitting

Spotlight

Wall light

Batten holders

Table lamps add decorative interest to a room and are a good way of providing accent lighting, on a coffee table, sideboard or at a bedside table for example. They should always be used in conjunction with other lights but should be positioned so that you cannot see the bulb itself.

Wall lights add character to a room, providing both general and mood lighting, by creating interesting pockets of light. Although they can add interest to a previously dull and flat wall surface, they can also show up any defects on a poorly finished wall, so be careful where and how you place them. Wall lights must be positioned above eye level and, like table lamps, you should not see the bulb itself.

Downlighters usually recessed in the ceiling, vary from those which give a wide general beam of light, to those giving a very narrow intense beam, used for highlighting specific objects. They give an uncluttered look to a ceiling, but will need to be recessed within the ceiling void, which is not always possible.

Lighting tracks and spotlights come in a very wide range of options and are used extensively throughout the home. However, they are also frequently misused, for example, a ceiling track with spotlights should never be used to replace a single pendant light, this would result in poor lighting with shadows and both direct and reflective glare. Tracks and spotlights are not suitable for providing general lighting but should be used to provide accent or mood lighting.

Uplighters are all those lights which direct light upwards, so that it is reflected back from the ceiling and adjacent walls. This form of lighting can be used to stunning effect, but it can also highlight a badly finished wall surface, so be careful where you use it.

Apart from the different types of light, you also need to understand the different light sources, known technically as lamps (although you would probably call them bulbs). There are three main types:

Fluorescent lighting, usually in the form of strip tubes, uses an ultra-violet light which reacts with chemicals painted on the inside of

Uplighters from the Mazda Interiors range used to stunning effect in a dining room

the tube to produce the light. It offers a high-light output for low-power consumption and is cheaper to run than tungsten filament lamps – provided they are not switched on and off too often. However, the light they give off is bluish and cold and glares uncomfortably. (Choose warm white for use in the home.) Best used as a functional light only.

Tungsten filament lamps are what we are most familiar with. They comprise a glass housing containing a filament, or bent wire, made from tungsten which can withstand being repeatedly heated up and cooled down. Wattage ranges from 10 watts for nightlights, up to 150 watts. Always make sure you don't use a more powerful lamp than specified by a light fitting or the shade may be damaged.

Tungsten halogen lamps contain halogen, an inert gas, which surrounds the tungsten filament. This increases the life of the lamp and casts a very bright, white light, more intense than ordinary tungsten lamps. There are two categories of tungsten halogen lamps: mains-voltage and low-voltage. Mains voltage uses the standard electrical current of 240 volts which runs through all lighting circuits in the UK. Low voltage requires a much lower voltage to run - usually 12 volts – and burns more efficiently, more brightly and for longer than tungsten filament lamps. The excess power is converted or transformed into more energy for the bulb by means of a transformer.

GLOSSARY

To help you unravel some of the mystique involved in lighting here's a guide to many of the technical terms used.

AC (Alternating current) *All the electricity supplied to our homes via the national grid is AC.*

Accent lighting *Highlighting a small object or feature with a beam of light.*

Amps or amperes *The rate of flow at which electricity is supplied to the home.*

Bayonet cap (BC) *Name given to the method of fitting a lamp into the light fitting.*

Bulbs *The popular name used for filament lamps, comprising a glass housing and coiled tungsten filament.*

Ceiling rose *Connects the central ceiling pendant flex to the mains.*

Colour rendering *The colour appearance given to objects by a lamp, as compared with their appearance by natural light.*

Crown silvered *Where the crown on the glass bulb housing is silvered so that light is thrown back to give glare-free light.*

Diffuser *The covering of a fluorescent tube which reduces glare and spreads the light over a wide area.*

Directional lighting *Lighting designed to illuminate an object or surface from a specific direction.*

Dimmer switch *A device which enables you to vary the amount of light given off from the bulb. They usually take the place of a conventional switch.*

Downlighter *A cylindrical ceiling fitting which directs light down and prevents glare. They can be ceiling-mounted or recessed, although the latter will require a space of around 150-220 mm (6-8") between the ceiling and the floor above.*

Earthing *Any metal light fitting should have an earth lead connection, unless all the metal parts are insulated from the user.*

Eyeball spot *Recessed downlighter which looks just like an eyeball and provides directional lighting. It swivels to direct light at any angle.*

Fluorescent lamps *A light source which does not have a filament. Gives five times as much light for the same number of watts as filament lamps.*

General lighting *Lighting designed to illuminate an entire room or area.*

Glare *Light which causes discomfort to the eyes. It's the equivalent to staring at the sun. It can be caused by accidental viewing of the light source itself (direct glare) or when the light bounces off an adjacent surface such as a wall or picture, (reflective glare).*

Halogen *An inert gas which is contained in a tungsten filament lamp to produce a very bright white light.*

Lamp *Correct technical name for a bulb.*

Lighting track *Wired metal track usually available in metre runs connected to a single light point or socket and fitted to the wall or ceiling. A number of spotlights can be clipped into the track anywhere along its length. This is a good way of getting more light without rewiring.*

Luminaire *Correct technical name for a light fitting.*

Pendant *Light which hangs from the ceiling.*

Picture lights *Either a tungsten filament tube attached to an angled wall bracket or slim fluorescent tube hidden by a baffle used to highlight a picture.*

Pullcords *The method used to switch lights on and off and usually found in a bathroom for safety reasons.*

Reflectors *Used in spotlights, downlighters and floodlights to produce a more concentrated light.*

Ring circuit *The wiring system which supplies electricity to the light and socket outlets. Most homes have two circuits one for the lights and one for the switch sockets.*

Rise and fall light *Adjustable light fitting, usually with a curly cable connected to a spring, which allows you to move a pendant light up and down.*

Screw cap (ES) *Refers to the method of fixing the bulb into the light fitting. Usually found on continental bulbs.*

Spotlights *Type of light fitting which produces a directional beam of light. The beams can be of different sizes and intensity. Ideal for work areas as they concentrate light on a particular spot.*

Switch sockets *Plug socket outlets which have a switch so that they can be turned on and off.*

Table lamps *Probably the most simple, decorative form of domestic lighting available in a wide variety of styles to suit your decor. The bulb in a table lamp should be about 1 metre (39") from the floor.*

Time switches *A useful plug-in device which can be used to turn lights on and off automatically, creating the impression that someone is in the house. Useful for security reasons.*

Touch switches *A lighting control which only needs to be lightly touched to switch a light on or off. Useful if your hands are full.*

Unit *The measurement of electricity.*

Uplighter *Light fitting which directs light upwards so that it is reflected off the ceiling and adjacent wall.*

Voltage *The pressure at which electricity is supplied. The UK domestic supply is 240 volts.*

Wallwashing *Method used to emphasise an area of a room with light by using several fittings.*

Wattage *The rate at which electricity is used.*

USING WOOD IN THE HOME

From stripped floorboards to timber panelling, solid wood kitchen units to robust shelving, there's a whole host of ways to use timber in the home. Timber can be used in so many ways around the home that it really ought to play a more important part in home decor, but its decorative value is only just starting to be realised. Whereas people are willing to buy teak table and chairs for their dining room, pine kitchen units or mahogany bedroom furniture, it has taken a long time for timber to be used creatively in its own right.

Timber, with its attractive grain, not only looks good in its natural state, covered with a coat of protective clear varnish, but it can be enhanced by staining and dyeing, offering a wide range of decorative possibilities. Of course wood can also be painted. This is becoming very fashionable, but does cover up a lot of the natural beauty. In addition, timber is durable and has good insulation properties helping to reduce a room's heat loss, so a timber-clad room can actually be – as well as feel – warmer than one which is just painted.

SOFTWOOD

Softwoods come from evergreen coniferous trees such as pine and spruce, and the timber which is produced from them and sold on the UK DIY market is predominantly European Redwood (sometimes called pine, deal, red deal or, in the lower qualities, knotty pine), or European Whitewood (sometimes called white deal, white pine or spruce). Softwoods tend to be less expensive than hardwoods and are the timbers which are commonly available from timber merchants and DIY stores.

Softwoods are used extensively throughout this country for most building purposes, such as floors and roofs as well as for window frames, doors, etc. There is now also a thriving market for high quality 'pine' furniture.

Most of the DIY softwood available will have been properly kiln dried before sale so that it is in the best possible condition when it reaches the merchant or retailer. However, there is a danger that they may not store it properly. It is important that the timber is dry before you use it in your home, so do not buy timber which feels damp to the touch; store it in your home for a few days or so before you start work to

Wicanders real-wood strip flooring

allow it to acclimatise, lay it flat so that there is no tendency for it to twist or warp.

Softwoods can be bought either rough-sawn or planed. Sawn timber will obviously be less expensive but, of course, is unsuitable for those situations where a good decorative surface is required. Sometimes you will see planed timber referred to as PAR (planed all round) or PSE (planed and square-edged). Remember that planing removes timber so if you see 100 × 50 mm (4″ × 2″) PAR timber it will almost certainly be 95 mm × 45 mm (3¾″ × 1¾″) in actual size, so make allowances for this when you are calculating how much timber you will need for a job.

Softwoods are available in a wide range of sizes, all of them sawn or planed to metric dimensions and lengths. Nominal sizes range from say 12 mm to 75 mm (½″ to 3″) thick and 12 mm to 225 mm (½″ to 9″) wide. It can also be bought in a wide range of profiles, such as decorative tongued and grooved boarding and mouldings, like skirting boards and picture rails.

HARDWOOD

Hardwood is more expensive than softwood and comes from the broad-leaf non-coniferous trees. The traditional hardwoods such as oak, teak, mahogany, etc., are well known, but nowadays there is a wide range of newer species available, Hardwoods are generally known for their strength and durability, especially for outdoor use, although, with the modern preservative treatment of softwoods, the difference nowadays is less obvious.

Hardwoods are known for their attractive grain and are used for decorative purposes, floors, shelves and for furniture. They are not so widely available on the DIY market as softwoods and in many places can only be bought subject to special order. One exception to this is a hardwood called ramin which is reasonably priced and is readily available in the form of high quality mouldings.

Hardwood is available in boards ranging in size from 25 × 150 mm (1″ × 6″) up to 100 × 100mm (4″ × 4″), and very large sizes can be obtained to special order. Proprietary hardwood flooring in ash and beech is available from a number of specialist flooring suppliers.

MAN-MADE BOARDS

As well as these natural timbers, there are a number of man-made boards which are used extensively in the home. They are:

Blockboard comprises a core of rectangular wood battens sandwiched between two softwood veneer surfaces by pressure bonding. It is used for jobs where structural strength is required, such as supporting a worktop or shelving. If the board will be seen and appearance is important, the edges will need to be covered with wood lipping.

Blockboard is usually sold in sheets 18 mm (¾″) thick, although it is also available in 12 mm and 25 mm (½″ and 1″) thicknesses.

Chipboard is made from chips of softwood which are bonded together with resin adhesive under pressure. Because of its method of construction, it is a very stable material and is unlikely to warp and bend unless exposed to damp conditions. It is usually sanded smooth on both sides; where necessary the edges can be filled and the surfaces primed for painting. Laminate- or melamine-covered chipboard is widely used in the kitchen and is also available in narrow boards which are used to make shelves. Several different grades are available including heavy-duty chipboard and flooring-grade chipboard.

Chipboard is vulnerable to moisture and although moisture-resisting grades are produced, these are not generally available to the DIY market. So do not use ordinary chipboard in conditions where it may get wet, for example in bathrooms or outside.

Chipboard comes in standard sheets measuring 2440 × 1220 mm (8′ × 4′). It's available in three thicknesses: 12, 18 and 25 mm (½, ¾ and 1″).

Hardboard is made from softwood pulp which is compressed into sheets; one side is smooth and shiny, the other rough and matt. It is not as strong as most other man-made boards, but is relatively inexpensive and can be used in many ways, to provide an underfloor for floorcoverings, to make small sliding doors, as a back for cabinets and cupboards and as a base for drawers.

As well as the standard sheets, there are several other types of hardboard available. **Peg board** is a perforated hardboard which can be used in the kitchen so that you can hang all your kitchen utensils from it. **Screening**, a decorative, pierced hardboard, which is available in a number of different designs, is ideal for making floor-standing screens or for using as a screen to cover up an ugly sight, a radiator for example. **Oil tempered hardboard** is a specially treated board which is suitable for a whole variety of exterior jobs.

Standard hardboard is 3·2 mm (⅛″) thick and comes in sheets 2440 × 1220 mm (8′ × 4′), but most stockists will keep smaller cut sheets, such as 1200 × 600 mm (3′ 11″ × 2′). Thicker boards are available.

Plywood is made by bonding several thin layers of wood veneer together under high pressure to form a sheet. It is particularly strong and many better quality plywoods are used to make furniture. The veneers (plies) always lie with their grain directions alternating, to give strength, and the number of layers used always comes to an odd number so that the grains of the two outer veneers run in the same direction. The outer veneers of decorative plywood are frequently hardwoods, such as birch, although other woods are also available, oak and sapele for example. Plywood is also readily available in construction quality, which is ideal for non-decorative uses indoors and out.

Plywood comes in standard sheets, ranging from 610 × 610 mm (2′ × 2′) up to 2440 × 1220 mm (8′ × 4′) and is available in thickness ranging from 3·2 mm to 25 mm (⅛ to 1″).

TIMBER PANELLING

Timber panelling is probably the most popular way of using timber in the home and many home owners have used panelling in their kitchen or bathroom or up the stairs, to great effect. As well as being a good insulator, wood, with its attractive graining, will give a room a stunning appearance, although additional interest and greater individuality can be created by staining or dyeing with one of a wide range of attractive translucent colours. Don't think you have to completely cover the boards with a stain or dye either, many imaginative patterns can be created, possibly using stencils, using stains and dyes which will give a totally individual look.

Apart from the decorative finish you can create with stains and dyes, the boards themselves can be arranged in a number of striking ways: fixed vertically, horizontally or diagonally, or any such combination You can use ordinary planed (PAR) square-edged boards for this job, but an attractive alternative finish is achieved by using tongued and grooved boards, as they permit fixing nails to be easily hidden from view. Many DIY stores stock tongued and grooved boards in pre-packaged quantities. They are usually 9 mm (⅜″) thick. However, for particular applications you may choose to use boards which are either 12 mm (½″) or 20 mm (¾″) thick.

When it comes to buying tongued and grooved boards there are several different types to choose from:

Shiplap, where one edge of each board slips under the 'tail' of its neighbour.

Narrow 'V' or **wide 'V'** tongued and grooved board, where one edge of each board has a tongue or lip which slots into the groove of its neighbour.

When buying tongued and grooved boards you will have to make allowances for the joins. For example, a board which may measure 95 mm (3¾″) overall width will only cover 88 mm (3½″) by the time the boards are slotted together. Remember also that although these pre- packaged boards should be fully dried out, it is always a good idea to store them in the room they are to be used in for a few days before you start work. This way they will adjust to the room's temperature and atmosphere before fixing.

FINISHES

For a number of reasons, whether for decoration or protection, it is likely that timber surfaces will need to be finished and there is an extremely wide range of proprietary products available on the market to choose from. As well as paint, you can choose wood dyes, varnishes and decorative stains.

■ In simple terms, if you want a natural wood finish your best bet is to varnish the surface. Polyurethane will protect the timber against dirt and moisture while providing a surface which is hardwearing and resistant to bumps and scratches. Ensure the surface is smooth (sanding is essential for good results) and make good any defects with a wood filler, making sure the filler matches the colour of the wood. Remove all traces of dust and wipe over with a damp cloth, then varnish according to the directions on the can. You can get varnish in high gloss, satin (semi-gloss) and matt finishes.

■ If you would like to colour the timber, use an appropriate wood dye topped with clear polyurethane varnish. Choose a colour that you won't tire of because, once applied, most dyes are virtually impossible to remove as the colour actually penetrates into the wood. Try out the dye on an off-cut before applying to ensure the finished result looks how you expect it to look. Alternatively, use a coloured varnish which does not sink into the timber, although in heavy wear areas the colour could eventually wear off.

■ To enrich the natural colour of the wood, use a wood stain. These are really intended for external use but look very attractive indoors as well. These are available in various wood hues, such as walnut, chestnut, maple, ebony, etc.

FIXING TIMBER PANELLING

Timber panelling makes a very attractive finish for walls and ceilings and is the ideal way of covering up a surface that is particularly uneven or in a poor condition.

It is a decorative way of boxing-in a bath or disguising unsightly pipework or wiring. Once fixed, the timber can be finished in a variety of stains, varnishes and colours.

Timber boards can be bought from most DIY shops as well as timber and builders' merchants. They come in a variety of widths, thicknesses and styles, frequently in pre-packaged quantities. Tongued and grooved boards provide the most popular timber cladding as the meeting edges of the boards are machined to produce a decorative profile. Types include Narrow 'V', Wide 'V' and Shiplap. Alternatively, if you want a more robust finish, you could buy plain square-edged boards (without tongues and grooves) which can give some very interesting effects.

Whatever you choose, always buy the correct number of boards needed to complete the job in one batch to ensure a perfect match and that all the tongues and grooves fit. Most boards will have been dried to a fairly low moisture content before you buy them. But, where possible, it is always a good idea to store them in the room they will be used in for a few days prior to fixing; this will allow the boards to adjust to the temperature and atmosphere.

When calculating the amount of timber you will need for a particular area, you will need to carefully check the covering width of the boards as this will be different from the actual width by the time they are slotted together. For example a 9 mm (⅜″) board may be 95 mm (3¾″) actual width, but have only 88 mm (3½″) covering width, similarly a 15 × 145 mm (⅝″ × 5¾″) board will have a covering width of 138 mm (5½″).

Equipment

Essential items:

■ tongued and grooved boards

■ 50 mm × 25 mm (2 × 1″) softwood battens

■ drill with wood bits, masonry bit and countersink

■ wallplugs and screws

■ screwdriver

■ spirit level

■ wood packaging

■ steel tape measure and pencil

■ try square

■ tenon saw

■ sandpaper

■ 32 mm (1¼″) panel pins (or screws or clips)

■ pin hammer

■ nail punch

■ mallet

■ wood filler

■ wood trim

■ stain or varnish

Optional:

■ electric drill (for wallplugs)

■ electric jigsaw

■ electrical orbital sander

Method

1. Prepare the wall for panelling. Skirting boards and picture rails can be removed, but as it is unlikely that they can be re-used, they may be left within the space formed by the battens.

2. To enable you to fix the panelling to the walls you will need to fit a framework made with timber battens. If you take time and care at this stage to fix the battens straight and true, you will get a better finished result. With masonry walls, fix the battens using masonry wallplugs and screws (masonry nails may be used as an alternative). On timber stud walls, the battens should be nailed or screwed through the plasterboard lining into the vertical wood studs. Make sure you avoid any concealed pipes or wiring.

3. Position the battens horizontally for vertical panelling or vertically for horizontal panelling. Vertical or horizontal battens are suitable for diagonal panelling.

4. The spacing of the wall battens is largely determined by the thickness of the panelling and by the rigidity required; panelling needs to be most rigid where it may be leant against, such as on a staircase wall. Battens should be fixed at about 400-500 mm (16-20") centres for 9 mm (3/8") board. Thicker boards may permit wider centres.

5. Fix the two extreme horizontal or vertical battens about 25-50 mm (1-2") from the floor/ceiling to enable easy nailing of the panelling. This will also prevent the boards splitting when nailing.

6. Once fixed the battens should form a level framework. Use a spirit level to check the battens are either truly vertical or horizontal.

7. If the wall to which the battens are fixed is very uneven it may be necessary to pack behind the battens with plywood or hardboard packs in order to get them flat and level.

8. Now start fixing the boards. Starting at one end of the wall, measure the length of board required. Measure off this length on the back of the board and mark with a pencil using the try square to ensure accuracy. Cut to length carefully with a tenon saw and sand off any rough edges.

9. Fixing the first board will depend on how you have decided to fix the remainder of the boards. They can be fixed to the battens by one of three methods. The simplest is face fixing, nailing through the surface of the board. However, the nail heads will remain visible or they will have to be punched below the surface and filled with a matching filler. (Boards can be screwed but these have to be exposed and look better in brass with cups under the heads.)

10. The better, but slightly more difficult, method is secret nailing, where the boards are fixed by driving panel pins through the tongue of each board, using a nail punch, in such a way that the groove of the next board hides the nail. This takes great skill to avoid splitting off the tongues on thinner boards. Of course, with this method the two extreme end boards must be face nailed.

11. The third method is using proprietary fixing clips, which slip into the board groove and are fixed to the battens by nailing through the tab. The clip is hidden when the next board is fixed.

12. If secret nailing, the first board should be fitted into the corner with tongue outermost. If using metal clips, make sure that the groove is outermost. With face fixing the boards can be either way round.

13. Face nail the first board into position making sure that it is vertical with the spirit level.

14. Build up the wall panelling by slotting boards together and fixing them by the desired method.

15. Hand pressure should be sufficient to push the boards together, but if any are a little warped, an offcut may be pushed over the edge of the offending board and then used as a buffer to tap home the board gently using a mallet. A temporary nail through the offcut into a batten will hold the board in position while nailing or fixing takes place.

16. It should be possible to buy tongued and grooved boards in sufficient lengths to avoid end jointing, but it may be necessary with large areas of horizontal panelling. Take care to stagger joints on adjacent boards to avoid continuous joint lines.

17. When you reach the other end of the wall cut the last board to size along its length using a tenon saw. If you have one, an electric jigsaw will make this job easier.

18. Fix the last board in place by face nailing.

19. At any external corners, boards may be overlapped or trimmed by one of a wide range of softwood trims now available.

20. If the wall/ceiling junction is uneven, this can be disguised by either fitting a softwood trim or coving.

21. Fix a new length of matching skirting board.

22. Finally fill any nail holes with matching wood filler. Allow the filler to dry and sand the whole area to a smooth finish. An orbital sander will make this job easier, but do not use a circular sander.

23. Stain or varnish as desired.

VARNISHING AND STAINING WOOD

Wood used on any interior surface should be varnished to protect it from knocks and stains and also to give it a sheen which will accentuate the grain. Depending on the finished effect you want, clear varnish is available in three sheen levels: gloss, satin and matt. As well as clear varnishes, you can also get a stain varnish – basically a varnish and dye combined – so you can change the wood's colour as you varnish. Wood dyes are also available on their own.

Whether you use a clear varnish or stain varnish, for the best results you need to make sure the timber surface is absolutely clean and smooth before you apply it. Ensure it's free of any oil, grease, wax or dust. Dust particles, no matter how minute, will show up once the varnish has dried and could ruin the finished effect. The method for varnishing wood may vary, depending on which proprietary product you use. Always read the instructions on the can carefully before you start.

Make sure you work with clean cloths and brushes. Don't use old paint brushes which could have traces of paint attached to them which could spoil the finish. The size brush you need depends on the job. For general work 12 mm (½"), 25 mm (1") and 50 mm (2") brushes are suitable. For floors use a 100 mm (4") brush.

Equipment

■ Medium and fine grade abrasive papers

■ White spirit

■ Lint-free cloth or rubber*

■ Varnish

■ Clean paint brush

■ Fine wire wool

■ Wax polish

■ Clean duster

Dulux wood varnishes and stains

* **A rubber** is made from a 300 mm (12") square clean white cotton rag which should be saturated in methylated spirit then wrung out until just damp. Dip a handful of cotton wool in shellac and squeeze out the excess. Wrap the cotton wool in the rag, twist excess cloth to form a grip. Use the smooth base pad.

Method

1. Make sure the surface is clean, dry and free of any dust. Previously treated wood, should always be sanded lightly with a medium grade abrasive paper in the direction of the grain, then wiped over with white spirit on a lint-free cloth.

2. Bare wood needs a priming coat. Thin varnish with 10% white spirit. Using a soft cloth pad or rubber* apply thinned varnish, rubbing well into the grain of the wood. Leave for at least six hours, ideally allow 24 hours to elapse between coats.

3. Gently rub the surface with a fine abrasive paper. Wipe over with white spirit on a lint-free cloth to remove any dust and grease.

4. Apply second coat of varnish with a brush in exactly the same way as you would apply paint. Load brush by dipping one third of the bristles into the liquid. Remove excess gently on the side of the container. Be careful not to cause any bubbles to form in the varnish, this could spoil the finished result if transferred to the timber.

5. If the surface is going to be subjected to hard wear, apply a third coat. Following the same procedure given above.

6. If you are not totally satisfied with the final result, dip very fine wire wool into wax polish. Using parallel strokes and following the direction of the grain, rub over the surface. Buff with a soft duster. This may remove a high gloss finish, but will give a surface with an attractive sheen and no obvious imperfection.

Safety

If you are varnishing a large area of timber, such as a wall or floor, it can cause an unpleasant build-up of fumes. Open all windows for ventilation and wear a gauze face mask.

As attractive as natural wood may be, there are many circumstances where you may prefer to stain it. Stains can be either natural wood hues, such as pine, chestnut or mahogany, or stronger colours such as red, green or blue. In many cases you can buy a combined varnish and dye and these products should be applied in exactly the same way as clear varnishes. However it is worth making a test strip on a spare piece of timber before you start so you know how many coats you need to apply to achieve the desired result.

To make a test strip use a spare piece of timber from the batch you will be staining. Paint the whole strip with a coat of stain. Allow this to be absorbed, then apply a second coat leaving a strip of the first coat showing. Continue in this way always leaving a strip of the previous application for comparison. If you are not using a combined stain and varnish, apply a coat of varnish to the test strip once the stain has dried to make sure you like the finished result. As some varnishes react

unfavourably with oil-based stains, always use products from the same manufacturer for the best results.

1. Your wood needs to be perfectly clean and free from grease, otherwise the stain may not take.

2. If using a water-based stain, sand the wood until completely smooth, then dampen the surface with a wet rag. Leave to dry then sand with fine abrasive paper. If using an oil-based stain, this treatment is not necessary, although the wood still needs to be clean and grease free.

3. Apply stain with a paintbrush, paint pad or a rubber*. As it is very fluid a rubber may give the best results as you'll be able to control runs on vertical surfaces more easily. A rubber is the best way to stain turned wood and rails.

4. When applying, do not brush out stains as you do when painting, but apply liberally and evenly always following the direction of the grain. For the best results it is important to blend the wet edges. Work quickly and complete the job in one go, otherwise the finished result could be patchy.

ADVICE

If you're looking for ideas and inspiration on how to use wood decoratively in the home, send off for a colourful 16-page boklet *The Ronseal Book of Colouring Wood* which shows some stunning decorative treatments. Write to: Consumer Services, Sterling Roncraft, 15 Churchfield Court, Churchfield, Barnsley, South Yorkshire S70 2LJ.

For DIY information on how to use wood in the home 'The Home Woodworking Campaign' has produced a range of five free colourful leaflets called *Make Yourself at Home with Timber*. These contain a variety of useful step-by-step projects for indoors and out. Write to The Home Woodworking Campaign, The Swedish Finnish Timber Council, 21/23 Carolgate, Retford, Nottinghamshire DN22 6BZ.

For advice on using and caring for hardwood, write to the National Hardwood Campaign, 44 Duke Street, St. James's, London SW1Y 6DD.

HOME SECURITY

Have you ever thought how safe your home is from burglars? In 1980 there were 284,375 known break-ins whilst in 1986 the figure had risen to over 900,000 and the signs are that it's not going to stop there. Unfortunately burglary is on the increase, so it's worth making sure that you do all you can to protect your home. In fact a little time and money spent on simple deterrents could save you a lot of anxiety and distress in the future.

Contrary to popular belief, most burglaries take place during the day, when the house is likely to be unoccupied. They are usually the result of a spur of the moment decision – an open window is an open invitation to the passing opportunist burglar who will want to get in and out as quickly as possible. In fact it is estimated that around 90% of all burglaries are carried out by teenagers aged between 14 and 17. Unlike the professional burglar, most of these criminals will be deterred by relatively simple window locks and bolts. Unfortunately there's little you can do to keep out the determined professional, particularly if you have something valuable to steal.

AVOIDING A BURGLARY

There are a number of precautions you should always follow to avoid your house being chosen as the target.

■ Always lock windows and doors every time you leave the house. Never leave a window open if you are going out - even in the middle of the summer. It might be tedious

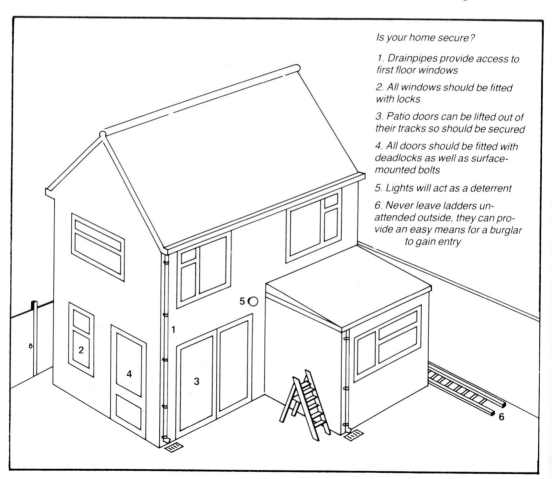

Is your home secure?

1. Drainpipes provide access to first floor windows

2. All windows should be fitted with locks

3. Patio doors can be lifted out of their tracks so should be secured

4. All doors should be fitted with deadlocks as well as surface-mounted bolts

5. Lights will act as a deterrent

6. Never leave ladders un-attended outside, they can provide an easy means for a burglar to gain entry

Protect yourself
nd your belongings...

... with the **WALK EASY**™ Personal Alarm
and TOPLINE Property Marking Kits

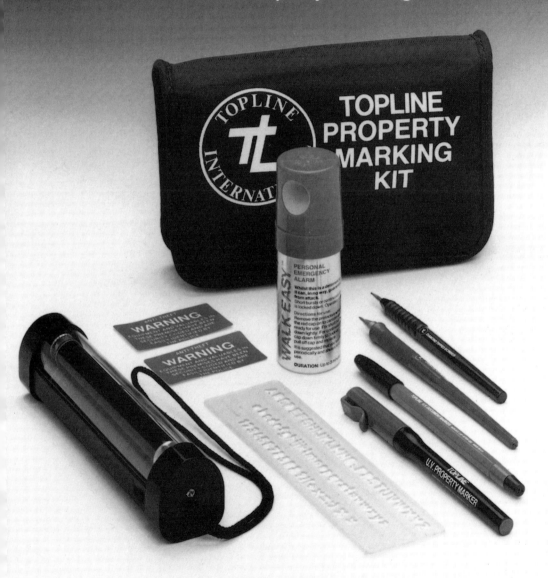

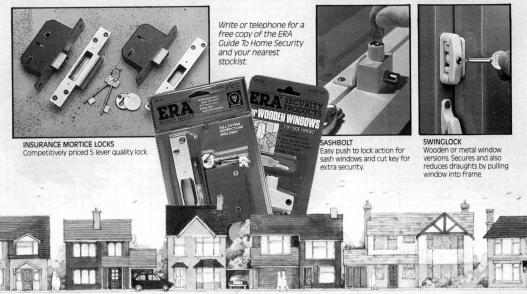

BRITAIN'S TIGHTEST SECURITY SYSTEM IS A PIECE OF PAPER.

If a company designs, installs or services electronic security systems, becoming a member of the BSIA is a tall order.

Because the Security Systems Inspectorate (SSI) ensures that to receive our certificate, any company has to have an ongoing commitment to excellence. Ongoing, because the company is checked annually and they're all committed to achieving BS5979 (central stations standard) and BS5750 (quality standard).

Certificate

BSIA

C B Porter

SECURITY SYSTEMS APPROVED INSPECTORATE

What's more, we have a special section for CCTV companies.

Any company that's a member of the BSIA can be relied on totally. So check and see that your security system comes via a BSIA member.

If it does, rest assured. If not, sound the alarm.

The British Security Industry Association, Security House, Barbourne Road, Worcester WR1 1RS. Telephone: 0905 21464.

making sure all the windows are locked and the house might be hot and stuffy when you return, but you may have prevented an opportunist burglar taking a chance. Don't leave open first-floor windows, burglars can easily climb drainpipes or climb on top of a porch or flat roof to gain access.

■ If you go out during the evening, try to give the impression that someone is still in the house. Draw the curtains and leave lights on in the living room and the kitchen. Ideally use a time switch to turn lights on and off at pre-programmed times.

■ Ensure the back of your house is totally secure. If it's not overlooked it could provide the perfect cover for a burglar to make an entry. The back of a house is one of the favourite entry points for a burglar.

■ An open garage door suggests no one is at home. If you store tools and a ladder in the garage a passing burglar could use them to make a break-in. Keep the garage door shut and if you keep a ladder in the garage make sure it's fixed to the wall and secured with a lock.

■ Darkness and shadows are the burglar's friends. A porch light will act as a deterrent, as will a floodlight fitted at the back of the house. Avoid large bushes near the front door, it could provide the perfect cover for an intruder.

■ Never leave keys under a mat or plant pot or hanging from a piece of string through the letterbox. Burglars know all the favourite hiding places. Don't put any form of identification on your house keys. Don't leave internal keys in the locks where they can be seen.

■ Always change the locks on external doors when you move into a new house or if you lose your keys.

■ If you are going away for more than a day cancel the milk and newspapers.

■ Ask a neighbour to push any 'free' newspapers or bulky mail through the door, to take in any large parcels left on the doorstep and to generally keep on eye on things.

Increasingly effective as a deterrent are the Neighbourhood Watch Schemes set up by groups of householders with the help of the police. After an initial meeting with the police, residents in a specific area keep an eye on each other's homes, reporting any unusual or suspicious happenings. Participants are also issued with window stickers and posters warning potential burglars that a Neighbourhood Watch Scheme is in operation. It has been shown that in areas covered by the scheme, the number of burglaries fall. Ask your local police station for details.

The next step in the battle against the burglar, is to try and make your house as difficult as possible to break into. All windows and doors should be fitted with secure locks, drainpipes painted with anti-climb paints and the garage, shed and any outhouse kept locked.

Free advice on choosing the right types of lock is available from the Crime Prevention Officer (CPO) attached to your local police station. He will come to your home and tell you which areas are most vulnerable and the types of lock to fit.

WINDOWS

The most vulnerable access points of any home are the windows. The average window catch or single hinge stay offers only slight resistance when the window is shut, whilst an open window offers a sneak thief easy access. A security lock will deter most potential intruders – even if the glass is broken to release the catch or stay – a window lock will still present an unwelcome obstacle.

There's a wide range of window locks available and what you choose will largely depend on the type of windows you have and the material of the frame, but it's unlikely to cost more than £5 per lock. Most locks are easy to fit and are usually supplied with all the necessary fixings, but do check that the frame it will be fixed to is in good condition – there's no point fixing a lock if the frame will easily give way.

Mortise-rack bolts are best suited to timber casement windows. They fit neatly into the side of the window and, at the turn of a special key, shoot a bolt into a second hole drilled in the edge of the frame.

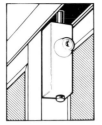
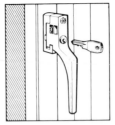

*All locks by Era
from J. E Reynolds*

*Multi-purpose bolt suitable for
patio doors and french windows*

*Lockable
window latch*

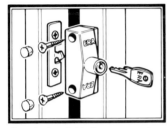
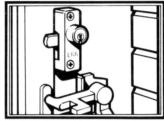
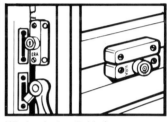

*Snaplock suitable for casement
windows*

Metal window security lock

*Window lock suitable for
wooden casement and sash windows*

Sliding wedge locks for metal casement windows fit into the channel of the opening frame. Neat and unobtrusive, they can't be tampered with and are easy to fix.

Key-operated locks immobilise the handle or window stay of a casement window and are particularly suitable for metal-framed fanlights.

Pivoting locks are suitable for narrow-framed timber windows and come in two pieces: one part is screwed to the inside surface of the window, the other to the frame. When the window is shut they are locked together with a special key.

Sash windows are more difficult to secure. The best method is with a **sash lock** which screws on to the top of the lower sash. Or alternatively a **dual screw**, which fits into a hole drilled in the top rail or lower sash, is less obtrusive. Both are key-operated and work by shooting a bolt into a hole in the outer sash securing the two together.

Sliding patio windows can literally be levered out from their tracks, so should always be fitted with special **patio locks**. The lock is secured to both the top and bottom of the fixed frame and is key-operated, throwing a bolt into the sliding panel, which holds it in place. Most modern patio doors are supplied fitted with their own security locks. If your patio doors do not have an in-built security device, it may be difficult to secure one so you might have to try several different lock makes before you find one which fits. If you are thinking of installing patio windows check to make sure they come with their own security device system.

If you have louvre windows you'd be advised to replace them. The slats are very easy to take out and there are very few ways of making the louvres secure, bar sticking them together with an epoxy resin glue.

Double-glazing will make it more difficult for a burglar to get into your home, simply because he will have to get through two panes of glass. So if your window frames are not in very good condition, it could be worth fixing replacement windows for the security they'll give. Before buying, check to see if the replacement window is supplied with an integral locking system.

One security device for windows which is very popular on the Continent and gaining popularity in this country are **security shutters**. Fitted outside the window they comprise a blind of tough slats set into a shutter box with a guide rail on either side of the window. When you want to close the blind, a self-winding belt is operated and the slats roll down within rubber guide lines forming a secure barrier to potential burglars. The sight of the shutters alone should make burglars look elsewhere.

Security shutters will have to be made to measure to fit your windows exactly and professionally installed, so they are not cheap. But there are other benefits, such as improved insulation against heat loss and noise and protection against sunlight, thus reducing damage and fading to fabrics and furnishings. These benefits only occur when the blinds are down, so be prepared for your home to look like Fort Knox when the shutters are in use.

DOORS

It's likely that your front door will be fitted with some form of lock, but check that it's a security lock and not a single, spring-loaded rim latch.

The best front door lock is a good quality **mortise deadlock**, which will have a strengthened casing and hardened steel bolts to withstand drills and saws. It is designed to fit into a recess cut into the edge of the door and can only be opened by a special key, so once the door has been locked externally the bolt is set and can only be withdrawn by means of the key. If your front door has a glass panel and a burglar breaks it to try and open the door from the inside, a mortise deadlock will stay firm. If your door is not thick enough to accommodate the body of this type of lock fit a good quality **rim-mounted deadlock**. Whatever type of mortise lock you choose make sure it complies to British Standard 3621, which means it will have at least a five-lever movement, making it very difficult to be 'picked'.

Side and back doors, which are popular exits for thieves, should also be fitted with a deadlock — choose a model with a latch and handle as well.

In addition fit all external doors with **surface-mounted** or **key-operated security bolts** at the top and bottom of the door, whilst any outward-opening doors which have exposed hinges should be fitted with **hinge bolts** to prevent them being levered out.

French windows and double doors are difficult to secure and vulnerable to attack. Your best choice here is to fit four **mortise and rack bolts** (one into the top and bottom of each door) which lock down and upwards into the sill and head of the frame. Alternatively

you could fit four **surface-mounted key-operated push bolts**.

BURGLAR ALARMS

If you live in a high risk area or tend to be absent from your home a great deal, you might like to fit a burglar alarm. These range from simple DIY packages to complex professional systems with infra red or ultrasonic detection devices and offer a visible warning to would-be burglars so act as a useful deterrent. Whatever you choose it will only be as effective as the positioning of the components. To avoid any costly mistake get the advice of your local CPO.

As a guide, the more expensive, professionally installed systems should conform to BS 4737. Make sure it is fitted by a company on the National Supervisory Council for Intruder Alarms list of approved installers. Write to them at Queensgate House, 14 Cookham Road, Maidenhead, Berkshire SL6 8AJ ☎ 0628-37512. It is important to ensure that your home looks occupied at all times, particularly at night. Simple **24-hour time switches**, which plug into an ordinary socket, can be set to turn lights on and off at a given time every night. More sophisticated **seven-day switches** or **security light switches** will allow you to vary the time the lights go on and off from day to day. Even more sophisticated are devices incorporating a photo-electric cell which will automatically turn the lights on when it gets dark. Both indoor and outdoor versions are available.

Generally speaking it's not worth locking internal doors, if a burglar gets into your home he is likely to break them down. However, don't leave valuables lying around as an open invitation — the opportunist burglar will only spend a few minutes in the house.

For jewellery and other small valuables, consider a small safe. Video recorders, which are still regularly stolen, can be secured with one of the special anti-theft devices available. Other items could be property marked, that is engraved, etched or stamped with your post code or other distinguishing mark. Alternatively you can mark the items with an 'invisible ink' pen which only shows up under ultra-violet light. Whichever method you choose, you will, of course, have to advertise the fact so that the potential thief knows your property can be traced.

APPENDICES

GUIDE TO FABRICS AND FIBRES

A brief guide to the many different furnishing fabrics and fibres available for use in the home.

Acetate fibre is manmade from cellulose then treated with chemicals. Gives a cheap, soft yarn which drapes well and is often used to imitate silk. Resistant to moths and mildew. Can be mixed with other fibres, such as cotton, silk, viscose and wool.

Acrylic fibre is manmade from oil. Light and soft with a bulky feel. Of all manmade fibres it is the closest to wool. Absorbent, warm, resistant to mildew and moths, it is used for upholstery and curtain fabrics. Brand names include Acrilan, Courtelle and Dralon.

Baize fabric is woven from wool and named after the town of Baza in Spain where it was

The Pomander Collection — a range of printed linens from Osborne & Little

first made. A thick cloth with a napped surface, traditionally made in green and used to cover tables and line drawers.

Brocade fabric is heavy and ornate, with a multi-coloured or self- coloured raised design, often with metallic threads. The name is taken from the French verb 'brocart' meaning to ornament. Originally always made in silk, it can now be made from acetate, cotton, polyester and viscose. Best used for curtains.

Broderie anglais fabric is an embroidered cotton with lacy designs cut out of the cloth. Used to trim bedding and table linen.

Buckram fabric is a cheap cotton yarn, heavily impregnated with size to give it a stiff finish. Name taken from the town of Bokhara in Russia where is was first made. Used for pelmets or lampshades.

Calico fabric is the generic name for a plain, coarse cotton which was first made in Calicut in India. Now mainly used unbleached as a base cover for sofas.

Cambric fabric is an inexpensive, fine, firmly woven cloth made from bleached cotton. Often glazed on the right side, so slightly stiff. Used to cover duvets.

Candlewick fabric, with a thick tufted pile, is usually made from cotton or synthetic fibres. Used to be popular for bedspreads and bathmats.

Canvas fabric is made from coarse cotton or linen. Rugged and stiff it is the most popular fabric for outdoor living, deckchairs for example, and is often woven in stripes.

Cheesecloth fabric was originally used for wrapping cheese. Loosely woven, inexpensive cotton with a fine, open, crinkly weave, usually in a natural ecru colour. Can be used for informal curtains.

Chenille fibre, with a thick, nubbly pile, is made from cotton, viscose or silk. Used to be popular for curtains and tablecloths.

Chintz fabric is a plain-weave cotton, usually with a large printed design of flowers or birds, with a shiny glazed finish. The name comes from the Hindi word 'chint' which referred to the painted stained calico imported from the East to the UK in the 17th century. Used for

curtains and upholstery.

Corduroy fabric is made from cotton, acrylic or a blend of fibres with cut pile 'ribs' running along its length. Used for upholstery.

Cotton fibre is made from seed hairs which are collected, combed, carded and spun into yarn which is woven into a soft absorbent cloth. Can be used on its own or mixed with synthetics to make it more easy- care. Used for curtains, upholstery and various other furnishings.

Crash fabric is linen or cotton with a rough irregular surface. Comes from the Latin crassus meaning coarse. Used for towels and upholstery linings.

Cretonne fabric is a strong, printed or plain cotton used for curtains, loose covers and upholstery.

Damask fabric with an elaborate woven design, is similar to brocade, although it is not raised. Made from cotton, linen or viscose and used for upholstery, curtains and table linen.

Duck fabric is made from closely woven cotton or linen, it is a lightweight version of canvas and used for upholstery.

Dupion fabric is an imitation silk usually made from viscose with an irregular surface with the same sheen as silk. Used for curtains.

Felt fabric is made by pressing fibres together and bonding them with heat and moisture, usually made from wool or viscose. As it's non-woven it will not fray, although it's not washable. Used for lining drawers and covering pinboards.

Flannelette fabric is made from cotton or viscose to imitate wool. Has a soft, warm yarn with a nap surface and is used for sheeting.

Flax fibre comes from the inner bark of the flax plant, which is washed, combed and spun to make linen.

Flock fibre is cut, torn or ground fibres which are fixed to a background material to give a raised design. Usually used for wallcoverings.

Gingham fabric is made from firm, lightweight cotton or poly-cotton. The name comes from the Malayan 'gin-gan'. Hard-wearing, it is usually checked and used for tablelinen.

Glassfibre is a fibre which is totally non-absorbent so won't rot, although it may crack. Sometimes used for curtains.

Hessian fabric is made mainly from jute or hemp, which is woven and then dyed. Used in upholstery and makes a popular wallcovering.

Holland fabric is made from cotton or linen which is finished with size and oil for stiffening. Used in upholstery or for blinds.

Jacquard fabric is the name given to any cloth woven on a jacquard loom producing a complex design on one side only.

Jute is fibre which comes from the jute plant grown in India. Coarse, but not as durable as flax and hemp, it's used for sacking and carpet backing.

Kapok fibre resembles cotton, it comes from the seed pods of the Malayan kapok tree. Very light with a silky sheen, it is used as an upholstery filling.

Lace fabric is the name given to describe any elaborate, openwork construction made from cotton or manmade fibres. The name comes from the Latin 'laqueos' meaning to knot. Made as edgings as well as fabric widths and used for curtains, bedspreads and tablecloths.

Lawn fabric is very fine, smooth and light made from cotton or a cotton/manmade blend. Printed or plain it's used for curtains.

Linen fabric is woven from flax yarn, which has a slightly knobbly texture and is very strong and absorbent. Has a tendency to crease and will shrink unless treated. Rarely used for sheets nowadays, but is mixed with other fibres for furnishings and tablelinen.

Linen union is a fabric which contains more linen than any other fibre. Popular for upholstery and loose covers, although it tends to crease and doesn't resist abrasion well.

Matelasse fabric has a multi-weave which gives a quilted appearance. Comes from the French, meaning cushioned or padded, and may contain metallic threads. Made in cotton it may be used for curtains and bedspreads.

Milium fabric is the trade name for a type of insulated curtain lining made from cotton, acetate, viscose or nylon polyester which contains metallic fibres, to reflect heat back into the room.

Moire fabric has a wavy, rippled effect design usually in cotton or viscose. The name comes from the French verb 'moirer', meaning water.

Moquette fabric is probably one of the best-known upholstery fabrics. It has a pile surface, made from a manmade fibre, with a wool or cotton backing; the pile can be cut, left uncut, or be a combination of the two, to create a variety of patterns.

Muslin fabric is usually made in cotton with the look of a lightweight gauze, similar to cheesecloth, but finer. Very cheap, but it tends to shrink. Can be slightly stiffened and used for lightweight curtains.

Net fabric has an open mesh, either woven, knitted or knotted, made in cotton, silk, or manmade fibres and used for net curtains or sheers.

Ninon fabric is like voile, light and soft, but usually made from manmade fibres. Used for net curtains.

Nylon fabric is the accepted name for polyamide fibre which is produced from mineral sources. Non-absorbent and hardwearing, it doesn't drape well and attracts static, so is usually blended with other fibres, although it has excellent colour fastness, dyes well and is virtually crease-resistant. Brand names include Enkalon and Tendrelle.

Oilskin fabric has been treated with oil to make it wind-and waterproof. Mainly used as table and shelf coverings although it has virtually been superseded by more modern coated fabrics.

Panne is a crushed finish given to velvet.

Percale fabric has a close, plain-weave giving a firm smooth surface, usually in cotton. Hardwearing and used for sheets and duvet covers.

Polyester fibre is manmade from raw materials, derived from petroleum. Widely used to imitate wool, silk and cotton. Hardwearing and easy-care, it is not absorbent, but mixes well with other natural fibres. Brand names include Dacron, Terylene and Trevira.

Poplin fabric is made from a plain-weave cotton with a fine rib running from selvedge to selvedge, usually has a sheen. Originally made of silk and used for church vestments and hangings. The name comes from papeline a 15th century fabric woven in France. Used for curtains and loose covers.

PVC (polyvinylchloride) chemically produced material, used to coat one side of cotton and other base fabrics to give a waterproof finish. Used for tablecovers and aprons.

Repp fabric is made of closely woven cotton or synthetics with a pronounced rib effect. Strong but rather stiff, it is used for curtains and upholstery.

Sateen fabric is similar to satin, but made from cotton. Soft with a sheen, it is mainly used for curtain linings.

Satin, strictly speaking this refers to a type of weave which gives a smooth, shiny surface with a matt reverse; but it is also used to describe any shiny fabric woven in this way.

Scrim fabric is loosely woven, low-quality cotton cloth similar to cheesecloth, often stiffened and used as a backing or base for embroidery or upholstery lining.

Seersucker fabric which has a puckered, crinkly effect, is usually made in cotton or manmade fibres. Does not need ironing and creases do not show. Used for informal curtains and tablecloths.

Silk fibre is made from the cocoons of the silkworm which each consist of a continuous filament gummed together. Strong and luxurious, it is absorbent and dyes well, but can only be dry cleaned. May be used plain or hand-painted for cushions and bedcovers.

Spun silk fibre is made from silk 'scrap' - defective silk cocoons and waste silk – where the silk filament is not continuous, is bound and twisted together and spun like cotton. Although the fabric should be cheaper than silk, the process is fairly lengthy and expensive.

Synthetics are fibres or filaments produced from chemical materials as opposed to those made by man or occurring naturally.

Terylene, see polyester.

Ticking fabric is a hardwearing, closely woven cloth usually made from cotton or linen. Used for mattress or pillow covers, can also be used for upholstery.

Towelling fabric, with a looped pile cloth, is usually cotton or poly-cotton, which is soft and highly absorbent. Used mainly for towels.

Twill is a type of weave which produces diagonal lines on the right side of the cloth, usually running from left to right. Made from cotton or wool, it makes a thicker cloth than a plain weave.

Utrecht velvet fabric is a type of hardwearing velvet usually used for upholstery.

Velour fabric, the French word for velvet, it actually refers to a heavy, warm cloth with a short warp pile. Can be made from acrylic, cotton or nylon.

Velvet fabric has a cut pile no more than 3mm (1/8") in length, made from two warp yarns, one forms the background, the second the pile which is pulled up by wires. Made from cotton, silk and synthetics, it needs to be handled with care to prevent the pile from being crushed.

Viscose fibre is manmade from cellulose. Soft and absorbent it feels like wool and is warm to handle. Can be used alone or mixed with other fabrics.

Voile fabric has a light open-textured finish, made from cotton or polyester. Soft and transparent, it is used for lightweight curtains.

Warp is the name given to the threads running lengthways in woven fabric (parallel to the selvedges).

Weave is a pattern of interlacing warp and weft threads which form a fabric. Basically there are three types: plain, satin and twill.

Weft is the name given to the threads running widthways in woven fabric, at right-angles to the warp.

Wool fibre is the natural fibrous covering from sheep, goats, camels and rabbits which is washed, combed, carded and spun. Very warm, soft, tough and resilient, although it has a tendency to shrink. Often mixed .with manmade fibres which improves its wearing qualities. An excellent fabric for upholstery.

MEASURING UP WINDOWS

Whatever kind of window treatment you want, it's important that you measure up the windows correctly to enable you to calculate the amount of fabric required or the size of the blind which has to be ordered. Always use an expandable rule, as a fabric tape measure tends to stretch and won't give accurate figures.

MEASURING FOR CURTAINS

Curtains will look best if they're sill length or floor length. If you are having one of the modern styles, where the curtains drape in folds on the floor, the length will not be quite as critical.

METHOD

1. Always fix the curtain track or pole in position first.

2. For the length: decide how long you want your curtains to be then measure from the top of a track, or just underneath a pole, to the desired length, whether it's the sill (A), top of a radiator (B) or to the floor (C). Add on allowances for hems and headings, but deduct 10 mm (½") from the length for the sill-length or floor-length curtains, to allow for clearance.

3. For the width: multiply the length of the track or pole (D) by the required fullness of the desired heading tape. Some tapes require more fabric than others.

4. Divide this measurement by the fabric width, rounding the figure up to the nearest full number. This will give the amount of fabric widths required. Obviously if you have a pair of curtains, this figure should be halved to get the number of widths which have to be joined to make one of a pair. Half widths should always be joined to the outer edge of each curtain.

5. Multiply the curtain length by the number of fabric widths to determine the amount of fabric needed.

6. Make allowances for pattern matching, depending on the pattern repeat.

MEASURING FOR BLINDS

The way you measure up for blinds will vary slightly depending on what type it is and where it is to be hung. Blinds. are usually sited in a window recess, although you can also mount them to hang outside the window. Always use a metal expandable rule for measuring.

METHOD

Roller blind: for the width, measure horizontally from one side of the recess to the other (A). Deduct 30 mm (1¼") to allow for the pin and spring mechanism (B). Position the brackets about 30 mm (1¼") from the top of the recess. Measure the drop from the top of the track to the sill (C).

For a roller blind which is to be hung on a window with no recess, mount the blind on the window frame, if it is suitable. Alternatively, fix it on the wall beyond the frame. Measure across the width of the window, ensuring that the blind extends beyond the sides and top of the window (B).

Austrian blind: Austrian blinds hang from a track mounted inside the window recess. For the width, measure the length of the track. Measure the drop from the top of the track to the sill.

For an Austrian blind fitted inside a recess: fix track inside the recess.

For a window without a recess the track should extend 15 cm (6") beyond the edges of a plain window and should be flush with the edges of a moulded window frame. Measure as before.

Roman blind: Roman blinds are fixed to a batten fitted to the recess ceiling. For the width, measure the length of the batten. Measure the drop from the top of the batten to the sill.

For a Roman blind fitted inside a recess: fix a batten to the recess ceiling.

For a window without a recess, the batten will have to be supported at the sides, so position the supports above the window frame (C). Measure as before.

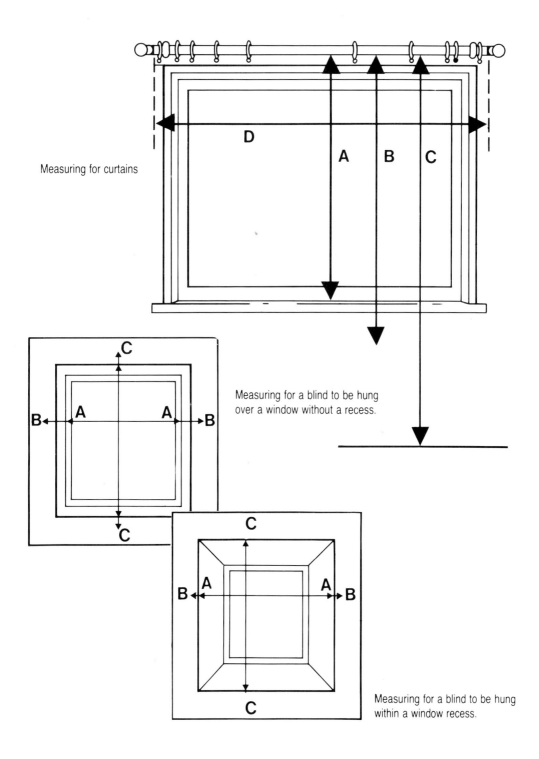

Measuring for curtains

Measuring for a blind to be hung over a window without a recess.

Measuring for a blind to be hung within a window recess.

DECORATIVE DETAILS

Cornices, ceiling roses, dado rails and panelling are all attractive ways of giving a room character and individuality. Wall panelling originated as far back as Tudor times, whilst decorative plasterwork, used to embellish walls and ceilings, became popular during the 18th century. All of these features can be added to your home, whatever its age, provided they are in keeping with the overall architectural style and decor – there's no point fixing traditional riches if your furnishings are modern in design, for example.

Most decorative details are traditionally made from fibrous plaster or wood, although they also come in a variety of materials, including polystyrene, glass fibre and polyurethane, and are available for simple DIY fixing. Here is a guide to the various products available and how they can be used:

Traditional wall panelling from W.H.Newson

Arch, usually pre-formed in a classical design, it comprises a fibrous plaster arch and supporting corbels and columns or pilasters (see below). Can be used instead of a door or as a decorative link between two rooms. Integral arches, made by fixing galvanised wire mesh moulds to the opening and then covering them with plaster, are a modern alternative.

Beams can be used to give a room a Tudor or cottage-style look. Available in solid wood, glass fibre or moulded polyurethane.

Centrepiece or **ceiling rose** is used to form a decorative surround for a ceiling light fitting, with the light flex passing through the centre. Available in polystyrene, polyurethane and fibrous plaster, they come in many different sizes and designs. They can be glued in place, although heavier centrepieces should be pinned for support, or screwed to the ceiling joists.

Columns are literally decorative columns used to frame a doorway, support an arch or, in generously proportioned houses, as a decorative feature in their own right. **Half columns** are also available.

Corbels are decorative supports usually used to provide the 'support' for an arch, although they can also be used on their own to provide a shelf for an ornament. They come in plaster, polyurethane or wood.

Cornices and coving are borders which are fixed where the walls join the ceiling to give a finished effect. They are mitred in the corners and come in a variety of designs and sizes in fibrous plaster, polystyrene, polyurethane and wood and are fixed with adhesive and/or galvanised nails. They can be painted to blend in with the ceiling and walls, or highlighted to stand out as a feature.

Dado rails, also known as chair rails, were originally designed to prevent chairs damaging the wall. They come in wood and are fixed about 90 cm (36″) up from the floor. Traditionally the area below the rail is covered with Anaglypta. They make an interesting visual break, particularly for a high wall. For a visual effect only consider using a paper or stencilled paint border.

Embellishments are all the decorative trims used to finish off fireplaces, doors and rooms, such as plaques, cameos, garlands and bows. They come in plaster, polyurethane and wood.

Frieze is a moulded, highly decorative border found between a cornice and picture rail, usually depicting a classical design of ancient Greece or Rome. They come in plaster or polyurethane.

Niche is a traditional style, pre-formed alcove, which makes a decorative 'hole in the wall' usually used to display ornaments. They come in fibrous plaster, polyurethane or wood.

Panelling literally gives the impression of wood panelling. It provides a good method of hiding a damaged wall, whilst giving sound and heat insulation. Traditional wood panelling is available, as well as 'fake' wood in polyurethane.

Panel moulding comes in strips which are used with decorative quadrant corners and corner blocks to form decorative fake panels on a wall. They provide a good way of adding interest to a large expanse of plain wall. They come in fibrous plaster, glass fibre and wood.

Picture rails are fixed to the wall three-quarters of the way up from the floor and used for hanging pictures with hooks. They also make a decorative item in their own right. Made of wood. **Plate rails** are slightly wider rails used for displaying plates, and are fixed at the same height.

Pilasters are square columns which partly project from a wall and are used with arches and corbels. They come in plaster, polyurethane or wood.

There are many companies offering these decorative details for DIY installation, including the large DIY outlets such as Sainsbury's Homebase and Wickes. However, if you want to match existing period mouldings, you would be advised to contact one of the many companies specialising in fibrous plaster mouldings. These include:

G. Jackson & Sons Ltd, Unit 19, Mitcham Industrial Estate, Streatham Road, Mitcham, Surrey CR4 2AJ. ☎ 01-640 8611

Locker & Riley Ltd., Capital House, Bruce Grove, Wickford, Essex SS11 8DB. ☎ 0268 561161

W.G. CROTCH LTD.

ORIGINALLY ESTABLISHED IN 1820

MANUFACTURERS OF FIBROUS PLASTER
Tel: Ipswich (0473) 250349
Fax: Ipswich (0473) 213180

A SMALL SELECTION FROM OUR STANDARD RANGE

A GUIDE TO TOOLS

Everyone needs a few basic tools to carry out all the diy jobs around the house. A really good toolkit is not something you can put together overnight – like most collections it will expand gradually over the years as the depth of your pocket or the breadth of your interest increases.

It's not necessary to spend a fortune on the contents of your DIY toolkit, but that doesn't mean you should seek out the cheapest examples either. As with most things, you get what you pay for and if a tool is cheap it's made from cheap materials – for example, poor quality steel which won't hold an edge or bends easily, with rough wooden handles which splinter and break at the first sign of heavy use. There's a lot of truth in the old adage 'a bad workman blames his tools' but bad tools won't do a good job anyway.

However, all collectors have to start somewhere and a few basic tools are a must for every householder. So what are you most likely to need and what should you be looking for?

Screwdrivers The tools you'll probably use most are screwdrivers. A set of eight of varying sizes – four slot-head, three crosshead (for Phillips or Pozidriv screws) and a small electrical screwdriver for plugs etc – will be more than adequate. Those with chrome-vanadium shafts will be the strongest and it's worth looking out for those with handles that can be fitted with a spanner for extra leverage on stubborn screws.

Power drills These days power drills are inexpensive and have made the hand drill all but redundant. The most basic type has only one speed, with a 300-400W motor and a 10 mm (⅜″) chuck, capable of drilling holes up to 20 mm (¾″) in wood or 10 mm (⅜″) in metal or masonry. Much more useful is a hammer action drill, which can literally hammer the bit into masonry helping to break it up. Even more versatile is a two-speed or variable-speed drill (slower speeds are better for metal and masonry), with a larger motor and a 12 mm (½″) chuck.

Bits Good quality drill bits are essential – cheap ones will blunt quickly. Black & Decker's Craftsman set contains all you'll need: ten high-speed steel bits for metal, six twist and three

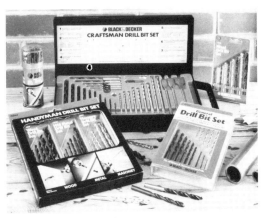

Black & Decker drill bits

flat wood bits, nine masonry bits, two glass/tile bits and a countersink for recessing screws.

Hammers One of the tools which comes in for a lot of abuse is the hammer. One of the most robust types is one with a steel shaft bonded to the head so that it won't work loose and with a comfortable rubber handle. A 16 oz claw hammer (the claw is used for removing nails and other levering jobs) will do for most jobs. A 4 oz pin hammer with a wooden shaft is best for more delicate work.

Saws To cut wood and other materials you'll need a selection of saws – use a hacksaw for metal and plastic. A 150 mm (6″)) bladed junior hacksaw for small jobs and a 300 mm (12″) one for bigger jobs.

For wood, use a tenon saw with between 14 and 16 teeth (or points) to the inch for making joints and other light cutting jobs. Use a panel saw with 10 to 12 teeth (points) per inch for cutting sheet and thick material. Be sure to try the handle of any saw for comfort before buying and remember that the more teeth per inch there are the finer and slower the cut.

Two tools can be used for smoothing, removing and shaping timber: the **plane** and the **surform**. A 250 mm (10″) smoothing plane is ideal for most DIY jobs and is not too heavy to use for long periods.

The surform is a rasp-like tool with replaceable blades which can be used on wood, plastics, soft metals and ceramics. A variety of shapes and sizes are available.

Chisels Chisels are also used for shaping, as

well as cutting, wood. A set of three bevelled-edge chisels 6 mm, 13 mm and 25 mm (¼", ½" and 1") will be adequate for light DIY use each with plastic or wooden handles – plastic may be more robust at the cheaper end of the market.

Files For shaping and smoothing metal you will need a set of files. Choose medium-smooth flat, round and half-round versions around 250 mm (10") for versatility.

Pliers One of the most versatile gripping tools to have around is a pair of combination pliers, which have toothed jaws for holding and sharp, toughened blades for wire cutting. A pair with insulated handles (useful for electrical work and comfortable to use) will cost from 5. Pliers are useless for turning nuts and bolts; a 150 mm (6") adjustable spanner is much better and will cope with nuts up to 20 mm (¾") across.

Measures Measuring equipment is a must and your toolkit should contain a 3 metre (10') steel tape measure with a locking device and metric and imperial scales for general measuring jobs; a try-square, for marking and determining right-angles; and a 300 mm (12") spirit level for finding true horizontals and verticals.

Finally you'll need some sort of **workbench** - using the kitchen table is guaranteed to make you unpopular. The deservedly popular Workmate, with its built-in vice, has a multitude of uses and takes up little storage space when folded up.

Once you've got your basic toolkit, take good care of it. If possible store tools on racks on the shed or garage wall – not all jammed together in the bottom of an old toolbox. If they're to be left for any length of time, treat metal parts to a light coating of penetrating oil to keep rust at bay (not files, which will clog). And don't put a tool to a use for which is wasn't intended – buy the right one instead.

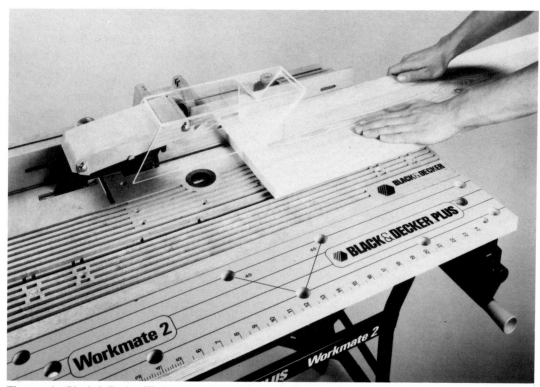

The popular Black & Decker Workmate with the Power Tool Table attachment

CALLING IN THE EXPERTS

Although a competent amateur can tackle most jobs around the home, there are times when it is necessary – and sensible – to call in a professional, for example if your home needs to be completely rewired or if you are planning to convert a spare bedroom into a second bathroom.

Some people will welcome such a challenge, but there's absolutely no point tackling such a job if you don't feel happy about what you're doing. After all, if things do go wrong it could cost you more than if you'd asked a professional to do the job in the first place. Remember, no one can tell you exactly when you need help, only you know that.

When it comes to calling in a professional, where exactly do you start? You need to be careful about following up advertisements or cards dropped through your letter box. Many good tradesmen do not need to advertise; they obtain more than enough work from personal recommendations. But how do you *know* that the person or company you select will do the job well? Anyone can set themselves up as a builder or plumber, whether or not they have any previous training or experience, and as a result there are many 'cowboys' about who will either take a deposit then disappear, or whose work is abysmally poor.

Over the years the Office of Fair Trading has received so many alarming stories regarding home improvement work carried out by contractors that it has compiled seven golden rules which you should always follow when you want to employ a contractor. They are:

1. **Before you start** Decide exactly what you want done. For larger jobs consider getting advice from an architect or surveyor.

2. **Council approval** Ask your local authority whether you need planning permission or Building Regulations' approval and whether you can get a grant towards the work.

3. **Shop around** Don't be rushed. Get estimates or quotations in writing from at least two firms.

4. **The firm** Find out as much as you can about the firm you plan to employ. Can it cope with the job? If in doubt, get a second opinion.

5. **Your contract** Make sure your contract is in writing and gives full details of prices, cancellation rights, guarantees and when the work will be started and finished. Check whether any sub-contractors are to be used and who is liable if things go wrong.

6. **Payment** Be careful about parting with money in advance, especially if you are asked to pay large deposits. Always query any price increases and ask why they were not included in the original estimate.

7. **If you have a problem** Act quickly and get advice from your local Trading Standards (or Consumer Protection) Department, Citizens' Advice Bureau or Consumer Advice Centre.

The Office of Fair Trading also offers further information regarding various aspects of home improvements in a free 12-page booklet simply called *Home Improvements* which is available from your local Citizens' Advice Bureau, local authority, or from the Office of Fair Trading direct:

Office of Fair Trading, Room 306, Field House, Breams Buildings, London EC4A 1PR. ☎ 01-242 2858.

Personal recommendation is always one of the best ways of finding a reliable contractor. Alternatively, contact one of the many professional organisations listed here.

ARCHITECTS

If you are planning any building work which involves major structural alterations or additions to your house, it would be advisable if you sought the advice of a qualified architect. RIBA has a free advisory service (the Clients' Advisory Service) and will provide a list of professionals working in your area.

Royal Institute of British Architects (RIBA), 66 Portland Place, London W1N 4AD. ☎ 01-580 5533.

BUILDERS

The Federation of Master Builders administers a warranty scheme to protect consumers against non-completion of work and any faults which may occur within two years of the work being carried out by any of their members. Write with a s.a.e for a list of registered builders in your area.

Federation of Master Builders, Warranty Department, 33 John Street, London WC1N 2BB. ☎ 01-242 7583.

DECORATORS

Members of the British Decorators' Association subscribe to a Code of Practice to ensure standards of workmanship. They will supply a list of members in your area.

British Decorators Association, 6 Haywra Street, Harrogate, North Yorkshire HG1 5BL. ☎ 0423 567292/3.

DOUBLE-GLAZING

All members of the GGF offer the safeguards of a Code of Ethical Practice and Deposit Indemnity Fund. They have a number of leaflets which are available, free of charge, relating to double-glazing, and can also supply a list of regional members.

Glass & Glazing Federation (GGF), 44-48 Borough High Street, London SE1 1XB. ☎ 01-403 7177.

ELECTRICAL

All members of the Electrical Contractors' Association carry out work which complies with the IEE Regulations. Consumers using an ECA member are protected against bad workmanship and non-completion of work by a consumer protection guarantee.

Electrical Contractors' Association (ECA), ESCA House, 34 Palace Court, London W2 4HY. ☎ 01-229 1266.

Electrical Contractors Association of Scotland, 23 Heriot Row, Edinburgh EH3 6EW. ☎ 031-225 7221.

The NICEIC was set up for the protection of electricity consumers against faulty, unsafe and defective installations. It furthers this aim by maintaining a Roll of Approved Contractors,

whose work is subjected to inspection. Copies of the Roll may be inspected at Electricity Board showrooms, or obtained direct.

National Inspection Council for Electrical Installation Contracting (NICEIC), Vintage House, 36/37 Albert Embankment, London SE1 7UJ. ☎ 01-582 7746.

HEATING

If you are having a gas appliance installed, it is essential that it is fitted by an approved contractor. The Confederation for the Registration of Gas Installers (CORGI) promotes safety standards and maintains a Register of Installers who all hold public liability insurance. A copy of your local CORGI Register is available for inspection in gas showrooms, or through CORGI regional offices.

Confederation for the Registration of Gas Installers, St. Martins House, 140 Tottenham Court Road, London W1P 9LN. ☎ 01-387 9185.

Members of the Heating and Ventilating Contractors' Association will give impartial advice on fuels and central heating systems. Consumers are protected by the Double Guarantee Scheme. HVCA also offer a number of free advice leaflets on all aspects of central heating. Contact them for a list of local members.

Heating and Ventilating Contractors' Association (HVCA), ESCA House, 34 Palace Court, Bayswater, London W2 4JG. ☎ 01-229 2488.

All members of the National Association of Plumbing, Heating and Mechanical Services Contractors are vetted before their membership is accepted; they operate a Code of Fair Trading as protection for the consumer. Contact them for a list of member firms.

National Association of Plumbing, Heating & Mechanical Services Contractors (NAPH & MSC), 6 Gate Street, London WC2A 3HX. ☎ 01-405 2678.

PLUMBING

The Institute of Plumbing is a professional

organisation whose main concern is to raise the standards of plumbing. They have a list of registered plumbers, which is available on request.

Institute of Plumbing, 64 Station Lane, Hornchurch, Essex RM12 6NB. ☎ 04024 72791.

SURVEYORS

The Royal Institution of Chartered Surveyors is a professional organisation with a high entry standard for members. Chartered surveyors will advise you on all aspects of extensions and home improvements and can provide invaluable help.

Royal Institution of Chartered Surveyors (RICS), 12 Great George Street, Parliament Square, London SW1P 3AD. ☎ 01-222 7000.

MISCELLANEOUS

British Chemical Dampcourse Association, 16a Whitchurch Road, Pangbourne, Reading, Berkshire RG8 7BP. ☎ 07357 3799.

Members include dampcourse installers and chemical manufacturers, all of whom are vetted before being allowed to join, and who subscribe to a Code of Practice. Write with a s.a.e. for a list of members.

British Wood Preserving Association, 6 The Office Village, 4 Romford Road, Stratford, London. ☎ 01-519 2588.

Offers free and impartial advice on all aspects of wood preservation. Will supply a list of member companies specialising in remedial work. Free and priced publications and video available.

Builders Merchants Federation, 15 Soho Square, London W1V 5FB. ☎ 01-439 1753.

The 'professional' distributors of building materials to the trade, who also welcome the public. They give expert advice on all aspects of home improvement as well as providing planning and installation services. A regional list of members is available on request.

Chipboard Promotion Association, Schauman UK Ltd, Stags End House, Gaddsden Row, Hemel Hempstead, Herts HP2 6HN. ☎ 058285 4661.

Will provide information and advice on all aspects of chipboard and its uses.

Home Woodworking Campaign, 21/25 Carolgate, Retford, Notts DN22 6BZ.

Sponsored by the Swedish/Finnish Timber Council to encourage everyone to use timber. They produce a series of free colour DIY project leaflets called *Make Yourself At Home With Timber.*

G. Jackson & Sons Ltd., Unit 19, Mitcham Industrial Estate, Streatham Road, Mitcham, Surrey CR4 2AJ. ☎ 01-640 8611.

Founded in 1780, Jackson's specialise in installing and refurbishing traditional fibrous mouldings and still retain many of the original moulds. Also offer new plasterwork such as friezes, cornices etc., for DIY or professional fixing. Provide many fireplace styles including Adam.

Kitchen Specialists Association (KSA), Information Office, 8 St Bernard's Crescent, Edinburgh EH4 1NP. ☎ 031-332 8884.

Members are kitchen specialists who display, design, supply and install kitchens. They have a Code of Practice and customers are protected by a consumer protection scheme. They offer a free consumer guide, *The Do's and Don'ts of Buying a Kitchen* suitable for anyone about to buy a new kitchen and operate a telephone Helpline at the above number.

National Hardwood Campaign, 44 Duke Street, St. James's, London SW1Y 6DD.

Will provide advice on the most suitable hardwoods for a particular application and can provide a free leaflet, *Caring for Hardwoods.*

Timber Research and Development Association (TRADA), Hughenden Valley, High Wycombe, Buckinghamshire HP14 4ND. ☎ 024024 3091.

Offers a number of data sheets on all aspects of timber and can offer advice on the use of timber in the home, on a fee-paying basis.

INDEX

ADVERTISERS INDEX